Engineering Code Confidence

Building Effective Quality Gates in CI/CD Pipelines

Engineering Code Confidence

ISBN: 978-1-0492-9290-8

Table of Contents

Introduction: The Night the Pipeline Betrayed Us

It was 2:00 AM on a Wednesday when Sarah's phone buzzed with that dreaded "Critical PagerDuty" alert.

She sat up groggily, already knowing it was going to be a long night. She was the lead engineer for the Checkout Team at RocketCart, a fast-growing e-commerce company known for its blazing fast release cycles. They had just moved to "continuous delivery," proudly shipping to production several times a day.

But something had gone wrong. Horribly wrong.

Half of their users couldn't check out.

As the war room Slack channel filled with emojis, blame-free questions, and quiet panic, the team worked backward through logs, metrics, and commits. Finally, someone named the culprit: a small code change meant to fix a rounding issue on currency conversions. It had passed the build. It had passed unit tests. It had even gone through a successful deployment. But it had silently broken international checkout for customers using non-standard currencies.

No one had caught it, not because they weren't smart or diligent, but because there was nothing in the pipeline designed to *catch* it.

"We didn't break production," muttered Dan from QA, "we just *automated* the breaking of production."

Silence.

And then: laughter.

It was the kind of gallows humour only sleep-deprived engineers can appreciate. But beneath the laughter was a sobering realization: **they had automated speed, not safety**.

The Postmortem That Sparked a Movement

The next day, bleary-eyed but clear-minded, the team gathered for a postmortem.

It wasn't the code that failed them, it was the *process*. Or rather, the lack of guardrails in the process.

They had CI/CD, sure. They had tests. But there was no system in place to say:

- "Hey, this code reduced test coverage in a critical area."
- "Your static analyser is flagging a possible logic flaw."
- "This change affects currency conversion. Are there integration tests for international carts?"
- "This change added a dependency with known vulnerabilities."

And so, the idea was born: what if our pipeline didn't just move code forward, but knew when to stop it?

They started small. A gate to block merges when code coverage dipped. A security scan that failed builds with high-severity CVEs. A policy that required passing integration tests for the payment service.

Week by week, their confidence grew. Failures in prod dropped. Confidence in releases increased. Devs even started pre-emptively fixing quality issues, because they *knew* the gate would catch them anyway.

Quality wasn't an afterthought anymore. It was built in.

The Moral of the Story

What the RocketCart team learned the hard way is something every team eventually stumbles upon: **moving fast is meaningless if you're moving blindly**.

CI/CD is like a bullet train. But without quality gates, you're running it on tracks with no signals, no brakes, and no one watching the switches.

Quality gates are not about slowing teams down, they're about making sure you arrive at the right destination, safely, every time.

And that's where this book begins: with a team that automated everything, except quality.

Now it's your turn to build pipelines you can trust.

Your Journey to Quality Governance Success

Writing this book has been a journey in itself. With more than two decades in the software industry, and over half that time spent writing, teaching, and reflecting on it - quality has always been a central theme in my work. Over the years, I've explored quality through many lenses: architecture, test automation, engineering practices, and delivery models. Each of these perspectives has shaped how I think about building reliable software at scale.

What I've learned, however, is that the most effective way to govern and sustain quality, especially across teams and large organizations, is not through isolated practices or frameworks, but through quality gates embedded directly into the development and deployment process. This realization didn't come overnight. It emerged through years of experimentation, failure, refinement, and success across multiple organizations, where quality gates proved to be the most practical and scalable mechanism for turning quality from an aspiration into a repeatable outcome.

Designing quality into architecture remains essential, and strong testing and automation are foundational to fast feedback. But the next evolution for organizations, and for quality professionals themselves, is learning how to operationalize these practices within teams, integrating them seamlessly into CI (Continuous Integration)/CD (Continuous Delivery) pipelines to drive quality proactively rather than reactively. This shift, from quality as an activity to quality as a built-in control, is what ultimately inspired this book. If you aren't familiar with the concept of CI/CD pipelines, I do explain them in more detail in the chapter titled *"Foundations of CI/CD Pipelines"*.

While this has been a long journey for me, my hope is that this book will significantly shorten that journey for you. I aim to provide enough foundational context around testing, quality, and delivery to make the material accessible, without requiring you to wade through volumes of additional literature. At the same time, many of these topics are intentionally covered at a high level, and readers will benefit most if they bring, or continue to develop, a working understanding of quality and testing practices as they progress through the book.

This book is not about prescribing rigid rules. It is about helping you understand how to think about quality gates, how to design them thoughtfully, and how to use them as a powerful enabler of modern, high-confidence software delivery.

This book begins by grounding the reader in what quality gates are and why they exist, framing them not as bureaucratic controls, but as practical guardrails that enable teams to move faster with confidence. We start by demystifying quality gates and placing them in the broader context of modern software delivery, helping readers understand how they evolved alongside CI/CD and why they have become essential in high-performing engineering organizations.

From there, the focus shifts to the foundations of CI/CD pipelines, establishing a shared understanding of how code flows from commit to production. This sets the stage for a deeper discussion on what "quality" actually means in software delivery, exploring its many dimensions, functional correctness, performance, security, reliability, and maintainability, and how these dimensions translate into measurable, enforceable signals within a pipeline.

With this foundation in place, the book explores the different types of quality gates, starting with static code analysis and test automation. These chapters show how early, automated feedback can prevent defects from ever reaching later stages, and how testing strategies - when treated as first-class gates - become one of the most powerful enablers of fast, safe delivery. Security, compliance, performance, and reliability gates are then introduced, illustrating how non-functional requirements can be continuously enforced rather than audited after the fact.

As the reader's understanding matures, the book moves beyond generic gating to explore custom and contextual quality gates. Here, quality gates become adaptive: shaped by risk, environment, change size, and business context. This naturally leads into designing effective gate policies and thresholds, where readers learn how to balance strictness and flexibility, avoid unnecessary friction, and align gates with real-world delivery needs.

The journey continues into the practical realities of pipeline orchestration and gate integration, showing how quality gates are implemented and managed across common CI/CD platforms. Observability and feedback loops are then layered in, reinforcing the idea that gates are not static rules but living systems that improve through visibility, metrics, and learning.

Recognizing that no system is perfect, the book addresses how to handle gate failures and exceptions gracefully, turning failures into learning opportunities rather than blockers. This feeds directly into continuous improvement, where readers learn how to evolve quality gates over time, respond to changing technologies and business goals, and avoid stagnation or gate fatigue.

Real-world case studies then bring theory into practice, highlighting both successes and failures from industry and extracting patterns that readers can apply in their own environments. From there, the focus widens to culture and organizational alignment, emphasizing that quality gates only succeed when teams, leadership, and incentives are aligned around shared ownership of quality.

The book culminates by guiding readers through building their own quality gate framework, synthesizing technical, cultural, and organizational insights into a cohesive approach tailored to their context. Finally, it looks ahead to the future of quality gates, exploring predictive, adaptive, and autonomous models that point toward self-regulating delivery systems.

Additionally, during this book I may drop many different technical terms that you might not be familiar with. Rather than explain everything in the chapters to preserve readability, you can navigate to the *"Terms and References"* section at the end of the book to unpack any concept you are unfamiliar with further. Or, AI and Google are fantastic resources to aid you here as well.

By the end of this journey, readers won't just understand how to implement quality gates, they'll understand why they matter, how to evolve them, and how to use them as a strategic advantage in modern software delivery.

We understand that different reads might be a different spaces on the CI/CD journey and as such, feel free to skip sections that you feel you might be comfortable with. While we've done our best to avoid too much repetition – there are periods where we do reexplain topics in different ways to ensure better flow for that chapter, remind the reader of specific concepts or unpack concepts explored earlier in more detail.

Introduction to Quality Gates

Purpose of chapter: In this chapter we will introduce to the concept of quality gates, explain what they are and why you will want to implement them in your delivery chain, looking at both the benefits they offer and the potential shortcomings that can occur should they be absent in your software.

The pace of the software world continues to accelerate, and speed has become a defining competitive factor. Software underpins nearly every modern organisation, enabling customer interactions, payments, and a wide range of value-added services. Without reliable applications or effective digital platforms, companies risk losing relevance in an increasingly digital-first landscape.

At the same time, organisations face significant pressure to maintain and evolve these systems. They must continue delivering value, ensure reliability, and innovate to stay ahead. This challenge goes beyond simply keeping systems running, it requires moving quickly while consistently delivering high-quality, always-available experiences.

And – as the team in the book's introduction learnt - the only way to do this effectively and at scale, is through the use of guardrails built into their CI/CD pipelines that allow code to be built, tested, deployed and delivered into production environments, but ensuring that the relevant testing and measures are in place to not cause any failures.

What are quality gates?

Quality gates are automated decision points in a CI/CD pipeline that verify a change meets agreed standards (such as test results, security posture, and operational readiness) before it can move forward. They exist to make the pipeline a source of trust: it should speed up delivery *and* prevent avoidable failures.

In practice, a gate either allows the change to progress or stops it with clear feedback so the team can correct the issue immediately.

The Purpose of Quality Gates

At their core, quality gates help teams move fast without breaking things. In high-velocity environments where code is integrated and deployed continuously, quality gates provide structured assurance that every code change:

- Meets coding standards and best practices
- Passes required automated tests
- Does not introduce security vulnerabilities
- Maintains acceptable performance
- Complies with organizational or regulatory policies

By embedding these checks directly into the delivery pipeline, quality gates reduce the risk of costly production issues, regressions, and security breaches.

Common Examples of Quality Gates

Quality gates can take many forms, each targeting a specific aspect of software quality:

- **Static Code Analysis Gate:** Ensures code adheres to coding standards and is free of critical issues.
- **Test Coverage Gate:** Blocks changes that decrease test coverage below a defined threshold.
- **Security Gate:** Scans for known vulnerabilities in dependencies.
- **Build Verification Gate:** Verifies that the code compiles successfully and passes all unit/integration tests.
- **Policy Gate:** Enforces rules like "no direct pushes to `main`" or "requires two code reviews."
- **Performance Gate:** Ensures performance benchmarks are not degraded by new changes.
- **Deployment Approval Gate:** Requires human review or compliance sign-off before production deployment.

Why quality gates matter in CI/CD

Below are the key reasons why quality gates are essential in a CI/CD context:

Catching Issues Early and Often

CI/CD encourages frequent, small code changes. Without guardrails, this can lead to a steady flow of flawed code reaching critical environments. Quality gates enforce checks immediately after code changes are integrated, catching issues such as:

- Broken tests
- Security vulnerabilities

- Poor code quality
- Performance degradations

By failing fast, teams can address problems before they propagate, saving significant time and effort.

Preventing Defects from Reaching Production

Every organization wants to avoid incidents in production. Quality gates help prevent:

- Costly rollbacks
- User-facing outages
- Embarrassing bugs or regressions

By enforcing automated standards, gates act as a final line of defence, ensuring only code that meets your team's definition of "ready" moves forward.

Promoting a Culture of Accountability and Quality

When developers know that every pull request or commit will be evaluated by automated quality criteria, it incentivizes better coding practices. Instead of relying on manual reviews or post-mortems, teams adopt a proactive mindset:

- Writing better tests
- Keeping dependencies up to date
- Fixing code smells early
- Thinking critically about risk

This shift-left approach embeds quality into daily habits, not just as an afterthought.

Enabling Safe, Confident Delivery at Scale

As teams scale, manual QA and review processes become bottlenecks. Quality gates allow teams to scale CI/CD pipelines without compromising trust by:

- Standardizing enforcement across all services / repos
- Reducing reliance on manual gatekeepers
- Providing fast, repeatable feedback loops

This increases developer confidence in the pipeline and reduces friction in the release process.

Supporting Compliance, Security, and Risk Management

In regulated industries or security-conscious environments, it's not enough for software to work, it must comply. Quality gates can be used to enforce:

- Licensing rules
- Secure coding practices
- Vulnerability thresholds
- Approval workflows

These checks provide an auditable, automated way to align delivery with organizational policies and external regulations.

Reducing Mean Time to Recovery (MTTR)

Even with high coverage and testing, incidents still happen. When quality gates are in place, they often reduce the blast radius of changes and allow teams to identify the root cause more easily, thanks to:

- Smaller, higher-quality deployments
- Reliable audit trails
- Confidence in upstream dependencies

This leads to faster rollbacks, better diagnostics, and shorter recovery times.

Enabling Continuous Improvement

Every failed gate is a learning opportunity. Over time, quality gates can be refined based on failure trends, improving:

- Test reliability
- Tooling precision
- Developer workflows

This feedback loop helps evolve your quality strategy alongside your product and team maturity.

Without quality gates, CI/CD becomes just a fast way to ship problems.

With them, you gain a powerful framework to balance speed with safety, enabling teams to innovate quickly without sacrificing quality. In the chapters ahead, we'll explore how to design, implement, and evolve quality gates to support every phase of the delivery lifecycle, from build and test to deploy and monitor.

The impact of skipping quality controls

The benefits are hopefully evident – but perhaps the best way to understand the benefits quality gates offer is to understand the impact of what could happen should they be absent in your delivery process.

Skipping quality controls, intentionally or due to process gaps, can feel like saving time in the short term. But in reality, it's akin to cutting corners on safety checks before launching a plane. Without quality gates in CI/CD, you expose your product, users, and business to significant risks. These risks compound as software complexity and deployment frequency increase.

Here's a breakdown of the most critical impacts:

Increased Production Failures

Without automated gates to catch regressions, faulty code can slip into production more easily, leading to:

- Application crashes
- Broken functionality
- Data corruption
- Customer disruptions

Every escaped defect not only damages your system, it damages trust in the pipeline and the development process.

Slower Recovery and Higher Cost of Fixes

Defects caught in production are exponentially more expensive to fix than those found in development or staging. When you skip controls like automated tests, linting, or security scans:

- Debugging becomes harder
- Root cause analysis takes longer
- Rollbacks are more frequent
- Developer morale suffers

In some organizations, mean time to recovery (MTTR) increases dramatically due to avoidable oversights.

Technical Debt and Quality Erosion

Unchecked code builds up technical debt, from bad naming and duplication to insecure dependencies and unstable APIs. Skipping quality gates means:

- Bad code practices go unchallenged
- Codebase becomes harder to maintain
- Performance bottlenecks creep in
- Complexity spirals, slowing future delivery

This is a silent, creeping impact that cripples long-term velocity and innovation.

Security Vulnerabilities and Compliance Violations

Skipping security gates, like dependency checks, static analysis, or policy enforcement, can open the door to:

- Known exploits being deployed
- Privilege escalation or injection attacks
- Non-compliance with data protection regulations (e.g., GDPR, HIPAA, POPIA)
- Expensive fines and brand damage

In regulated industries, lack of enforcement could even invalidate certifications or invite legal action.

Reputational Damage and Customer Churn

Production bugs and outages impact more than systems, they impact people:

- Customers lose trust
- Stakeholders lose confidence
- The business loses credibility

All it takes is one "hotfix weekend" that could have been avoided by a basic quality gate to shake faith in your product and engineering team.

Eroded Developer Confidence and Culture

When quality gates are missing, developers often:

- Lose trust in the pipeline
- Feel pressure to deliver without safety nets
- Resort to tribal knowledge instead of shared practices
- Get blamed for problems that automation should have prevented

This leads to burnout, siloed behaviour, and a drop in engineering morale, ultimately hurting collaboration and retention.

Broken Feedback Loops

Quality gates provide structured, fast feedback. Without them, issues surface:

- Too late in the cycle (if at all)
- With vague or missing context
- With inconsistent triage or follow-up

This undermines continuous improvement and leads to reactive firefighting instead of proactive engineering.

Skipping quality controls might feel like a shortcut to speed, but it's a fast lane to fragility. Without gates to ensure consistency, quality, and compliance, CI/CD becomes a liability rather than an asset. Quality gates are not overhead - they're investments in trust, stability, and sustainable velocity.

In the following chapters, we'll explore how to implement quality gates that deliver real value without slowing your teams down, ensuring that every deployment is both fast and safe.

Real-world scenarios and failures

Quality gates aren't theoretical, they are battle-tested guardrails forged in the heat of real software failures. Many of today's most infamous incidents trace back to missing or ineffective quality controls in software delivery procedures that could've been prevented due to the better implementation of quality gates.

Here are some real-world scenarios that highlight why quality gates matter, and what happens when they're absent. Please understand though that we are not doing this to shine a negative light on these companies.

These scenarios occur at thousands of other companies on a regular basis and it's only to the credit of these companies raising attention to them and fixing these concerns that we can write about it. They have learnt the lesson, remediated, and hopefully others can now learn as a result. Something which shows a strength rather than a weakness:

The Knight Capital Meltdown (2012)

What happened:

Knight Capital, a major trading firm, deployed new software to their production environment. One server didn't get the update due to a missed deployment control, resulting in a rogue algorithm executing trades.

Impact:

- $460 million lost in 45 minutes
- Stock market disruption
- Company was forced to sell itself

What was missing:

- Deployment verification gate
- Environment consistency checks
- Guardrails for fail-safe rollbacks

GitLab's Accidental Database Deletion (2017)

What happened:

An admin accidentally deleted a production database during a routine troubleshooting task. Due to missing backup validation and automation, the team scrambled to recover data for hours via outdated backups.

Impact:

- 6 hours of outage
- Lost data from ~5,000 projects

- Trust damage in a DevOps-centric company

What was missing:

- Backup integrity check gate
- Role-based access enforcement
- Change control gate in CI/CD for high-risk actions

Toyota's 2023 Global Factory Shutdown

What happened:

A software update disrupted Toyota's production ordering system. A capacity miscalculation led to failed deployments across multiple systems, halting manufacturing across Japan.

Impact:

- 14 production plants shut down
- Estimated cost in tens of millions
- Global supply chain disruption

What was missing:

- Load testing or stress testing gate
- Staging validation before production deployment
- Auto-scaling/resilience gate validation

AWS Outage due to Bad Configuration Push (2020)

What happened:

An internal configuration change to AWS Kinesis caused cascading failures across dependent services like Netflix, Slack, and Zoom. It stemmed from a single update that passed through without proper validation.

Impact:

- Widespread service outages
- Operational chaos across multiple platforms
- Erosion of trust in cloud reliability

What was missing:

- Infrastructure-as-code validation gate
- Canary deployment strategy
- Regression detection gate with rollback criteria

Healthcare.gov Launch Debacle (2013)

What happened:

The U.S. health insurance exchange site launched without proper performance and integration testing. Users encountered broken forms, timeouts, and crashed sessions.

Impact:

- Political backlash
- Emergency intervention by third-party tech teams
- Months of recovery effort

What was missing:

- Performance testing gate
- End-to-end functional testing
- Load simulation and monitoring integration

Facebook Outage due to BGP Misconfiguration (2021)

What happened:

An internal network update misconfigured Facebook's BGP routing tables, essentially erasing the company's presence from the internet.

Impact:

- 6 hours of global outage
- WhatsApp, Instagram, and Messenger all down
- Estimated $60 million in revenue loss

What was missing:

- Configuration review and approval gate
- Network impact simulation
- Failsafe controls on production changes

Key Takeaways from These Failures

Looking at all these above failures, below is a key summary of things that went wrong and how implementing quality gates could've solved these problems had they been in place:

Failure Theme	Quality Gate That Was Missing
Unsafe or partial deployments	Deployment verification, environment parity checks
Human error in prod changes	Role-based access, approval gates
Lack of testing at scale	Load/stress test gates
Broken recovery plans	Backup validation, failover simulation

Configurations gone wrong	Infra-as-code review, change approval
No gradual rollout	Canary/release ring gating, monitoring

The Pattern: Failures Are Preventable

Each of these disasters shares a common trait: they could have been prevented or minimized with automated quality gates. The cost of missing a gate can be staggering not just in money, but in trust, reputation, and resilience.

Conclusion: From Pain to Prevention

These stories aren't just cautionary tales, they're motivation to design robust pipelines that reflect hard-won lessons. The organizations that recover fastest are those who learn, adapt, and automate safeguards into every step of the delivery lifecycle.

There is no silver bullet in the software development world and quality gates alone won't solve all your problems. However, they do provide a good foundation for software delivery to be built on-top of.

In the next sections of this book, we'll explore how you can do exactly that, without grinding velocity to a halt. But first, we need to start at the beginning and understand CI/CD pipelines a little more for those unfamiliar with them. And for those that are, you could potentially learn something new too.

Foundations of CI/CD Pipelines

Purpose of Chapter: In this chapter will explore the concept of CI/CD pipelines in more detail – explaining what they are how they are structured and can add value to any software's delivery processes. We will unpack the different processes and steps of a typical CI/CD deployment process so that we can lay the foundation for how to integrate quality gates into them.

Modern software development demands speed, stability, and scalability. Continuous Integration and Continuous Delivery/Deployment (CI/CD) address these demands by automating how code is built, tested, and released. At its core, CI/CD is not just a set of tools, it's a culture and a workflow built on automation, collaboration, and continuous feedback.

At a technical level, CI/CD works by automatically triggering a pipeline whenever a change is made to the codebase. For example, a developer commits a small change to a Git repository. This commit triggers a CI pipeline that checks out the code, compiles or builds the application, and runs automated tests such as unit and component tests. If any of these steps fail, the pipeline stops and provides immediate feedback to the team, preventing faulty code from progressing further.

If the CI stage succeeds, the CD portion of the pipeline takes over. The validated build is packaged into a deployable artifact, such as a container image, and pushed to an artifact or container registry. The pipeline may then automatically deploy this artifact to a non-production environment (for example, a test or staging environment), where additional checks like integration tests, security scans, or performance validations can run.

Once all required checks pass, the same artifact can be promoted to production, either automatically or with a manual approval step. Because every step is scripted and repeatable, deployments are consistent and low-risk. This technical flow allows teams to release changes frequently, with confidence that each change has been built, tested, and verified in a standardized and automated way.

CI/CD encourages teams to integrate small, frequent changes into a shared codebase and to validate those changes automatically. Each change is built and tested as early as possible, allowing issues to be detected when they are easiest and least costly to fix. Instead of large, risky releases, software is delivered in smaller, incremental updates that can be deployed more confidently and more often.

For development teams, this approach reduces manual effort and uncertainty while increasing transparency and trust in the delivery process. Automated pipelines provide fast feedback on code quality and system health, enabling teams to focus more on solving problems and delivering value rather than managing releases.

Over time, CI/CD helps teams move faster without sacrificing quality, supports better collaboration across roles, and creates a more predictable and resilient path from idea to production.

What Is CI/CD?

If you're unfamiliar with the concept of CI/CD pipelines, we will attempt to unpack them in more detail at a foundational level. If you are, perhaps, more experience – you may choose to skip over some of these sections and move onto some of the more technical parts of this chapter hat you may be unfamiliar with.

CI/CD stands for:

- **Continuous Integration (CI):** Developers integrate code into a shared repository frequently, ideally multiple times a day. Automated builds and tests validate each integration.
- **Continuous Delivery (CD):** Validated code is automatically packaged and prepared for release to a staging or production environment.
- **Continuous Deployment (CD):** Every validated change is deployed automatically to production without human intervention.

Note: Continuous Delivery ends with a manual approval for production; Continuous Deployment skips that gate entirely. These terms are used interchangeably in the industry and outside of that final deployment step – all processes are exactly the same.

Core Principles of CI/CD

CI/CD is underpinned by a set of core principles that guide how teams design, implement, and continuously improve their delivery pipelines. These principles go beyond tooling and focus on creating fast, reliable feedback, reducing risk, and enabling teams to deliver high-quality software with confidence. When applied together, they form a cohesive approach that supports both rapid development and long-term system stability.

The principles below describe the foundational practices that make CI/CD effective in real-world environments. They emphasize early validation, automation, consistency, and incremental change, helping teams detect problems sooner, respond faster, and maintain a predictable path from development through to production.

- **Automated Feedback Loops**: Rapid feedback from builds, tests, and monitoring tools helps developers catch issues early.
- **Shift-Left Testing**: Testing is integrated early in the pipeline, not left to the end of development.
- **Fail Fast, Fix Faster**: Quick detection of integration failures minimizes the time and cost of fixing bugs.
- **Version Control Everywhere**: Everything from code to infrastructure configurations is stored and versioned in source control.
- **Small, Frequent Changes**: Smaller commits reduce complexity, risk, and make issues easier to trace and fix.
- **Pipeline as Code**: Pipelines themselves are treated as versioned, testable artifacts, improving reproducibility and auditability.
- **Environment Parity**: Consistent configuration across dev, staging, and production ensures predictable outcomes.

Typical CI/CD Workflow Overview

CI/CD isn't just about moving faster. It's about moving safely at scale, reducing manual effort, catching problems earlier, and delivering features to users faster with higher confidence.

Understanding the key stages in the process is essential for building a reliable and efficient DevOps pipeline. These stages work together to support automated, repeatable, and quality-driven software delivery.

Each stage plays a distinct role in validating code, detecting issues early, enforcing standards, and ultimately delivering features safely and quickly to users. For now we are simply introducing the stages and will unpack some of them in more detail when we discuss the quality gates relevant to them.

Continuous Integration (CI) – Key Stages

The Continuous Integration (CI) stage is composed of a series of well-defined steps, each with clear triggers, objectives, and quality measures. Its primary focus is the continuous introduction of code changes and the early validation of those changes through automated build, test, and analysis activities. By enforcing quality checks at this stage, teams ensure that new code is consistently compiled, tested, and verified before it progresses to downstream environments.

This early feedback loop helps detect defects, security issues, and integration problems as soon as they are introduced, reducing rework, protecting pipeline stability, and establishing a strong foundation for reliable and confident deployments.

Source Code Management

- **Trigger:** A change is pushed to a shared code repository (e.g., Git).
- **Goal:** Kick off the CI process automatically based on a branch strategy (e.g., main, develop, or feature branches).

Build

- **Purpose:** The application code is compiled or packaged.
- **Artifacts Created:** Executables, Docker images, libraries, or other deployable units.
- **Key Considerations:**
- Ensure build reproducibility.
- Fail fast if dependencies are missing or compilation breaks.

Static Code Analysis / Linting

- **Purpose:** Check code against formatting standards, security guidelines, and style rules.
- **Goal:** Blocks builds if critical violations exist (e.g., security or reliability issues).

Unit Testing

- **Purpose:** Test individual functions or components in isolation.
- **Automation:** Tests are run automatically after every build.
- **Success Criteria:** All unit tests pass with acceptable code coverage (often enforced by a quality gate).

Code Coverage Analysis

- **Purpose:** Measures how much of the code is exercised by tests.
- **Goal:** Enforce a certain coverage of automated test execution in the above step before proceeding to later steps.

Security & Dependency Scanning

- Purpose: Checks code and dependencies for any potential security violations or vulnerabilities.
- **Goal:** Identify vulnerable libraries or misconfigurations.

Integration Testing

- **Purpose:** Validate how different components work together. Unit tests will test the code in isolation. This step will test deployed versions of the code to ensure they work correctly. Contract testing can and should also take place here for greater efficiency in the pipeline process.
- **Goal:** Catch early-stage misalignments in logic or data flow.

Artifact Packaging & Publishing

- **Purpose:** Packaged builds are versioned and stored in an artifact repository (e.g., Artifactory, Nexus, DockerHub).
- **Significance:** Artifacts serve as the deployable units in CD.

Continuous Delivery / Deployment (CD) – Key Stages

The Continuous Delivery (CD) stage extends the assurances established in Continuous Integration by ensuring that validated code is always in a deployable state. This stage focuses on packaging, integration, and environment-level verification, applying progressively stricter quality gates such as integration testing, security scanning, performance validation, and infrastructure compliance checks.

While deployments may still require an explicit approval, Continuous Delivery ensures that every change has passed the necessary technical and quality controls to be safely released at any time. By enforcing consistent, repeatable validation across environments, this stage reduces release risk, improves predictability, and builds confidence that software can be deployed reliably when the business is ready.

Continuous Deployment represents the highest level of automation in the delivery pipeline, where every change that passes all defined quality gates is automatically released to production without manual intervention. In this stage, quality gates serve as the primary control mechanism, replacing human approvals with data-driven validation such as SLO checks, canary analysis, security policies, and real-time observability signals.

Continuous Deployment emphasizes fast feedback, resilience, and safe automation, relying on techniques like progressive rollouts, automated rollbacks, and monitoring-driven decision-making to manage risk. When implemented effectively, this approach enables teams to deliver value to users rapidly while maintaining high standards of reliability, security, and quality.

Acceptance/Smoke Testing

- **Purpose:** Verify that a basic set of functionalities work in an environment close to production.
- **Environment:** Staging or test environments.
- **Outcome:** Stop or proceed based on pass/fail criteria.

Environment Provisioning

- **Purpose:** Spin up infrastructure using Infrastructure-as-Code (IaC) or preexisting containers and environment files.
- **Outcome:** By using consistent environment configuration, it ensures consistency across dev, test, and prod.

Configuration Management

- **Purpose:** Manages the configuration of the different environments /pipeline builds based on certain parameters.
- **Outcome:** Ensure application configuration matches the environment settings securely and correctly.

Deployment to Staging

- **Purpose:** Automatically deploy the artifact to a non-production environment, so that additional testing can be executed
- **Outcome:** Environment built for the execution of End-to-end (E2E), UI, load, performance, and security testing.

Approval Gates (for Continuous Delivery)

In a health pipeline process, approval gates should general exist to ensure the process and their necessary rules execute correctly. These can be automated directly into the previous stages, though in many highly regulated organisations – these should form separate steps of their own for certain approval processes.

- **Human-in-the-loop:** Stakeholders or QA leads review test results or business metrics before releasing to production.
- **Common Criteria:** Business readiness, change management, release scheduling.

Deployment to Production

Your pipelines should also contain the correct deployment procedures for eventually deploying code into production. Depending on the deployment process, as mentioned in the above approval gate step, this will be either manually or automatically triggered:

- **Continuous Delivery:** Manual approval initiates deployment.
- **Continuous Deployment:** Automatically happens if all gates pass.

There are also different strategies and approaches to follow in deploying code. Which approach you take is often dependent on the architecture of your software or required approach to the necessary feature delivery

- **Blue-Green Deployment** – A release strategy that runs two identical environments (blue and green), switching traffic to the new version only once it has been fully validated to minimize downtime and risk.
- **Canary Releases** – A technique where a new version is gradually rolled out to a small subset of users first, allowing teams to monitor performance and catch issues before a full release.
- **Rolling Updates** – A deployment approach that incrementally updates instances of an application over time, ensuring continuous availability while replacing old versions with new ones.
- **Feature Flags** – A mechanism that allows teams to enable or disable features at runtime without deploying new code, providing flexibility for testing, gradual rollouts, and quick rollbacks.

Post Deployment Validation

Once code is deployed. It is important to run checks both immediately following the deployment and for periods afterwards to ensure that the system continues to operate as expected post the deployment.

- **Purpose** – To verify that the deployment has not introduced regressions, performance issues, or instability, and that the system behaves as intended in the production environment.
- **Outcome** – Increased confidence in release quality, early detection of issues, and the ability to respond quickly before users are significantly impacted.

Summary Table

The table below highlights how quality and control evolve from Continuous Integration to Continuous

Delivery/Deployment, mapping early code-level validation in CI to environment, release, and operational safeguards in CD.

CI Stage	CD Stage
Source Code Commit	Environment Provisioning
Build	Configuration Management
Static Code Analysis / Linting	Staging Deployment
Unit Testing	Automated Acceptance Testing
Integration Testing	Manual Approval (CD only)
Code Coverage Enforcement	Production Deployment
Security Scanning	Monitoring & Feedback
Artifact Packaging	Rollback Readiness

Each stage enforces discipline, accountability, and automation. Together, they enable development teams to:

- Catch issues early
- Deliver features faster
- Reduce manual handoffs
- Achieve consistency and compliance
- Improve developer confidence and end-user experience

Where Do Quality Gates Fit in the Pipeline?

Quality gates are strategically placed at multiple stages in the CI/CD pipeline. Here's how they typically map to the flow. We will go through what the different quality gates are for the different steps in a typical pipeline, but more details will be unpacked further in the book:

1. Post-Commit / Pre-Build (Optional, Early Guardrails)

- **What's gated:** Commit message conventions, linting, or pre-commit hooks.
- **Tools:** Git hooks, Husky, pre-commit frameworks.
- **Why:** Prevent low-quality or non-compliant code from entering the repo.

2. Post-Build (CI Phase)

This is one of the most common places for quality gates.

Quality Gates Applied:

- **Static Code Analysis:** No new critical/severe issues.
- **Code Coverage:** Thresholds met (e.g., 80% overall, 100% for new code).
- **Security Scans:** No critical or high vulnerabilities.
- **Test Results:** 100% unit test pass rate.

Tools:

- SonarQube
- Checkmarx, Fortify, Snyk
- Codecov, JaCoCo, Istanbul

3. Pre-Deployment to Staging (CD Entry Point)

At this gate, we determine whether the artifact is good enough for end-to-end validation.

Quality Gates Applied:

- Integration tests must pass.
- Build must be signed and verified.

- Artifact must be approved (e.g., via GitOps or Jira workflow).
- Container image must be scanned and signed.

4. Pre-Deployment to Production

This is the final and most critical quality gate, ensuring only release-ready code goes live.

Quality Gates Applied:

- Acceptance tests must pass (automated or manual).
- Business stakeholders may need to approve.
- Load / performance thresholds are met.
- Observability dashboards are green from staging validation.
- A rollback plan must be in place.

Visual Mapping Example

Below is a visual mapping of the different quality gate stages that can be found in a typical CI / CD pipeline:

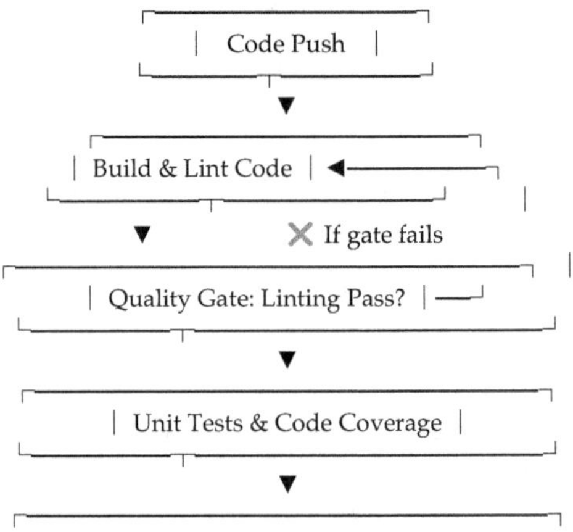

```
| Quality Gate: Test/Coverage? |
└──────────┬─────────────────────┘
           ▼
┌────────────────────────┐
| Artifact Creation   |
└──────────┬─────────────┘
           ▼
┌────────────────────────┐
| Deploy to Staging    |
└──────────┬─────────────┘
           ▼
┌──────────────────────────────────────┐
| Quality Gate: E2E, Performance, OK? |
└──────────┬───────────────────────────┘
           ▼
┌────────────────────────┐
| Manual Approval (CD) |
└──────────┬─────────────┘
           ▼
┌──────────────────┐
| Production |
└──────────────────┘
```

Why Quality Gates Are Strategically Placed

Quality gates are intentionally positioned at different points in the CI/CD pipeline to balance speed, confidence, and risk. Placing the right checks at the right stage ensures that problems are detected as early as possible, while more comprehensive validations are applied only once the software has proven a basic level of stability. This staged approach prevents unnecessary delays and keeps feedback relevant to the type of change being made.

In the early stages, quality gates focus on fast, low-cost checks such as linting, formatting, and unit tests. These validations run quickly and provide immediate feedback to developers, helping them correct basic issues before they propagate further down the pipeline. Catching problems here avoids wasted effort and keeps the pipeline flowing smoothly.

Mid-stage gates introduce deeper quality controls, including code coverage thresholds, security and dependency vulnerability scans, and more extensive integration tests. At this point, the goal is to ensure that the change not only works in isolation but also meets broader quality and security expectations. These checks act as a safeguard against technical debt and hidden risks.

Late-stage quality gates are designed to protect end users and the business. End-to-end tests, performance validations, and deployment readiness checks confirm that the system behaves correctly under real-world conditions. Combined with rollback strategies and monitoring hooks, these gates reduce the likelihood of customer-facing issues and ensure that, if something does go wrong, it can be quickly detected and addressed.

- **Early stages**: Catch basic issues fast (e.g., linting, unit tests).
- **Mid stages**: Enforce deeper quality checks (e.g., coverage, vulnerabilities).
- **Late stages**: Mitigate risk to end users (e.g., E2E testing, performance validation, rollback readiness).

The summary table below shows how quality gates are applied progressively across the pipeline, ensuring that the right checks are enforced at the right stage, from early code validation to production readiness and risk control.

Pipeline Stage	Example Quality Gates
Post-Commit	Code linting, commit message checks
Post-Build (CI)	Static analysis, unit test pass rate, coverage
Pre-Staging Deployment	Artifact integrity, integration tests

Pre-Production Deployment	Acceptance tests, approvals, rollback plan

Tooling overview

Modern CI/CD pipelines rely heavily on automation tools that integrate with quality gates to enforce code standards, run validations, and control release flows. Here's a high-level overview of popular CI/CD platforms and how they support quality gate implementation. For now, we will just touch on some of the scripts and tools at a very high-level with a deeper dive into the script files and some of the tools in more detail later in the book.

Jenkins

Overview:

- One of the most widely adopted open-source automation servers.
- Highly extensible via a massive plugin ecosystem.

How It Supports Quality Gates:

- **Pipeline as Code**: Declarative pipelines (Jenkinsfile) allow inserting conditional quality checks.
- **SonarQube Plugin**: Integrates with Jenkins to enforce code quality thresholds.
- **JUnit Plugin**: Visualizes and fails builds based on unit test results.
- **Security Scanners**: Integrations like Checkmarx or OWASP Dependency-Check.

Example (groovy script):

```
stage('Quality Gate') {
  steps {
```

```
    script {
      def qg = waitForQualityGate()
      if (qg.status != 'OK') {
        error "Quality gate failed: ${qg.status}"
      }
    }
  }
}
```

GitHub Actions

Overview:

- GitHub-native CI/CD solution.
- Uses YAML-defined workflows to automate build, test, and deploy steps.

How It Supports Quality Gates:

- **Job Status Checks**: Jobs can be set to fail on unmet conditions (e.g., test failures, linting).
- **Code Scanning**: Native integration with CodeQL for security analysis.
- **Third-Party Actions**: Supports tools like SonarCloud, Snyk, Trivy, and others.

Example:

```yaml
yaml
jobs:
  quality-checks:
    runs-on: ubuntu-latest
    steps:
      - name: Run Tests
        run: npm test
      - name: Enforce Code Coverage
        uses: codecov/codecov-action@v3
```

GitLab CI/CD

Overview:

- Fully integrated CI/CD with Git repository management.
- YAML-based .gitlab-ci.yml defines all pipeline stages.

How It Supports Quality Gates:

- **Quality Gate Integration**: With tools like SonarQube, Code Climate, or native SAST/DAST tools.
- **Pipeline Rules**: Use rules or only/except to dynamically control execution based on gate results.
- **Approval Gates**: Built-in manual approval stages and environment-specific approvals.

Example:

```
code_quality:
  stage: test
  script:
    - sonar-scanner
  allow_failure: false
```

Azure DevOps

Overview:

- Microsoft's end-to-end DevOps platform.
- Offers CI/CD via **Azure Pipelines**, with YAML or visual designer support.

How It Supports Quality Gates:

- **Pre-deployment Approvals**: Manual or automated gates based on tests, metrics, or external systems.
- **Built-in Extensions**: Integrates with SonarQube, WhiteSource, Checkmarx, and more.

- **Branch Policies**: Combine build validation and quality gate enforcement in pull requests.

Example:

```
- task: SonarQubePrepare@5
  inputs:
    SonarQube: 'MySonarQube'
    scannerMode: 'CLI'
- task: SonarQubeAnalyze@5
- task: SonarQubePublish@5
```

Other Notable Mentions

Tool	Notes
CircleCI	Fast, cloud-native, supports quality gate enforcement via orbs.
Travis CI	Easy setup, supports gates with test/lint conditions.
TeamCity	JetBrains solution with plugins for inspections and test thresholds.
Bamboo	Atlassian CI/CD with Jira integration, supports test/gate stages.

Each tool can enforce quality gates in different ways, some rely on external integrations (e.g., Jenkins + SonarQube), while others (e.g., GitLab and Azure DevOps) provide native gate capabilities including automated test checks, security scans, and approval workflows.

Choosing the right tool and configuring your quality gates effectively can drastically reduce software defects, streamline compliance, and build a stronger DevOps culture.

Looking further across the CI/CD Tools Landscape

We've briefly spoken about pipeline tools themselves here. However, across all phases, the CI/CD tooling landscape is quite broad and diverse – often requiring teams to integrate information from many different tools to properly build in their governance measures and quality gates.

This table highlights the most commonly used tools across each stage of the CI/CD lifecycle, showing how version control, automation, quality gates, deployment, and monitoring come together to enable reliable, end-to-end software delivery.

Stage	**Common Tools**
Version Control	Git, GitHub, GitLab, Bitbucket
CI/CD Orchestration	Jenkins, GitHub Actions, GitLab CI, CircleCI, Azure DevOps
Build/Package	Maven, Gradle, npm, Docker
Test Automation	JUnit, PyTest, Cypress, Selenium, Postman
Quality Gates	SonarQube, Checkmarx, Fortify, ESLint
Deployment	ArgoCD, Spinnaker, Helm, Terraform, Ansible
Monitoring	Prometheus, Grafana, Datadog, Sentry

Conclusion: The Balance between speed and quality

At its core – CI/CD pipelines help teams to get the speed of consistent test execution paired with early error detection – along with enforcing struct quality governance. It allows software to be deployed – and if done right – not break much in the process. Understanding their role and learning to master their implementation is a key skill that allows any development team to succeed.

For the next chapter, we will look at ways of defining quality when it comes to software delivery – which allows us to better assess how we can then begin to insert effective quality gates into them.

Defining Quality in Software Delivery

Purpose of chapter: To establish different definitions of quality and show they can be applied to the software delivery process. We will also look at how these different quality definitions can align with specific business needs, look at how we can measure each aspect of quality effectives and then how to find the right balance between speed and quality strictness that is required for effective CI/CD integration.

Before we can meaningfully integrate quality gates into a CI/CD pipeline, we must first unpack what software quality actually means in a modern delivery context. Quality is often treated as an abstract or subjective concept, something that is "felt" by users or debated by teams after defects appear. In reality, quality in CI/CD must be explicit, measurable, and actionable. If quality cannot be expressed as signals that a pipeline can evaluate, then it cannot be consistently governed, automated, or improved.

In the context of CI/CD, software quality is best understood as the degree to which a system continuously meets its intended functional and non-functional expectations at every stage of delivery. This includes correctness of behaviour, reliability under load, security of data and execution, maintainability of the codebase, and the ability to safely evolve the system over time.

Each of these dimensions contributes a different kind of value: functional quality ensures the software does what it promises; performance and reliability protect the user experience; security safeguards trust and compliance; and maintainability enables teams to move quickly without accumulating excessive risk or technical debt.

Crucially, quality in a CI/CD process is not a single checkpoint or a final approval step, it is a continuous set of validations applied as code moves from commit to production. Different stages of the pipeline are responsible for different aspects of quality, and not all quality signals are equal in terms of timing, cost, or impact. For example, catching a logic error during a unit test provides far more value than discovering it during a production incident.

Likewise, detecting a vulnerable dependency early in the pipeline is significantly cheaper and safer than responding to a post-release security breach. CI/CD forces us to think about quality not just in terms of outcomes, but in terms of when and how quality is validated.

This is where the concept of quality gates becomes essential. Quality gates act as the translation layer between abstract quality principles and executable pipeline logic. They formalize what "good enough" means at each stage of delivery, based on the type of change, the risk involved, and the expectations of the business.

Without a clear definition of quality, gates become arbitrary, overly strict, or inconsistently applied. With a shared understanding of quality, gates become powerful enablers - protecting the system, guiding teams, and reinforcing good engineering behaviour without slowing delivery.

Defining software quality for CI/CD, then, is not about perfection. It is about intentional trade-offs, visibility, and consistency. It is about deciding which quality signals matter most, when they should be evaluated, and how they collectively reduce risk while enabling speed. Once these principles are clearly articulated, quality gates stop being obstacles and start becoming the backbone of a reliable, scalable software delivery system.

Different Aspects of Software Quality

Quality is a multi-dimensional concept in software engineering, extending far beyond just "does it work?". Quality gates are designed to check across a range of quality dimensions, ensuring that each code change is not only correct but also reliable, secure, maintainable, and performant. Understanding these dimensions helps teams craft better gates and establish well-rounded quality criteria.

We do not unpack these different definitions of quality in a lot of detail, but do encourage you to explore other resources should you wish to understand the topics in more detail.

Functional Quality

What It Is: Ensures that the software behaves as intended according to defined requirements, acceptance criteria, and user stories. It focuses on validating that features work correctly from both a technical and user perspective, covering everything from individual code paths to complete user journeys. In a CI/CD context, functional quality is typically validated through automated tests at multiple levels, providing fast feedback that helps teams detect defects early and maintain confidence that new changes do not break existing behaviour as the system evolves.

How It's Validated:

- **Unit Tests**: Validate small code units in isolation.
- **Integration Tests**: Confirm modules work together correctly.
- **End-to-End Tests**: Simulate real user scenarios to verify functionality.

CI/CD Gate Example:

- Block merges if unit test pass rate < 95%.
- Require all critical test cases to pass before deploying to staging.

Performance Quality

What It Is: Assesses how well the system performs under various loads and usage conditions, speed, scalability, and responsiveness. It ensures that the application remains stable and efficient as demand increases, and that performance characteristics such as response times and throughput stay within acceptable limits.

Within a CI/CD pipeline, performance quality helps teams detect regressions early and prevents changes that may function correctly but degrade the overall user experience when the system is under real-world conditions.

How It's Validated:

- **Load Testing**: Simulate concurrent users or transactions.
- **Stress Testing**: Push system to limits to identify breaking points.
- **Response Time Monitoring**: Capture real-time performance metrics.

CI/CD Gate Example:

- Reject deployment if API latency exceeds 200ms under load.
- Flag regressions compared to previous performance benchmarks.

Security Quality

What It Is: Verifies that the application is resilient against security threats, vulnerabilities, and data leaks throughout its lifecycle. It focuses on identifying weaknesses in code, dependencies, and runtime behaviour that could be exploited by attackers, as well as ensuring sensitive data is properly protected.

In a CI/CD context, security quality is enforced through automated scanning and validation, allowing teams to detect and address risks early, reduce exposure, and maintain trust without slowing down delivery.

How It's Validated:

- **Static Application Security Testing (SAST)**: Analyses source code for vulnerabilities.
- **Dynamic Application Security Testing (DAST)**: Simulates attacks on a running application.

- **Dependency Scanning**: Identifies risks in third-party libraries.

CI/CD Gate Example:

- Fail the build if high-severity vulnerabilities are found in dependencies.
- Block promotion if OWASP Top 10 issues are detected during scanning.

Maintainability

What It Is: Focuses on how easily the software can be updated, extended, debugged, and understood by future developers. It emphasizes clean code, consistent structure, and manageable complexity so that teams can continue to evolve the system without introducing unnecessary risk or technical debt. In a CI/CD pipeline, maintainability quality is reinforced through automated analysis and standards enforcement, ensuring that speed of delivery does not come at the expense of long-term sustainability.

How It's Validated:

- **Code Complexity Metrics**: Cyclomatic complexity, duplication.
- **Linting/Static Analysis**: Enforces coding standards.
- **Code Coverage**: Measures how much code is tested.

CI/CD Gate Example:

- Reject PRs with >15% duplicated code.
- Require code coverage to stay above 80%.

Reliability

What It Is:: Measures the system's ability to function correctly under predefined conditions over time. It focuses on stability, fault tolerance, and predictable behaviour, ensuring that the software continues to function even as usage patterns change or components fail. Within CI/CD, reliability quality is reinforced by detecting flaky tests, monitoring error rates, and validating deployment behaviour, helping teams prevent unstable changes from progressing through the pipeline.

How It's Validated:

- **Flaky Test Detection**: Identifies intermittent failures.
- **Error Rate Monitoring**: Tracks exceptions or crashes.
- **Availability Metrics**: Uptime, mean time to failure (MTTF).

CI/CD Gate Example:

- Prevent promotion if known flaky tests are present.
- Alert teams if error rate exceeds threshold during canary deployment.

Portability and Compatibility

What It Is:: Determines whether the application can operate across environments, platforms, browsers, or infrastructure configurations. It reduces the risk of environment-specific defects by validating that the software can be built, deployed, and run reliably wherever it is intended to operate. In CI/CD pipelines, this quality dimension helps teams catch inconsistencies early, preventing "works on my machine" issues from reaching later stages or production.

How It's Validated:

- Cross-Browser Testing
- OS and Device Compatibility Suites
- Containerization Tests (e.g., Docker run consistency)

CI/CD Gate Example:

- Require validation in Chrome, Firefox, and Safari before merging.
- Block promotion if Docker image fails health checks on staging.

Usability

What It Is:: Addresses the user experience, how intuitive, accessible, and user-friendly the software is. Unlike other quality dimensions, usability can be more difficult to quantify and automate, and is often shaped by organizational standards and design maturity. In CI/CD, usability quality is typically validated through a combination of automated checks, such as accessibility and UI analysis, and informed human judgment, making it a complementary quality signal rather than a strict gating mechanism.

How It's Validated:

- UI/UX Testing Tools (e.g., Lighthouse)
- Accessibility Testing (A11y)
- Heuristic Review Automation

CI/CD Gate Example:

- Warn or block promotion if accessibility scores fall below WCAG 2.1 AA thresholds.

Summary Table

The table below summarizes the key dimensions of software quality and shows how each can be objectively validated and enforced through automated checks and quality gates within a CI/CD pipeline.

Quality Dimension	What It Is	How It's Validated in CI/CD
Functional Quality	Ensures the software behaves as expected according to defined requirements, acceptance criteria, and user stories.	Unit tests Integration tests End-to-end (E2E) tests
Performance Quality	Evaluates system speed, responsiveness, scalability, and behaviour under load.	Load testing Stress testing Response-time and throughput monitoring
Security Quality	Verifies resilience against vulnerabilities, attacks, and data exposure risks.	Static Application Security Testing (SAST) Dynamic Application Security Testing (DAST) Dependency and container scanning
Maintainability	Measures how easy the system is to understand, modify, and extend over time.	Code complexity and

		duplication metrics Linting and static analysis Code coverage analysis
Reliability	Assesses the system's ability to operate correctly and consistently over time.	Flaky test detection Error-rate monitoring Availability and stability metrics
Portability & Compatibility	Ensures the application runs consistently across environments, platforms, and systems.	Cross-browser testing OS and device compatibility testing Container and image validation
Usability	Evaluates how intuitive, accessible, and user-friendly the application is. Often harder to quantify and typically implemented as a complementary gate.	UI/UX analysis tools (e.g., Lighthouse) Accessibility (A11y) testing Automated heuristic evaluations

Aligning quality with business goals

In high-performing engineering teams, quality isn't just a technical metric, it's a strategic enabler. When quality efforts, including quality gates in CI/CD pipelines, are directly aligned with business goals, they help drive customer satisfaction, market competitiveness, regulatory compliance, and long-term sustainability.

Bridging this gap between engineering and business priorities ensures that quality initiatives deliver measurable value, not just internal reassurance.

Why Alignment Matters

Without alignment, quality initiatives risk becoming isolated "engineering concerns" that slow delivery or create tension between product, engineering, and leadership. With alignment, quality becomes a shared responsibility that:

- Reduces risk to revenue and reputation
- Improves time-to-market and customer experience
- Supports strategic objectives like innovation, scalability, and compliance

Mapping Quality to Business Objectives

The table below highlights how investing in quality gates and automated validation directly supports broader business objectives. By embedding quality into CI/CD pipelines, organizations translate technical excellence into measurable business outcomes, improving speed, trust, compliance, and long-term scalability while aligning teams around shared goals.

Business Goal	How Quality Supports It
Faster time-to-market	Automated quality gates reduce manual reviews and catch issues early
Customer trust and retention	High functional and performance quality prevents outages and bugs that drive churn
Regulatory compliance	Security and audit-related gates ensure adherence to laws like GDPR, SOC 2, HIPAA
Cost efficiency	Preventing defects early in CI/CD avoids expensive rework and reduces incident response time

Scalability and innovation	Maintainability and reliability gates ensure systems are built for future growth
Cross-team collaboration	Clear, codified quality expectations align engineering, QA, product, and security teams

Making the Link Tangible in CI/CD

To truly align, quality gates should be framed in business terms when discussed with leadership. For example:

Engineering Language	**Business Translation**
"All code changes must pass security scans."	"This prevents vulnerabilities from entering production, reducing breach risk."
"We enforce performance thresholds in our pipeline."	"This ensures our product remains fast and responsive as usage grows."
"We require 85% test coverage before release."	"This improves reliability and reduces incidents, saving support and dev time."

Adapting Quality Gates to Business Priorities

Business goals evolve, so should your quality strategy. For example:

- A startup might accept more risk and reduce gates to optimize speed.
- A regulated enterprise must prioritize compliance gates, even if it slows delivery.
- A growth-stage product may focus on scalability and performance gates.

CI/CD systems should be configurable to reflect these shifts:

- Use environments (e.g., staging, production) with different gate thresholds
- Add/remove gates based on business lifecycle phase
- Review gate effectiveness regularly in product/engineering planning cycles

Measuring Success

To gain sustained support for quality gates, teams must demonstrate their value in terms the business understands. While pipeline metrics and test results are useful internally, leadership engagement is driven by outcomes that reflect risk reduction, customer impact, and financial performance. Measuring and reporting quality gate effectiveness through business-aligned indicators helps shift the conversation from "process overhead" to "measurable value."

One of the clearest signals is **Mean Time to Recovery (MTTR).** By comparing MTTR before and after introducing automated quality gates, organizations can show how early detection and prevention reduce the time required to diagnose and recover from incidents. Faster recovery not only minimizes customer impact but also lowers operational costs and reduces the strain on engineering teams during outages.

Customer-reported incidents and defect leakage rates provide another powerful lens. A reduction in production defects reaching end users demonstrates that quality gates are successfully intercepting issues earlier in the delivery lifecycle. This directly correlates to improved customer trust, fewer support escalations, and stronger product reputation, outcomes that resonate well beyond engineering teams.

Change failure rate, one of the core DORA metrics, is especially valuable for connecting quality gates to delivery performance. Effective gates reduce the likelihood that a change will cause a production incident, rollback, or hotfix. Tracking this metric over time helps demonstrate that quality gates do not slow delivery, but instead enable teams to deploy more frequently with greater confidence and lower risk.

Another key measure is tying quality outcomes to **revenue impact** makes the value unmistakable. Major defects, outages, or security incidents often have direct financial consequences, from lost transactions and SLA penalties to reputational damage and customer churn. By correlating prevented failures or reduced downtime with estimated revenue protection, organizations can clearly show that quality gates are not just technical safeguards, but strategic business enablers.

Together, these measures help position quality gates as an investment in resilience, customer experience, and long-term business performance, making it far easier to secure buy-in from both leadership and delivery teams.

Quality as Business Value

When quality is treated as a business asset rather than a development afterthought, it enhances every dimension of product delivery. Quality gates in CI/CD are not just checks, they are automated expressions of what the business values most: trust, speed, reliability, and reputation.

By aligning your quality strategy with strategic business outcomes, you ensure that every test, scan, and review is driving the organization forward, not just keeping it safe.

Metrics that matter

In CI/CD pipelines, quality gates help enforce standards, but metrics make them measurable, actionable, and visible. By tracking the right metrics, teams can validate whether their gates are improving outcomes or just slowing delivery. More importantly, these metrics provide a shared language between engineering and the business, linking software health to organizational success.

Why Metrics Matter

- **Drive data-informed decisions**: Metrics help identify bottlenecks, technical debt, or quality regressions early.
- **Demonstrate value of quality gates**: With measurable outcomes, you can justify why certain gates exist and how they help.
- **Support continuous improvement**: Trends over time tell whether quality initiatives are improving or need adjustment.

Key Categories of Quality Metrics

Not all metrics are created equal, and it is essential to understand the purpose and context of each metric before using it to assess quality or performance. Metrics viewed in isolation can be misleading, often telling an incomplete, or even inaccurate, story about how teams and systems are truly performing.

A single data point rarely captures the complexity of modern software delivery. Instead, meaningful insights emerge only when multiple, complementary metrics are considered together across different categories, allowing patterns, trends, and trade-offs to become visible.

Equally important is the consistency of the data being measured. Metrics are only valuable when they are based on reliable, repeatable inputs. If teams interpret metrics differently, follow inconsistent processes, or use varying definitions for success, comparisons quickly lose their meaning.

For this reason, organizations must invest in aligning terminology, tooling, and measurement approaches across teams and pipelines. Establishing shared standards and common baselines ensures that metrics can be interpreted correctly, discussed constructively, and used to drive informed decisions rather than confusion or misalignment.

Ultimately, metrics should serve as signals for learning and improvement, not as blunt instruments for judgment. When used thoughtfully, consistently, and in combination, they provide a balanced view of quality, delivery health, and risk, forming a reliable foundation for effective quality gating and continuous improvement.

Throughout this book, we'll revisit a small set of core metrics in different contexts because the same signals often matter at multiple stages of a pipeline. To keep the narrative readable, we'll avoid re-explaining the basics each time and focus on what changes in meaning and usage from stage to stage.

Code Quality Metrics

These are metrics that can be used to measure the quality of the code itself and should ideally be run as early as possible on every single pull or merge request to ensure that the quality can be assessed early and remediated as soon as possible.

Metric	What It Measures	Why It Matters
Code coverage	Percentage of the codebase executed by automated tests	Indicates how well critical paths are validated and helps identify untested, higher-risk areas
Cyclomatic complexity	The number of independent paths through the code	Highlights overly complex or hard-to-maintain logic that is more prone to defects
Code duplication	Amount of repeated or copied code across the codebase	Increases maintenance effort and the likelihood of defects being replicated in multiple places
Linting violations	Count and severity of style or best-practice violations	Improves readability, consistency, and early detection of potential bugs or anti-patterns

Example Quality Gate: Block merges if code coverage drops below 85%.

Testing Metrics

These are metrics often applied to the testing itself and look at how different aspects of the code or application responded to adhering to the expected test outcomes. This information should be tracked every time tests are executed across all levels (unit, component, integration, end-to-end, etc)

Metric	What It Measures	Why It Matters
Test pass/fail rate	Proportion of tests that succeed versus fail in a pipeline run	Indicates whether recent changes have introduced functional regressions
Test execution time	Total time taken to run the automated test suite	Directly impacts CI/CD speed and the timeliness of developer feedback

Flaky test rate	Percentage of tests that fail intermittently without code changes	Affects trust in test results and can mask real defects
Regression failures	Failures in tests covering previously working functionality	Reveals unintended side effects of new changes and gaps in regression coverage

Example Quality Gate: Block deployment if critical regression tests fail or flaky rate >5%.

Pipeline Health Metrics

These are metrics that look at the health of the pipeline process itself and can identify how successfully the code is meeting the different pipeline criteria and possibly identify where improvements are needed in the code, testing or design itself. This information should be tracked in each pipeline execution and assessed over a certain period of time.

Metric	What It Measures	Why It Matters
Build Success Rate	Overall stability of CI/CD builds	Identifies recurring build failures and ensures confidence in automated pipelines
Build Duration	Time taken from commit to build completion	Helps pinpoint inefficiencies and optimize pipeline speed for faster feedback
Deployment Frequency	How often changes are successfully deployed	Reflects team agility and the ability to deliver value quickly to customers
Change Failure Rate	Frequency of post-deployment issues or rollbacks	Highlights risks in code quality, testing, or gate effectiveness and informs improvement efforts

Example Quality Gate: Alert if build duration increases 20% week over week.

Security and Compliance Metrics

These metrics assess the level of security or compliance risks are found in the code at any given time. But can also be tracked over a set period of time to identify long-term behaviours and attitude towards security and compliance violations.

Metric	What It Tells You
Vulnerabilities Detected	Security risks in custom or third-party code
Open CVEs (Critical/High)	Compliance gaps and breach risks
Secrets Scanning Results	Risk of exposed credentials or tokens

Example Quality Gate: Fail builds with critical security vulnerabilities or exposed secrets.

Performance and Reliability Metrics

These are metrics that look at how code and applications respond different at certain performance or load conditions. These can be measured either frequently at a code level using small-level load tests or towards the end of a deployment period against the broader system at a load or stress perspective to understand how the system and components respond in varying conditions.

Metric	What It Tells You
Response Time	Application performance from user perspective
Error Rate	Backend/service-level reliability
Uptime / Availability	Stability of the deployed product
MTTR (Mean Time to Recover)	Resilience in the face of production issues

Example Quality Gate: Block promotion if response time regression >10% from baseline.

Making Metrics Actionable

Effective use of quality metrics relies not just on collecting data, but on making it visible, actionable, and part of regular team conversations. Dashboards help visualize trends over time, making quality signals easy to understand and share across teams. Clearly defined thresholds turn these signals into enforceable quality gates, removing ambiguity around what constitutes a pass or fail. Alerts ensure that breaches of key thresholds are surfaced quickly, enabling teams to respond before issues escalate. Finally, reviewing these metrics during sprint reviews and retrospectives helps teams connect quality outcomes to delivery decisions, reinforcing a culture where data informs continuous improvement rather than reactive firefighting.

- **Dashboards**: Use tools like Grafana, DataDog, or SonarQube to visualize trends and share insights.
- **Thresholds**: Define pass/fail criteria clearly for automated gates.
- **Alerts**: Set up notifications when key thresholds are breached.
- **Retrospectives**: Review metrics in sprint reviews to connect quality and delivery outcomes.

Balancing Metrics

It's important to avoid "metric overload" or chasing vanity numbers. Focus on actionable, relevant, and team-aligned metrics:

- Don't chase 100% code coverage, ensure critical paths are covered.

- Use test duration not to punish slowness but to optimize parallelism or flakiness.
- Track security findings not just by count but by risk level and resolution time.

Summary Table

This table highlights how different categories of engineering and pipeline metrics translate technical signals into clear business value, helping organizations connect day-to-day delivery health with strategic outcomes.

Metric Type	Examples	Value to the Business
Code Quality	Coverage, complexity, duplication	Maintainability, cost reduction
Testing	Pass rate, execution time, flakiness	Release confidence, faster feedback
Pipeline Health	Build success, deploy frequency	Delivery speed and efficiency
Security	CVEs, secrets, dependency risk	Compliance, risk mitigation
Performance	Response time, error rate, uptime	User satisfaction, revenue protection

Tracking the right metrics, and acting on them, ensures quality gates are not roadblocks, but guardrails that help your teams move fast *and* safely.

Quality vs. velocity: Finding the balance

In software delivery, teams constantly face the challenge of balancing two competing priorities: shipping fast and shipping well. On one side is velocity, the need to deliver features, fixes, and updates quickly to stay ahead of market demands. On the other is quality, the need to ensure that those changes are reliable, secure, and maintainable.

Too much emphasis on velocity can lead to technical debt, production incidents, and customer dissatisfaction. Over-indexing on quality, on the other hand, can result in slower releases, bottlenecks, and missed business opportunities.

Finding the right balance is not just a technical goal, it's a strategic imperative.

The Tension Between Speed and Safety

This comparison highlights the natural tension between velocity and quality priorities, helping teams understand where balance is needed to deliver fast and sustainably.

Velocity Priority	**Quality Priority**
Rapid releases and quick feedback	Thorough validation and risk mitigation
"Fail fast" mindset	"Prevent failure" mindset
MVP-focused feature delivery	Sustainable and reliable systems
Shorter cycles, more iterations	Fewer defects, less rework

The trick isn't to pick one, it's to enable both, with the right processes, tooling, and cultural mindset.

How Quality Gates Help Balance the Two

Quality gates, when well-designed, are not blockers. They are automated enablers of safe speed. They inject quality checks at key points in the CI/CD pipeline, allowing teams to move fast without breaking things.

Quality Gates that Support Both Speed and Safety:

- **Static code analysis** during pull requests → catches issues early without manual review overhead
- **Automated test suites** in CI → ensures regressions are caught instantly
- **Security scanning** in build pipelines → prevents vulnerable code from being released
- **Performance baselines** in staging → ensures response times don't degrade unnoticed

The key is to ensure these gates are:

- **Fast** (optimized for performance)
- **Reliable** (low false positives/flaky failures)
- **Targeted** (focused on business-critical areas)

Practical Strategies for Balance

Below are some good strategies to follow that can align different metrics, gates and strategies to find a balance between speed and quality.

Shift Left, But Not Too Far Left

Start validating quality early (unit tests, linters, code reviews), but avoid duplicating checks at every stage. Balance depth with efficiency.

Prioritize Risk-Based Quality

Not all code needs the same scrutiny. Critical paths (e.g., authentication, payments) need higher standards than internal dashboards or MVP experiments.

Automate What Slows You Down

Manual QA, security checks, and performance tests can be bottlenecks. Automating these as quality gates ensures they happen without delay.

Set Clear, Context-Aware Thresholds

- Fast-moving teams may allow lower test coverage thresholds at first, then gradually raise them.
- Performance thresholds can be flexible in dev environments but strict in production pipelines.

Monitor, Adapt, and Iterate

Continuously review the effectiveness and impact of your quality gates. Are they:

- Catching defects before release?
- Blocking velocity unnecessarily?
- Scalable as the team/product grows?

If not, adjust thresholds, add exemptions, or reconfigure their timing in the pipeline.

The Metrics Lens

Balancing quality and velocity becomes easier when you're measuring both:

Velocity Metrics	**Quality Metrics**
Deployment frequency	Defect leakage rate
Lead time for changes	Test pass/failure rate
MTTR (Mean Time to Recover)	Flaky test rate
Cycle time	Security vulnerabilities resolved

Use these metrics to negotiate trade-offs, not escalate conflicts.

Culture is the Final Balancer

Technology and metrics help, but mindset is essential. Organizations that successfully balance quality and delivery speed tend to foster a culture where failures are treated as learning opportunities rather than blame exercises, allowing teams to improve systems instead of hiding problems.

Quality is considered early in the design process, with QA and testing expertise influencing architectural and product decisions rather than being applied only after development is complete. Developers are empowered to take ownership of both the code they write and the quality outcomes it produces, while close collaboration between product, security, and engineering ensures that quality gates reflect shared goals rather than siloed concerns. Together, these cultural practices transform quality gates from restrictive controls into trusted enablers of continuous delivery.

Organizations that balance quality and speed well tend to:

- Treat failures as learning opportunities, not blame games
- Involve QA early in design, not just post-development
- Empower developers to own both code and quality
- Encourage collaboration between product, security, and engineering

The Balance is a Moving Target

There is no static "right" balance between quality and velocity, it shifts with your:

- Product maturity
- Market pressures
- Customer expectations
- Team structure

What matters is having a CI/CD pipeline that is flexible enough to adapt, with quality gates that protect what matters most without slowing down what doesn't.

When done right, quality doesn't reduce velocity, it amplifies confidence, accelerates recovery, and builds long-term momentum.

Conclusion: Quality is a reflection of the entire organisation

In this chapter, we explored what quality means in the context of modern CI/CD pipelines, reframing it as a set of measurable, multi-dimensional signals rather than a vague or subjective concept. By breaking quality down into functional, performance, security, reliability, maintainability, and usability dimensions, we established a common language for discussing quality and a foundation for making it visible and actionable within the delivery process. Most importantly, we showed that quality in CI/CD is not achieved through a single checkpoint, but through continuous validation applied at the right time, in the right way, to reduce risk while enabling speed.

With this understanding in place, the next chapter shifts from *what quality is* to *how it is enforced*. We will explore the different types of quality gates that can be implemented within CI/CD pipelines, examining where they fit, what they protect against, and how they vary across stages of delivery. This transition marks the point where quality moves from theory into practice, where abstract quality principles are translated into concrete, automated controls that guide software safely from commit to production.

Types of Quality Gates

Purpose of chapter: In this chapter we look at the different types of quality gates that can be set up, where they apply in the delivery process, and what signals they use to enforce quality. We focus on why specific gates matter and how to use them effectively, setting a foundation for the deeper, implementation-focused chapters that follow.

This chapter builds on the earlier foundations by surveying the major gate categories and the kinds of evidence they rely on (tests, coverage, security findings, and performance signals). The focus is on how to think about placement and purpose, so you can later implement each gate with the right level of strictness and the least friction.

Pre-commit and commit-level checks

Pre-commit and commit-level checks are the first line of defence in a CI/CD pipeline. These gates are designed to catch issues early, before code even hits the main branch or enters the CI environment. By embedding quality at this stage, teams significantly reduce the cost of defects, prevent bad code from spreading downstream, and maintain fast feedback cycles.

- Pre-commit checks run *before* a developer's changes are committed to the local repository.
- Commit-level checks are triggered *after* a commit, often in the form of server-side validations such as Git hooks or remote repository checks.

Both types aim to enforce coding standards and correctness at the earliest possible stage, acting as automated quality gatekeepers on every change.

Examples of Pre-Commit Checks

These typically run locally on the developer's machine using tools like Git hooks or plugins:

- **Linting and Code Formatting**: Enforces code style consistency (e.g., using a variety of linting tools like ESLint, Prettier, Black, or Pylint).
- **Static Code Analysis**: Scans code for common bugs, complexity, and security issues (e.g., SonarLint, Flake8).
- **Secrets and Credential Scanning**: Detects hardcoded API keys or passwords (e.g., GitLeaks, TruffleHog).
- **Test Stubs or Unit Test Runs**: Runs a small set of unit tests to catch glaring issues before committing.
- **Spell Check or Doc Validation**: Ensures documentation or commit messages meet standards.

Examples of Commit-Level Checks

These checks are typically enforced by source control or CI platforms when a code commit is made – following successful validation by any pre-commit checks:

- **Signed Commits**: Verifies that commits are GPG-signed for authenticity and traceability.
- **Commit Message Validation**: Enforces conventional commit rules (e.g., "feat:", "fix:", "chore:") for consistent changelogs and automation.
- **Change Size or Scope Checks**: Blocks commits that are too large or lack associated issue references.
- **License or IP Scanning**: Ensures committed code doesn't violate licensing policies (e.g., FOSSA, Black Duck).

Why They Matter

- **Catches problems early**, reducing cost of fixing bugs later.
- **Improves developer discipline** and consistency across teams.
- **Reduces CI noise**, ensuring that only valid code gets pushed into shared branches.
- **Encourages faster feedback loops**, which is critical in agile environments.

Best Practices

Below are some best practices to consider when looking to implement commit-level checks:

- Don't overload pre-commit hooks, keep them fast to avoid developer frustration.
- Use tooling that works cross-platform and can be easily adopted across your team.
- Enforce checks through pull request policies or branch protections in your SCM.
- Provide clear remediation steps if checks fail, frictionless experience encourages adoption.

- Automate setup with shared tooling configs in the repository (e.g., `.pre-commit-config.yaml`).

Pre-Commit Checks and Developer Experience

Pre-commit checks are not just about preventing defects; they're also about improving developer experience by catching issues immediately, in context, and with clear remediation steps. When implemented thoughtfully, they raise quality without adding meaningful friction.

Build verification gates

Once code is committed and pushed, it moves into the build phase of the CI/CD pipeline. Here, build verification gates serve as critical quality checkpoints that determine whether the codebase is stable, valid, and safe enough to proceed to further stages like testing, deployment, or release.

These gates ensure that the software can compile, run, and integrate cleanly, and that key quality criteria have not been violated in the process.

What Are Build Verification Gates?

Build verification gates are automated CI checks that validate the integrity of a build right after code is pushed. If any check fails, the pipeline stops immediately and returns actionable feedback.

Common Build Verification Gates

Below are some of the common types of build verification gates you will find and their intended purpose:

Compilation or Build Success

- Verifies that the code compiles or builds correctly.
- Ensures all dependencies are resolved, and no syntax errors are introduced.
- Applies to all languages and compiled frameworks.

Dependency Checks

- Scans for known vulnerabilities in third-party libraries (e.g., OWASP Dependency-Check, Snyk, Dependabot).
- Flags outdated or deprecated packages.

Unit Test Execution

- Runs all unit tests to catch regressions in isolated logic.
- Can include coverage thresholds to enforce test quality (e.g., 80% minimum).

Static Code Analysis

- Applies in-depth analysis tools thar scan the code and look for any easily identifiable concerns.
- Checks for code smells, complexity issues, and maintainability violations.

Code Coverage Validation

- Ensures a minimum percentage of the code is covered by tests.
- Helps teams identify untested or risky areas of the application.

Artifact Integrity Checks

- Verifies that generated artifacts (JARs, Docker images, binaries) are complete, signed, and versioned correctly.
- May include checksum validation or reproducibility checks.

Build Time Limits

- Ensures that the build does not exceed an acceptable duration, signalling inefficiency or potential issues (e.g., infinite loops, flaky dependencies).

Why Build Verification Gates Matter

The below are key reasons why teams should consider introducing build verification gates into their software delivery process:

- **Prevent broken builds** from advancing to test or staging environments.
- **Catch regressions and instability** caused by recent commits.
- **Ensure confidence** in each integration point, allowing for rapid feedback.
- **Maintain consistency** in build artifacts and outputs across environments.
- **Protect the CI pipeline's downstream stages** (e.g., deployments, automated testing) from being triggered unnecessarily.

Real-World Failures Prevented by Build Gates

- Stopping a deployment due to an expired dependency or corrupted artifact.

- Halting release because a key service module fails to compile with updated interfaces.
- Catching a drop in test coverage due to rushed code before the team merges it.
- Detecting a license-violating open-source library before packaging it into a customer build.

Best Practices for Build Gates

Below are some bet practices to consider when looking into implement Build Gates into your process:

- Make all gates automated and deterministic, no manual intervention required.
- Fail fast and provide clear, actionable feedback to developers.
- Use caching and parallelism to keep builds fast and efficient.
- Version and store build artifacts for traceability and reproducibility.
- Treat a failed build gate as a priority, resolve it before continuing work.

The Build Is the Contract

In CI/CD, the build is the contract between developers and the system. If that contract is violated, through unstable code, failed tests, or insecure dependencies, the system must reject it. Build verification gates ensure that only high-quality, production-worthy code makes it past this first serious checkpoint.

Test gates (unit, integration, E2E)

After code has successfully passed build verification, it moves into a critical phase of validation: automated testing. This is where test gates play a pivotal role.

These gates ensure that new code behaves as expected and that it hasn't broken existing functionality. They help establish trust in the pipeline by providing clear, automated feedback on the functional correctness of the application across multiple levels of abstraction.

What Are Test Gates?

Test gates are automated checks that run one or more test suites (unit, integration, and/or end-to-end) and stop the pipeline on failure. Each layer provides a different kind of assurance, from fast code-level validation to end-to-end confidence in real user flows.

Type of Test	Scope	Speed	Purpose
Unit	Individual functions or methods	Fast	Catch logic bugs early
Integration	Interactions between modules or services	Moderate	Detect broken connections or contracts
End-to-End (E2E)	Full user workflows and system interactions	Slower	Validate real-world behaviour across systems

Test gates enforce the requirement that each change must pass all applicable levels of automated tests before proceeding further in the pipeline.

Key Types of Test Gates

Below is a high-level view of the different types of testing gates that focus on different aspects of testing the code, components and the entire solution.

Unit Test Gates

- Run fast, isolated tests on individual components or functions.
- Often paired with coverage thresholds (e.g., "must retain 80% test coverage").
- **Tools:** JUnit, xUnit, Mocha, Jest, NUnit, etc.

Integration Test Gates

- Validate interactions between components, modules, or external services.
- Ensure APIs, databases, queues, and contracts are working together correctly.
- **Tools:** Postman, pytest, Spring Test, TestContainers, etc.

E2E Test Gates

- Simulate real user scenarios from start to finish, across the UI and backend.
- Catch UI regressions, broken flows, or misconfigured environments.
- **Tools:** Cypress, Selenium, Playwright, TestCafe, etc.

Failing a Test Gate Should Mean: STOP.

Test gates are non-negotiable quality barriers. If any test suite fails, the pipeline must halt. Failing tests often indicate:

- Regressions introduced by recent code changes
- Incomplete features or incorrect assumptions
- Flaky test code (which also needs to be addressed)

By catching these early, teams avoid costly production incidents and protect end-user experience.

Test Gate Use Cases

- Catching a business logic bug missed by a unit test, via an integration test
- Validating a login workflow from the front-end to the database via E2E tests
- Ensuring a service's API still conforms to its contract after a refactor
- Detecting a race condition between services due to parallel test execution

Best Practices for Test Gates

- **Fail fast, but diagnose easily**: Output should clearly indicate which test failed and why.
- **Run tests in parallel** where possible to reduce CI time.
- **Categorize and prioritize**: Fast-running, high-value tests should block earlier in the pipeline.
- Use **test tagging** or **dynamic pipelines** to run only relevant tests per change.
- Regularly **review and retire brittle or flaky test,** they erode confidence in the test gate.
- Invest in **test data management and stable environments** for integration/E2E reliability.

Balancing Depth vs. Speed

While unit tests are lightweight and fast, integration and E2E tests are heavier. This makes test gate design a balancing act:

- Don't delay all test types until the end, introduce early smoke or sanity tests.

- Consider parallel pipelines or staged testing (e.g., run unit tests early, full E2E tests later).
- Fail early and cheaply with lightweight checks before running the expensive ones.

Test Gates Build Confidence in Every Commit

Test gates serve as automated reviewers, continuously validating that every change meets the expected behaviour at every layer. When integrated well, they improve developer confidence, reduce manual testing effort, and become a cornerstone of reliable, scalable CI/CD pipelines.

Code quality/static analysis gates

Beyond compiling code and passing tests, one of the most crucial, yet often overlooked quality gate categories is code quality and static analysis. These gates are designed to analyse the structure, readability, maintainability, and security of code before it ever gets deployed or even tested at runtime.

Static analysis gates automate early feedback on code health, and help enforce coding standards and prevent technical debt from accumulating.

What Are Static Analysis Gates?

Static analysis gates evaluate code without executing it, using rules and metrics to flag maintainability, correctness, and security concerns. In this chapter we treat them as a gate category; the dedicated static analysis chapter goes deeper into tooling, configuration, and implementation patterns.

They typically check for:

- Code smells
- Complexity and duplication
- Security vulnerabilities (e.g., injection risks)
- Maintainability issues
- Violations of coding standards

Why These Gates Matter

Even if your code compiles and passes tests, it may still be fragile, overly complex, or insecure. Static analysis helps identify:

- Hard-to-read or unmaintainable logic
- Poor design patterns or anti-patterns
- Unused or redundant code
- Critical security flaws (e.g., SQL injection, buffer overflows)

By adding this gate early in the CI pipeline, you reduce long-term technical debt and make future enhancements safer and faster.

Tools Commonly Used

Below are some of the most commonly used tools that can perform these static analysis scans. This is not an exhaustive list, but simply some of the more popular options you can find.

- **SonarQube/Veracode/Deepsource**: Industry standard tools offering deep code insight, maintainability ratings, and support for many languages.
- **ESLint / TSLint**: JavaScript and TypeScript linters enforcing code consistency.

- **Checkstyle / PMD / SpotBugs**: For Java, providing rules for formatting, complexity, and potential bugs.
- **Bandit**: Static analysis for Python with a security focus.
- **CodeQL**: GitHub's code analysis engine that queries source code like a database to find vulnerabilities.

These tools often integrate directly with all CI platforms to enforce real-time feedback loops.

Security and Compliance Checks

Modern static analysis also includes security scanners to identify:

- Hardcoded secrets or credentials
- Use of unsafe APIs
- Dependency vulnerabilities
- License compliance issues

Tools like SonarQube's Security Hotspots, Snyk, and OWASP Dependency-Check fall into this expanded static analysis category.

Common Static Gate Criteria

These are some quality thresholds you might enforce:

- Maintainability rating must be A or B
- No new critical or blocker issues
- Code duplication under 5%
- Code coverage not reduced by the commit
- Cyclomatic complexity stays under a given limit
- No security hotspots introduced

Failing any of these conditions results in the pipeline blocking the change from progressing further.

What Happens Without These Gates?

When these gates are absent from the build process, the following risks could likely surface:

- Code becomes difficult to test or refactor, stalling delivery velocity
- Teams inherit legacy debt they're afraid to touch
- Developers unknowingly introduce security vulnerabilities
- Critical bugs hide behind layers of unreadable or duplicated logic

Even small violations, if ignored consistently, compound into a system that's expensive to maintain and fragile to evolve.

Best Practices

Below are some best practices to consider when implementing static gates into your process:

- Start small: don't enforce all rules immediately; phase them in as your team matures.
- Use "new code" quality gates, enforce stricter rules on new or changed code, not legacy.
- Set up pull request comments or dashboards for visibility.
- Educate the team on what violations mean and how to fix them.
- Combine static analysis results with your code review workflow to reinforce shared standards.

Measuring Code Quality Is Measuring Dev Health

Code quality gates are about more than style, they measure the sustainability, readability, and reliability of the software you're building. And in CI/CD, that means catching issues before they slow down the entire pipeline.

Security gates

With software security a growing concern in an ever more interconnected and vulnerable landscape, security can no longer be an afterthought or a separate phase, it must be baked into every step of software delivery. That's where security gates come in: automated controls embedded within the CI/CD pipeline to catch vulnerabilities early, reduce risk, and enforce compliance.

What Are Security Gates?

Security gates in CI/CD are automated checks that evaluate software for known and unknown vulnerabilities using a combination of static, dynamic, and dependency analysis techniques. They help enforce secure coding practices, block insecure code from being deployed, and reduce the attack surface of your applications.

Security gates typically include:

- SAST (Static Application Security Testing)
- DAST (Dynamic Application Security Testing)
- Dependency / Software Composition Analysis (SCA)
- Secret Scanning
- Infrastructure-as-Code (IaC) Security Scanning

Below these are outlined in more detail.

SAST – Static Application Security Testing

- Analyses source code, bytecode, or binaries without running the application.
- Identifies code-level vulnerabilities like SQL injection, XSS, insecure API usage, and hardcoded credentials.
- Fast and integrated early in the pipeline.

DAST – Dynamic Application Security Testing

- Tests running applications to find vulnerabilities in real-time behaviour.
- Simulates attacks from an external perspective (e.g., a hacker probing your app).
- Useful for identifying issues like broken authentication, insecure session management, and misconfigurations.

Dependency Scanning / SCA

- Scans libraries and dependencies for known vulnerabilities (CVEs).
- Checks for outdated packages, transitive risks, and license issues.
- Should be enforced at every build to avoid publishing exploitable components.

Secrets Detection

- Identifies accidentally committed secrets, tokens, passwords, or keys.
- Blocks secrets from reaching shared repositories or pipelines.

IaC Security Scanning

- Analyses Terraform, CloudFormation, or Kubernetes manifests for insecure configurations.
- Blocks deployments with risky defaults like open ports, broad IAM roles, or missing encryption.

When to Enforce Security Gates?

- **SAST and Secrets Scanning**: As early as pre-commit or during build.
- **Dependency Scanning**: At build and regularly throughout the SDLC.
- **DAST and IaC Scanning**: After deployment to test/staging environments.

Each of these gates can be triggered at different stages of the pipeline to shift security left, while still covering runtime behaviours later in the pipeline.

Benefits of Security Gates

Introducing security gates early in the delivery lifecycle helps teams catch issues when they are cheapest to fix, most visible to developers, and least risky to the business.

- Prevent security flaws before they're deployed
- Reduce cost and complexity of late-stage fixes
- Enable compliance with standards like OWASP Top 10, NIST, PCI DSS, ISO 27001
- Increase developer awareness of secure coding practices
- Catch misconfigurations and vulnerable dependencies before they become liabilities.

Best Practices

The following best practices help teams embed security seamlessly into CI/CD pipelines while keeping feedback fast, actionable, and trusted.

- Automate and integrate security scans into every CI/CD run.
- Use baseline thresholds to block builds with high-severity vulnerabilities.
- Fail fast: notify developers immediately when risks are found.
- Whitelist known safe exceptions and suppress false positives intelligently.
- Regularly update scanners to keep up with the latest CVEs and rule sets.
- Visualize security posture in dashboards for transparency and risk tracking.

What Happens Without Security Gates?

Without security gates embedded in the CI/CD pipeline, organizations are forced into a reactive posture where risks are discovered too late and at the highest possible cost. Instead of preventing issues early, teams spend time firefighting avoidable incidents, scrambling to meet compliance requirements, and responding to vulnerabilities only after they've reached production. Over time, this erodes customer trust, increases legal and regulatory exposure, and creates reputational damage that far outweighs the effort of building security in from the start.

- Vulnerabilities slip into production unnoticed.
- Teams reactively firefight incidents that could've been prevented.
- Compliance becomes manual and painful.

- You risk customer trust, legal penalties, and reputational damage.

Modern breaches often stem from basic oversights, known vulnerabilities, leaked secrets, or unsafe third-party code. Security gates are your automated first line of defence.

Security gates are foundational to DevSecOps, integrating security as a shared responsibility across development and operations. When security checks are part of the same automated system that runs tests and builds, they become unavoidable, consistent, and scalable.

Performance/regression gates

While functional correctness is essential, it's not enough for software to *work,* it must also *perform well* under expected loads and conditions. That's where performance and regression gates come in. These quality gates evaluate the non-functional behaviour of an application, ensuring that performance characteristics like speed, scalability, and responsiveness are preserved as the software evolves.

These gates help teams avoid releasing code that, while correct, introduces performance degradation or instability in production environments.

What Are Performance/Regression Gates?

Performance and regression gates are automated controls in the CI/CD pipeline that measure and enforce performance thresholds. These checks are designed to:

- Detect degradation in response times, throughput, or latency
- Catch resource overuse (CPU, memory, I/O)
- Identify regressions introduced by recent code changes
- Simulate real-world traffic to validate scalability
- Maintain SLAs and SLOs

These gates help answer the question: *"Did this change make things slower, heavier, or less scalable?"*

Key Metrics Evaluated

Performance gates typically track:

Metric	What It Measures	Why It Matters
Response time (avg, p95/p99)	How long the system takes to respond to requests under load	Reflects user-perceived performance and helps catch latency regressions early
Throughput	Number of requests or users handled per unit of time	Indicates system capacity and efficiency under expected or peak load
Error rate	Percentage of failed or erroneous requests	Signals stability issues that may surface only under load
CPU utilization	Percentage of CPU resources consumed	Helps detect compute saturation and scaling limitations
Memory utilization	Amount of memory used during execution	Identifies memory leaks or inefficient resource usage
Startup and boot time	Time taken for services to start and become ready	Affects deploy speed, auto-scaling behaviour, and recovery time

GC pauses	Duration and frequency of garbage collection pauses	Highlights runtime inefficiencies that can cause latency spikes
Database query time and load	Execution time and concurrency of database queries	Exposes backend bottlenecks that often dominate end-to-end performance

These metrics can be compared against baseline benchmarks or previous build data to detect regressions.

Common Tools for Performance Gates

Below is a list of common tools that can be used to assist with measuring software performance and build in the appropriate gates:

- **JMeter / Gatling / k6**: Load testing tools to simulate traffic and measure response time
- **Locust**: Python-based load test framework
- **Artillery**: Lightweight performance testing for HTTP and WebSocket APIs
- **New Relic / Datadog / Dynatrace**: Integrated APM tools for runtime observability
- **Lighthouse / WebPageTest**: For front-end and browser-based performance validation
- **Prometheus + Grafana**: Custom metric monitoring and threshold alerting

These tools can run synthetic tests or monitor live metrics during test/staging deployments.

Where These Gates Fit in the Pipeline

Performance gates are usually integrated at later stages of the CI/CD pipeline due to their resource-intensive nature:

Types of Quality Gates

1. Post-deployment to a test/staging environment
2. Pre-release validation stage
3. Nightly or scheduled performance testing

In high-performance systems, you may even run per-commit smoke performance tests to detect major regressions early.

What Happens Without These Gates?

Without effective performance gates in place, teams lose early warning signals about system degradation, allowing avoidable performance issues to reach production and turning CI/CD pipelines from confidence builders into sources of risk.

- Releases that introduce performance bottlenecks or unscalable code go unnoticed
- Customer-facing apps become slower, leading to poor user experience
- Infrastructure costs increase due to inefficient resource usage
- Teams waste time firefighting performance issues in production
- Trust in CI/CD declines as releases become risky

Without performance gates, velocity often comes at the expense of system health and customer satisfaction.

Balancing Performance Testing with Delivery Speed

Performance tests can take time and be costly to run. To keep your pipeline efficient:

- Run quick sanity performance tests early in the pipeline (e.g., startup time, API latency)

- Run full load and soak tests periodically (e.g., nightly, before releases)
- Use baseline thresholds to detect regressions without blocking on minor variance
- Use performance budgets, predefined maximums for load time, latency, etc.
- Visualize trends to track gradual degradation over time

Best Practices

To ensure performance gates provide meaningful protection without slowing delivery, teams should adopt a set of disciplined best practices that balance realism, consistency, and continuous feedback across the pipeline.

- Define realistic baselines and SLOs per service or endpoint
- Use version control for test scripts to track performance assumptions
- Run performance tests in consistent, isolated environments
- Tag performance issues in your backlog to address them like bugs
- Integrate alerts for performance drift post-deployment using APM

From Reactive to Proactive Performance

Performance gates move teams from reactive firefighting to proactive optimization. They create a safety net that ensures code changes do not sacrifice speed, responsiveness, or scalability.

By continuously validating performance as part of CI/CD, teams can deliver fast *and* reliable software.

Manual approval gates (e.g., human review in CD)

Even in highly automated CI/CD, some releases benefit from explicit human judgment, particularly for production, regulated environments, or high-risk changes. Manual approval gates create a deliberate pause where a designated approver decides whether the release should proceed.

Manual approval gates serve as a final checkpoint to ensure that what's being delivered aligns with business, compliance, and operational expectations.

What Are Manual Approval Gates?

Manual approval gates require one or more designated individuals (for example, a release manager, QA lead, or product owner) to approve a deployment before it continues.

These gates are typically enforced:

- Before deploying to production or regulated environments
- When promoting artifacts to a higher-level environment (e.g., staging → prod)
- As part of go-live checklists or change control processes

In most CI/CD platforms (GitHub Actions, GitLab CI, Azure DevOps, etc.), these are implemented using approval steps, environments with checks, or manual intervention jobs.

Why Manual Gates Matter

Even in a fully automated pipeline, there are scenarios where automation can't fully capture:

- **Business context** (e.g., feature readiness, coordination with a marketing release)
- **Risk-based decisions** (e.g., known issues, last-minute fixes)
- **Compliance or regulatory obligations** (e.g., sign-offs required by auditors)
- **Customer impact considerations** (e.g., downtime coordination, peak traffic times)

Manual gates introduce a layer of accountability and flexibility, giving teams time to validate that everything is in order before critical steps.

Common Use Cases

Below are some common use cases where manual gates will often apply and be required for teams:

- Release approval by a product or delivery manager
- Change advisory board (CAB) approvals for regulated deployments
- QA or test lead review of test results in pre-production
- Security team sign-off for high-sensitivity applications
- Business readiness check before a public launch

Who Should Approve?

Approvers are typically individuals who:

- Understand the scope and impact of the release

- Can interpret test results, release notes, or exception reports
- Are accountable for stakeholder communication and coordination

Roles often involved include:

- Release Managers
- DevOps Engineers
- QA Leads
- Product Owners or Managers
- Security Officers
- Business Representatives

Trade-offs and Risks

While manual gates enhance control, they can also:

- Slow down delivery if not well-coordinated
- Introduce bottlenecks in otherwise automated workflows
- Encourage rubber-stamping if approval becomes routine
- Delay fixes for production incidents

To avoid this, manual gates should be used strategically, not universally. Automate wherever possible and reserve manual review for high-risk, compliance-critical, or customer-impacting deployments.

Best Practices

Manual approval gates can be powerful safeguards when used intentionally, but without clear structure they quickly become bottlenecks, these best practices help ensure approvals add accountability and confidence rather than delay and ceremony.

- Clearly define when manual gates are required and why
- Limit approvals to appropriate environments only (typically staging → production)
- Use templated checklists to ensure consistency and thoroughness
- Document who approved what and when for traceability
- Monitor approval gate response times to avoid unnecessary slowdowns
- Encourage accountable, not performative, approvals

A Human Layer of Confidence

Manual approval gates aren't about slowing things down, they're about adding confidence where automation isn't enough. In fast-moving teams, these gates can serve as critical alignment points between engineering, business, and operations.

They remind us that, while automation accelerates delivery, software is still a human endeavour, and some decisions still need a human touch.

Policy gates (e.g., branch protection, role-based approvals)

Policy gates enforce "how work happens" in your delivery system: who may change what, what reviews are required, and which conditions must be met before merging or deploying.

These gates don't just prevent mistakes, they enforce discipline, promote transparency, and protect against risky or unauthorized actions.

What Are Policy Gates?

Policy gates are automated (and sometimes manual) rules that prevent changes from progressing unless governance requirements are satisfied, typically enforced in source control, CI, or deployment tooling.

They typically operate at the source control level (Git), CI pipeline level, or in deployment tools.

Key Examples of Policy Gates

Branch Protection Rules

Prevent direct changes to important branches in the chosen code repository tooling (e.g., main, release) by enforcing:

- Mandatory pull request (PR) reviews
- Status checks (e.g., tests must pass before merge)
- Linear history (no force pushes or merges without PRs)
- Required code owner approval
- Enforcement of signed commits

Role-Based Access and Approvals

Define who is allowed to trigger deployments, approve pull requests, or manage specific environments based on roles such as:

- Developers
- QA/Testers

- Security Analysts
- Release Managers
- Admins

Ensures separation of duties and aligns with compliance or audit requirements (e.g., SOX, HIPAA).

Mandatory PR Templates and Checklists

Policies that enforce structured and complete pull requests:

- Linked ticket or issue required
- Justification for changes
- Security or testing notes
- Business impact statement

Helps ensure consistency and review readiness.

Required Pipeline Conditions

Policies that prevent builds or deployments unless all the following are true:

- Test coverage threshold is met
- Linting and formatting pass
- All secrets checks are cleared
- All approvers have signed off

These gates automate enforcement of your team's standards.

Artifact Promotion Rules

Prevent untested or unsigned artifacts from being promoted across environments. For example:

- Only artifacts signed and tested in staging can go to production
- Artifacts must pass a vulnerability scan before being published

Why Policy Gates Matter

Without enforced policies:

- Unsafe or unreviewed code can be merged or deployed
- Production deployments can occur without traceability
- Individuals may bypass critical testing or security processes
- You increase the risk of human error, security violations, or compliance breaches

Policy gates create clear expectations, guardrails, and enforceable standards that protect both your product and your people.

Common Platforms That Support Policy Gates

- **GitHub**: Branch protection rules, required reviews, status checks, CODEOWNERS, role-based environment approvals
- **GitLab**: Protected branches/environments, required approvers, pipeline policies
- **Azure DevOps**: Branch policies, required reviewer configuration, RBAC on pipelines and environments
- **Bitbucket**: Merge checks, branch restrictions, required builds

These tools offer GUI and YAML-based enforcement, giving teams flexibility in how they define and apply policies.

Best Practices

Policy gates provide guardrails for safe and consistent code delivery, these best practices ensure they guide development effectively without creating unnecessary friction or bottlenecks.

- Apply branch protection to critical branches (main, release, hotfix)
- Use CODEOWNERS to assign reviewers based on file or feature ownership
- Enforce that all pipelines pass before allowing a merge or promotion
- Define policies as code (e.g., in GitHub repo settings or GitLab .gitlab-ci.yml)
- Review policy gate configurations regularly as teams and projects evolve
- Use policy gates not to block progress, but to guide teams toward safe delivery

When Policy Gates Are Missing…

Without policy gates in place, teams risk introducing errors and security issues into production, while also losing traceability and confidence in their delivery process.

- Production outages may stem from unreviewed changes
- Sensitive data or credentials may be leaked due to missing checks
- Teams struggle to trust the process, leading to finger-pointing and fire drills

- Compliance audits become difficult due to poor traceability

Policy gates provide the structure and accountability needed in any mature software delivery organization.

Policy as Code, Governance by Design

Policy gates embody the principles of "policy as code" and governance by design, building safeguards directly into the tools and workflows developers use every day. When implemented well, these gates foster speed with safety, collaboration with clarity, and compliance with confidence.

They don't slow you down, they make sure you're going the right way, fast.

Conclusion: Quality Gates can be applied everywhere

In this chapter, we explored the various types of quality gates that can be applied throughout a CI/CD pipeline, highlighting how different gates serve different purposes at different stages of delivery. From early commit-level checks to test, security, performance, and environment-specific gates, we saw that effective quality gating is not about a single control point, but about layering protections that progressively reduce risk as changes move closer to production. By understanding where each type of gate fits and what kind of quality signal it enforces, teams can design pipelines that provide fast feedback early while applying stricter controls only where they add the most value.

With this broader landscape established, the next chapter takes a deeper dive into one of the earliest and most foundational forms of quality gating: static code analysis. We will examine how static analysis gates help enforce coding standards, detect defects and vulnerabilities early, and improve maintainability before code is ever executed. This chapter will move from conceptual understanding into practical application, showing how static code analysis becomes a powerful first line of defence in building high-quality, scalable CI/CD pipelines.

Implementing Static Code Analysis Gates

Purpose of Chapter: In this chapter we unpack the nature of static code analysis gates further. Looking into more detail at how they work, understanding their usage, what they need to measure and show to best implement them effectively. We will also look at the tools involved in these stages a little more and some of the pipeline scripts that can help define your quality gates in these phases of the deployment process.

Now that we've surveyed the main types of quality gates, we'll start going deeper into how to implement them. We'll begin with static code analysis - one of the fastest, most scalable ways to catch defects, maintainability issues, and security risks before code ever runs.

What is Static Code Analysis?

Static code analysis involves automatically reviewing code against predefined rules and patterns without running the software. This is often done using linters, style checkers, complexity analysers, and security scanners.

Static code analysis gates fail the pipeline if critical issues are found, such as:

- Unused or unreachable code
- Violations of naming or formatting standards
- High cyclomatic complexity
- Code duplication
- Unsafe patterns (e.g., SQL injection risks, hard-coded credentials)

Why Use Static Analysis Gates?

Static gates are very good at catching issues close to when the code is written, allowing fer quick and inexpensive remediation that helps improve delivery speed and quality later on.

- Catch issues early, before they become bugs or vulnerabilities
- Enforce consistent coding standards across teams
- Reduce technical debt accumulation
- Improve readability and maintainability
- Identify security risks before code is even deployed

Because they run quickly and don't require deployment, static gates are ideal pre-build or commit-level checks.

Common Static Analysis Tools by Language

There are a variety of tools that can do this effectively – most of the chapter opensource solutions are language specific while for teams and organisations that that require cross-language coverage in this area – there are a large number of professional tools that can be utilised.

Language	Tools
Java	SonarQube, PMD, Checkstyle, SpotBugs
JavaScript/TypeScript	ESLint, TSLint, Prettier
Python	pylint, flake8, Bandit
C#/.NET	Roslyn Analysers, StyleCop, FxCop
Go	golangci-lint, go vet
C/C++	cppcheck, Clang Static Analyzer
Cross-language	SonarQube, Codacy, Semgrep, CodeClimate, DeepSource

When Static Gates Are Missing…

Static gates are very good at catching some important issues early and when they are missing or not operating effectively, you run the risk of the following challenges:

- Style and quality become inconsistent across the codebase
- Small mistakes go unnoticed, leading to production defects
- Security vulnerabilities may creep in unnoticed (e.g., via insecure coding)
- Time is wasted on manual reviews for issues that could be automated
- Refactoring becomes difficult due to unstructured or duplicated code

Best Practices

Below are some best practices to consider when implementing static gates:

- Enforce static checks on every pull request
- Classify issues (e.g., Blocker, Critical, Info) and define pass/fail thresholds
- Integrate tools into IDE and CI/CD pipeline for consistent feedback

- Treat warnings as educational, but enforce high-severity rules strictly
- Provide clear, actionable feedback in PRs or dashboards
- Combine with code coverage and security scanning for full-spectrum visibility

Choosing the Right Static Code Analysis Tools

Not all tools are created equal, and the best choice depends on your language stack, team structure, compliance needs, and developer workflow. Here's how to choose wisely:

Language and Ecosystem Compatibility

Start by selecting tools that:

- Support your primary programming language(s)
- Integrate easily with your build system or CI tool
- Provide plugins or integrations for your IDE and version control platform

Example: ESLint is a better fit for JavaScript teams than general-purpose scanners like SonarQube.

Scope of Analysis

Determine what kind of checks you need and the tools you need for them:

- **Style enforcement** (naming, formatting) → ESLint, Prettier, flake8
- **Bug detection** → SpotBugs, PyLint, cppcheck
- **Security scanning** → Bandit, Semgrep, CodeQL

- **Complexity and maintainability** → SonarQube, CodeClimate
- **License compliance** → FOSSA, WhiteSource

Some tools provide multi-dimensional coverage, while others specialize.

Integration with CI/CD and Developer Workflow

When selecting tools to support quality gates, it is important to prioritize solutions that integrate naturally into the CI/CD workflow rather than adding friction to it. Tools should run automatically as part of the CI pipeline, ensuring that quality checks are applied consistently and without relying on manual intervention. Inline feedback within pull requests is especially valuable, as it allows developers to see and address issues in context, close to the code they are changing. Seamless integration with common CI/CD platforms ensures that quality gates can be adopted across teams without requiring custom or brittle implementations.

In addition, effective tools should provide APIs, dashboards, or reporting mechanisms that make quality data visible and actionable beyond individual pipeline runs. This enables trend analysis, alerting, and integration with broader observability and governance practices. Conversely, tools that require excessive manual setup, depend heavily on local execution, or fail to scale with increasing pipeline complexity often become bottlenecks. Such tools undermine the very goal of automation and should be avoided in favour of solutions that grow alongside both the pipeline and the organization.

Choose tools that:

- Run automatically in your CI pipeline
- Provide inline feedback in pull requests
- Integrate with your chosen CI/CD tooling
- Offer APIs or dashboards for reporting and alerting

Avoid tools that require too much manual setup or can't scale with the pipeline.

Customization and Rule Management

When evaluating static analysis and quality gate tools, it is important to look for flexibility in how rules and thresholds can be configured. Fine-grained control allows teams to tune checks based on the type of code, risk profile, and maturity of the system, rather than relying on one-size-fits-all defaults.

The ability to define project- or team-specific policies ensures that quality gates align with local standards and delivery realities, while mechanisms to suppress known false positives or manage justified exceptions prevent unnecessary noise. This flexibility helps teams trust and adopt quality gates, reinforcing good engineering practices without turning automated analysis into a rigid or obstructive enforcement mechanism.

Look for:

- Fine-grained rule configuration and thresholds
- Ability to define project-specific policies
- Options to suppress false positives and manage exceptions

This helps align the analysis with team norms rather than enforcing rigid defaults.

Security and Compliance Requirements

For many organizations - particularly those operating in heavily regulated industries - security and compliance risks are significant, and the requirements to address them must be deliberately reflected in the rules enforced within delivery pipelines through quality gates.

If working in regulated environments, choose tools that:

- Include secure coding rule sets
- Offer audit-ready reports
- Support integration with SBOMs (Software Bill of Materials) and vulnerability databases
- Can be used offline or on-prem (for air-gapped environments)

Cost and Licensing

Static analysis tooling spans a wide spectrum of options, from lightweight open-source tools to fully managed enterprise platforms, and choosing the right solution requires balancing cost, capability, and impact on developer productivity.

- Many tools have open-source versions (ESLint, pylint)
- SaaS tools like Codacy, CodeClimate, and Snyk Code offer convenience but may come at a cost
- For enterprise needs, consider commercial tiers with dashboards, security, and support. Tools like Semgrep, CodeQL, or SonarQube Enterprise offer robust compliance support.

Weigh cost against coverage, ease of use, and impact on team productivity.

Choosing Smart, Scanning Early

Static analysis gates are foundational to a quality CI/CD pipeline. When implemented thoughtfully, with the right tools for your tech stack and workflow, they become an early warning system that prevents downstream problems and ensures high-quality, consistent, and secure code.

Don't treat static analysis as a formality, treat it as a development best friend that helps you deliver clean code, faster.

Integrating Static Analysis into a CI/CD Pipeline

By integrating static analysis into your CI/CD pipeline, you ensure that every change is automatically checked for quality issues, providing fast feedback to developers and maintaining high code standards.

Configuring the Tool

Once a tool is selected, it needs to be installed and configured in your environment. There are a wide number of different tools that do this – but for the sake of this example, we will look at the use of a Python linter called Pylint and how it can be added to a pipeline file:

```
pip install pylint
```

You can customize rules and thresholds by creating a configuration file, typically generated via:

```
pylint --generate-rcfile > .pylintrc
```

This configuration allows teams to define which issues are critical, which are warnings, and which can be ignored.

Integrating Static Analysis into CI/CD

The next step is to automate the static analysis as part of your pipeline. This ensures that code is checked on every push or pull request, providing immediate feedback to developers. Here's a GitHub Actions example for a Python project:

```
name: CI

on:
  push:
    branches: [ main ]
  pull_request:
    branches: [ main ]

jobs:
  lint:
    runs-on: ubuntu-latest
    steps:
      - name: Checkout code
        uses: actions/checkout@v3

      - name: Set up Python
        uses: actions/setup-python@v4
        with:
          python-version: 3.11

      - name: Install dependencies
        run: |
          python -m pip install --upgrade pip
          pip install pylint

      - name: Run Pylint
        run: |
          pylint your_package_name --exit-zero
```

In this particular script, the --exit-zero allows the pipeline to complete even if Pylint detects issues. Removing it will fail the build on lint errors, enforcing stricter quality control. We will explain more on different sort of thresholds that can be used in the next part of this chapter.

The pipeline can also easily be extended to generate reports or integrate with dashboards for team visibility.

Defining code quality rules and thresholds

Code quality gates are only as effective as the rules and thresholds behind them. These determine what constitutes acceptable code and define the criteria that must be met for code to proceed through the pipeline.

Whether it's enforcing code style, catching bugs, or preventing performance bottlenecks, defining clear, consistent rules and meaningful thresholds is critical to building trust in quality gates and ensuring they align with business goals.

What Are Code Quality Rules and Thresholds?

- **Code quality rules** are specific checks applied to your codebase, such as "no unused variables", "methods must not exceed 50 lines", or "SQL statements must be parameterized".
- **Thresholds** are the pass/fail criteria attached to these rules, such as "no more than 2 critical issues", or "test coverage must be ≥ 80%".

These rules and thresholds become gatekeepers, automatically preventing low-quality code from merging or deploying.

Types of Code Quality Rules

Code quality rules help maintain readability, reliability, and security across a codebase, ensuring that new contributions meet team standards and reduce long-term maintenance costs.

Rule Type	Example	Purpose
Style and Formatting	Enforce naming conventions, indentation	Improves readability and consistency
Complexity	Limit cyclomatic complexity or nesting depth	Prevents difficult-to-maintain code
Code Duplication	Detect copy-pasted or repeated logic	Reduces maintenance overhead
Best Practices	Discourage use of eval(), use const	Encourages secure and reliable code
Security	Detect hard-coded secrets, injection risks	Prevents vulnerabilities
Test Coverage	Require coverage thresholds by module	Ensures confidence in test reliability
Documentation	Require comments for exported functions	Supports maintainability

These rules are enforced through static code analysis, linting tools, and CI integrations.

Setting Quality Thresholds

Thresholds create quantifiable limits for acceptable code quality. These should be:

- **Realistic**: Based on your current baseline and goals
- **Enforceable**: Automatically checked during CI runs

- **Adjustable**: Evolving with the team and codebase

Examples:

- No blocker / critical issues allowed
- No more than 5 code smells per file
- Code duplication < 3%
- Test coverage ≥ 80%
- No security vulnerabilities of medium or higher severity
- Build time must be < 10 minutes

How to Define and Enforce Rules in Practice

Below are some simple guidelines on how to apply these rules in your respective delivery processes:

- **Start with baseline scanning**: Use automated tools to analyse your current codebase, then review the default rule set and overall score.
- **Tailor rules to your team**: Disable what's irrelevant, strengthen what matters, and introduce project- or directory-specific overrides where needed.
- **Set clear CI pass/fail thresholds**: Define gating conditions (e.g. fail the pipeline if the security rating drops below B) and integrate them into your CI/CD pipeline.
- **Evolve incrementally**: If your codebase has existing issues, focus on new code first and gradually improve using a "ratcheting" approach where each improvement becomes the new baseline.
- **Align with business priorities**: Emphasise security for sensitive systems, maintainability for legacy-heavy codebases, and balance speed with quality through automation, linting, and test coverage.

Examples of Rules and Threshold Configurations

Below are some brief examples of different configurations found in different tools and how they can easily be set in the respective pipeline script:

SonarQube Example (in yaml):

```
qualityGate:
  coverage: 80
  code_smells: < 10
  duplicated_lines: < 3%
  blocker_issues: 0
```

ESLint Example (for JavaScript – using JSON):

```
"rules": {
  "no-unused-vars": "error",
  "complexity": ["error", { "max": 10 }],
  "max-lines-per-function": ["warn", 50],
  "no-console": "warn"
}
```

GitHub Action Example (in yaml):

```
- name: Run SonarCloud Scan
  run: sonar-scanner -Dsonar.qualitygate.wait=true
```

Best Practices

When applied thoughtfully, code quality gates reinforce good engineering habits without overwhelming teams, helping standards evolve alongside the codebase rather than becoming a source of friction.

- **Treat critical and blocker issues as non-negotiable**: These represent real risk and should always prevent unsafe changes from progressing.

- **Regularly review thresholds to reflect evolving code health and team maturity**: What's strict early on may be too lenient later (or vice versa).
- **Use dashboards and PR comments to surface quality violations**: Make issues visible where developers already work to speed up remediation.
- **Educate developers on what the rules mean and why they matter**: Understanding intent builds buy-in and better long-term behaviour.
- **Avoid overloading teams with too many failing rules at once**: Introduce or tighten rules gradually to prevent fatigue and disengagement.

What Happens Without Clear Rules and Thresholds?

Without clear, agreed-upon rules and thresholds, quality becomes a matter of opinion rather than a shared standard, undermining both trust in the pipeline and confidence in each release.

- **Developers may skip or ignore quality concerns** – Ambiguity makes it easier to rationalize shortcuts or defer fixes.
- **Teams end up arguing over subjective code quality issues** – Lack of standards shifts discussions from facts to personal preference.
- **The pipeline becomes noisy and unreliable** – Inconsistent or poorly defined checks lead to false positives and alert fatigue.
- **Security or performance issues sneak into production** – Gaps in enforcement allow real risks to pass unnoticed until they cause impact.

A well-defined rule set and threshold strategy transforms code quality from opinion to objective, enforceable practice.

Quality Gates Start with Clarity

Quality isn't just about running tools, it's about knowing what you're measuring and what "good enough" looks like. By defining clear, thoughtful code quality rules and thresholds, you empower your pipeline to guide development, enforce discipline, and build confidence in every release.

Managing false positives and technical debt

As organizations adopt quality gates in their CI/CD pipelines, they inevitably encounter false positives and face the challenge of existing technical debt. Both can undermine confidence in the gating process, slow down development, and lead to resistance from teams if not handled thoughtfully.

Effectively managing these issues is essential for sustainable pipeline governance, team buy-in, and continuous improvement of code quality.

What Are False Positives?

A false positive occurs when a quality gate or static analysis tool flags an issue that is:

- Incorrect (e.g., a valid piece of code is misidentified as a bug)
- Not relevant in a specific context
- Technically valid but intentionally written that way due to business or architectural constraints

Left unchecked, false positives lead to:

- Developer frustration
- Gate fatigue (people ignore the warnings)
- Bypassing or disabling gates altogether

Strategies to Manage False Positives

To maximize the effectiveness of static analysis, it's important to tune rulesets thoughtfully. Overly aggressive or irrelevant rules can create noise and reduce developer buy-in, so align rules with your language version, frameworks, and coding standards. Categorize issues by severity, using warnings for low-risk concerns and errors for critical problems, to focus attention where it matters most.

Suppression mechanisms should be used judiciously. Developers may annotate code to bypass specific rules, but only after peer review, and suppressed issues should be tracked to prevent misuse. For legacy systems, it's often practical to establish a baseline, accepting existing violations while enforcing stricter checks on new or modified code. Many tools support filtering to focus on new code.

Equally important is educating the team on why rules exist and how to address violations, differentiating between opinion-based and risk-based rules. Continuous improvement is supported by collecting feedback, regularly reviewing false positives and involving developers in refining the ruleset ensures the static analysis strategy remains practical, effective, and aligned with team workflows.

In summary:

Tune Your Rulesets

- Disable overly aggressive or irrelevant rules.

- Align rules with language versions, frameworks, and coding standards.
- Use "warning" severity for low-risk issues and "error" for critical ones.

Use Suppression Mechanisms Wisely

- Allow developers to annotate specific code with comments (e.g., `// eslint-disable-next-line`) only after peer review.
- Track suppressed issues in dashboards to avoid abuse.

Maintain a Baseline

- For legacy systems, accept current violations as the "baseline" and apply strict gating only to new or modified code.
- Tools like SonarQube and CodeClimate allow "new code" filtering.

Educate Teams

- Help developers understand why rules exist and how to address them.
- Clarify which rules are opinion-based vs. risk-based.

Collect Feedback

- Regularly review false positive patterns and tune rules accordingly.
- Involve developers in refining the gating strategy.

What Is Technical Debt?

Technical debt refers to shortcuts or suboptimal solutions made during development, often to meet deadlines or due to limited resources. While sometimes necessary, over time this debt can:

- Slow down development velocity
- Increase defect rates
- Make the codebase harder to maintain and evolve

When quality gates are introduced, they often expose this technical debt, leading to thousands of warnings, smells, or test gaps.

Strategies to Manage Technical Debt

Effectively managing technical debt requires a deliberate strategy that separates it from day-to-day delivery. By tracking debt in a dedicated backlog and classifying it by severity, impact, and system area, teams can maintain visibility and make informed decisions without disrupting regular development work.

Introducing a debt budget helps keep technical debt within acceptable limits, such as capping duplicated code or complexity, with progress measured through tools or custom dashboards. Incremental remediation is key: adopting the "Boy Scout Rule," developers clean up small issues whenever they touch code, gradually improving the system over time.

Quality gates are essential to prevent new debt from accumulating, enforcing standards on new code even if legacy code does not comply. Prioritization ensures focus on high-risk areas, modules that are frequently changed, business-critical, or historically prone to defects. Finally, recognizing and rewarding improvements through dashboards, code reviews, or retrospectives encourages long-term commitment to code quality and fosters a culture of continuous improvement.

In summary:

Separate Debt from Day-to-Day Delivery

- Track debt in a dedicated backlog.
- Classify by severity, impact, and system area.

Introduce a Debt Budget

- Set an allowable threshold (e.g., "no more than 2% duplicated code").
- Measure progress with tools like SonarQube, CodeClimate, or custom dashboards.

Fix Debt Incrementally

- Apply the **"Boy Scout Rule"**: always leave the code better than you found it.
- Clean up small issues as part of regular feature development or bug fixes.

Use Quality Gates to Prevent New Debt

- Gate new code against the current standard, even if older code doesn't meet it.
- Prevent "debt drift" by enforcing minimum test coverage or maximum complexity.

Prioritize High-Risk Areas

Focus debt remediation on modules that are:

- Frequently changed
- Business-critical
- High in complexity or defect rate

Reward Improvements

- Make progress visible through dashboards, code reviews, or retrospectives.
- Acknowledge teams or individuals contributing to long-term quality.

Balancing Reality and Rigor

You don't need to fix every problem right away. A successful strategy is realistic, prioritized, and designed for long-term evolution, not overnight transformation.

The key is to make quality a moving forward goal:

- Don't let debt grow unchecked.
- Don't let tools overwhelm your team.
- Use quality gates to protect today's code while cleaning up yesterday's gradually.

Best Practices at a Glance

Challenge	Strategy
False Positives	Tune rules, apply suppression carefully, gather feedback
Technical Debt	Baseline old code, track debt separately, fix incrementally

Developer Frustration	Educate teams, automate feedback, make progress visible
Pipeline Noise	Prioritize actionable issues, avoid over-alerting

Quality gates should never feel like a barrier, they should feel like a trusted guide. By managing false positives and addressing technical debt with intention, you can ensure that your gates build confidence, foster better code, and evolve with your team's needs.

Automating code reviews

Code reviews are a critical part of software development, they help catch bugs, ensure consistency, and improve code quality. However, manual reviews can be time-consuming, inconsistent, and prone to human error, especially under pressure. Automating parts of the code review process allows teams to scale quality enforcement, reduce bottlenecks, and free up reviewers to focus on logic and design rather than repetitive formatting or style issues.

What Is Automated Code Review?

Automated code review refers to the use of tools that analyse code automatically during or immediately after a commit or pull request. These tools apply predefined rules to detect:

- Code style violations
- Potential bugs or anti-patterns
- Security vulnerabilities
- Poor documentation
- Unmet test coverage or complexity thresholds

The results are typically integrated directly into your code hosting platform, surfacing issues as comments or quality summaries in pull requests.

A Sample Workflow

To better explain the code review process – below is a simple step-by-step workflow of how this would typically work in most scenarios:

1. Developer pushes code.
2. CI/CD pipeline:
    - Runs linting, tests, static analysis
    - Posts results as inline comments or checks
3. Developer fixes flagged issues
4. Human reviewer focuses on business logic, design, and tests
5. CI enforces gating thresholds before merging

What Can Be Automated?

Not everything can be automated, though the below table does highlight the important things that can be automated in the code review process:

Category	Examples of What Can Be Checked
Style & Formatting	Indentation, naming conventions, import order
Linting	Language-specific issues (e.g., unused vars, typos)
Security	Injection risks, secrets in code, unsafe libraries
Complexity	Large functions, deep nesting, cyclomatic complexity
Test Coverage	Code added/modified without adequate test coverage
Documentation	Missing docstrings/comments for public APIs
Performance Smells	Inefficient loops, N+1 queries

Benefits of Automating Code Reviews

Automating code reviews offers significant advantages for teams aiming to maintain high-quality standards while scaling development. One key benefit is consistency at scale: every commit is evaluated against the same rules, eliminating reviewer bias or accidental oversights. Automation also provides a faster feedback loop, giving developers instant insights into issues before human review, which accelerates development and reduces rework.

By handling routine checks such as formatting, naming conventions, and basic style rules, automated code reviews reduce reviewer fatigue, allowing human reviewers to focus on higher-value concerns like architecture, business logic, and user experience. Automation ensures objective enforcement of coding standards and thresholds, embedding quality directly into the CI/CD pipeline rather than leaving it to individual judgment. Additionally, it supports improved onboarding by helping new developers understand team expectations without the need to memorize informal standards, fostering quicker integration and consistent code quality across the team.

- **Consistency at Scale**: Every commit is held to the same standard, no reviewer bias or oversight.
- **Faster Feedback Loop**: Developers get instant feedback on their code before waiting for human review.
- **Reduced Review Fatigue**: Reviewers can focus on architectural, business logic, and UX concerns instead of code formatting or naming.
- **Objective Enforcement**: Enforces coding standards and thresholds as part of the pipeline, not someone's opinion.

- **Improved Onboarding**: New developers understand expected standards without needing to memorize team preferences.

Best Practices

Below are some basic best practices that can be adopted to achieve success in this area:

- **Run Automated Checks Pre-PR**: Integrate automated review tools into pre-commit hooks or CI so issues are flagged before a PR is even submitted.
- **Fail CI on Critical Issues**: Treat linting or security failures as gating criteria in CI.
- **Combine with Manual Reviews**: Don't replace manual reviews, complement them. Let automation handle the repetitive, objective checks.
- **Customize Rules**: Tailor linters and analysers to your team's specific conventions and risk profile.
- **Provide Clear Feedback**: Use tools that offer in-line annotations or actionable summaries directly on the PR.

Watch Out For...

While automated tools and processes offer many benefits, teams should be mindful of potential pitfalls. Overwhelming developers with hundreds of issues at once can be counterproductive; it's better to start with a manageable set of rules and gradually raise standards over time. Similarly, false positives can frustrate developers and waste effort, so tools should be regularly tuned to ensure the feedback is meaningful and actionable.

Finally, it's important not to rely solely on automation. Some aspects of code quality, such as design decisions, naming clarity, or architectural consistency, still require human judgment and thoughtful review. Balancing automated checks with human oversight ensures that quality practices are effective without becoming burdensome or rigid.

- **Overwhelming Developers**: Don't surface hundreds of issues at once. Start small and incrementally raise standards.
- **False Positives**: Tune your tools regularly to avoid developer frustration and wasted time.
- **Relying Only on Automation**: Some issues, like poor design decisions or unclear naming, still require human judgment.

Automating code reviews is not about replacing developers, it's about augmenting them. By automating repetitive, rule-based checks, teams improve code quality, accelerate delivery, and foster a more productive and focused review culture.

Conclusion: Your code quality is your first line of defence

Static code analysis plays a critical role in maintaining code quality by acting as an early, automated gate in the CI/CD pipeline. By enforcing coding standards, detecting potential bugs, and providing consistent, objective feedback, it ensures that only code meeting agreed-upon quality thresholds progresses through the delivery process. Effective implementation - including tuned rulesets, incremental remediation, and thoughtful integration with developer workflows - helps teams reduce technical debt, improve maintainability, and accelerate feedback loops without overwhelming developers.

Building on this foundation, the next chapter explores test automation as a quality gate, extending the principles of early, automated verification to functional behaviour. While static analysis focuses on the structure and safety of code, test automation ensures that the system works correctly, reliably, and meets user expectations before it reaches production. Together, these gates form a complementary approach to embedding quality throughout the software lifecycle.

Test Automation as a Gate

Purpose of chapter: We will now look at how using the results of test execution runs can be utilised as effective quality gates. We will look at how to implement dynamic scans where tests are actually run and the results checked along the way. We will explore some basic strategies that will help to make these tests more effective so that they don't impact your delivery pipelines negatively in slowing down performance or through flakiness.

Testing serves as a critical quality gate, ensuring that only code that meets functional, performance, and reliability standards is deployed to production. By embedding tests directly into the pipeline, teams can automatically verify that new changes do not break existing functionality and that new features behave as expected. This automated verification provides fast, repeatable feedback, allowing developers to identify and fix issues early - before they escalate into costly defects in production.

Automation is essential for this process because manual testing cannot keep pace with the rapid cadence of modern software delivery. Automated tests, ranging from unit and integration tests to end-to-end and performance tests, can be executed on every commit or pull request. This ensures consistent enforcement of quality standards across the team, reduces the risk of human error, and allows developers to focus on higher-value work such as design, architecture, and user experience improvements.

Moreover, automated testing enables continuous feedback and early detection of regressions, which is especially important in environments with frequent releases or multiple teams contributing to the same codebase. By making test results immediately visible through dashboards and reports, teams gain actionable insights into code health, coverage, and potential problem areas. In this way, test automation not only enforces quality but also drives a culture of accountability and continuous improvement throughout the software lifecycle.

Test Pyramid Strategy and Its Role in Gating

Not all tests are created equal, and not all should be treated equally within your gating strategy. That's where the Test Pyramid comes in.

The Test Pyramid is a conceptual model that helps teams structure their automated tests efficiently by placing more emphasis on fast, low-level tests (like unit tests) and fewer, slower end-to-end (E2E) tests. When applied as part of a gating strategy, the pyramid ensures fast, reliable, and cost-effective feedback, improving both test confidence and pipeline performance.

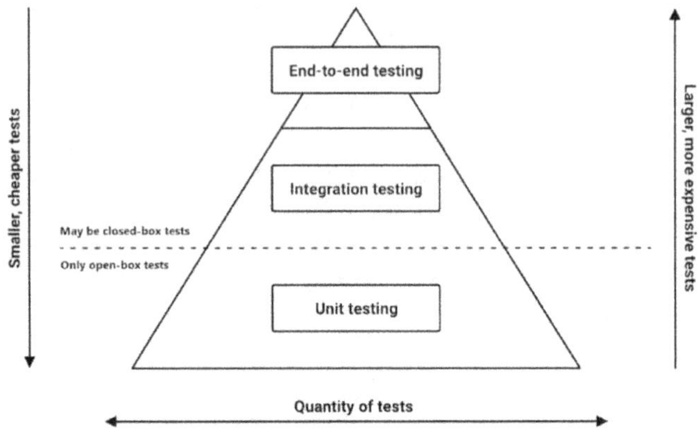

What Is the Test Pyramid?

The Test Pyramid, first popularized by Mike Cohn, visualizes a layered testing strategy. While it might be over simplistic – it provides a good representation on the importance of how testing should build on the foundation of lower levels and be used as precursor for ensuring that less time is spent on more expensive forms of testing:

Unit Tests (Base of the Pyramid)

- **Scope:** Individual functions, methods, or small components tested in complete isolation from external dependencies.
- **Speed:** Very fast (typically milliseconds), enabling frequent execution on every code change.
- **Volume:** High, forming the largest portion of the test suite.
- **Goal:** Ensure the correctness of business logic and edge cases early, providing fast feedback to developers and preventing defects from propagating further down the pipeline.

- **Why it matters:** Unit tests are cheap to write, easy to maintain, and act as the first line of defence against regressions.

Integration Tests (Middle Layer)

- **Scope:** Interactions between multiple components or systems, such as services, APIs, databases, message queues, or external dependencies.
- **Speed:** Moderate, slower than unit tests due to system setup and I/O, but still suitable for automated CI execution.
- **Volume:** Medium, focused on critical integration points rather than exhaustive coverage.
- **Goal:** Validate that components work correctly together and that contracts, data formats, and communication paths behave as expected.
- **Why it matters:** Integration tests catch issues that unit tests cannot, such as configuration errors, schema mismatches, and broken service interactions.

End-to-End (E2E) Tests (Top Layer)

- **Scope:** Complete application flows from the user's perspective, often spanning UI, backend services, and data layers.
- **Speed:** Slow (seconds to minutes per test) due to full system orchestration and environment dependencies.
- **Volume:** Low, carefully curated to cover only the most critical user journeys and business scenarios.
- **Goal:** Ensure that real-world user workflows and business-critical paths function correctly in a production-like environment.
- **Why it matters:** E2E tests provide the highest level of confidence before release but should be used

sparingly due to their cost, fragility, and execution time.

There are additional layers in this testing pyramid, such as component and contract testing, which are important in their own right. However, for the purposes of this book and chapter, we will focus on the three layers discussed above. From a technical perspective, these three represent the most distinct approaches, while the other layers can generally be considered extensions or variations within one of them.

The Role of the Pyramid in Gating

Each layer of the test pyramid plays a distinct and deliberate role as a quality gate within the CI/CD pipeline. Their position in the pyramid reflects a balance between execution cost, feedback speed, and confidence gained. When used together, these gates progressively increase assurance while minimizing wasted time and resources.

Unit Test Gates (Fastest and First)

- **Execution timing:** Run on every commit or pull request to provide immediate feedback.
- **Purpose:** Act as the first and most critical quality gate, catching the majority of logic and implementation errors as early as possible.
- **Impact:** Prevent broken or incomplete code from advancing into slower, more expensive pipeline stages.
- **Behaviour:** Enforce a "fail fast" mindset, if basic correctness is not met, the pipeline stops immediately.
- **Value:** Keeps feedback loops tight and protects overall pipeline efficiency.

Integration Test Gates

- **Execution timing:** Run on branch merges, nightly builds, or scheduled pipelines, depending on system complexity.
- **Purpose:** Validate how services, components, and dependencies interact (e.g., APIs, databases, message brokers).
- **Impact:** Gate against regressions that occur across system boundaries rather than within isolated units.
- **Behaviour:** Ensure stable interfaces, contract adherence, and correct data flow between components.
- **Value:** Builds confidence that the system works as a cohesive whole before full end-to-end validation.

End-to-End (E2E) Test Gates

- **Execution timing:** Run before promotion to staging or production environments.
- **Purpose:** Validate a small set of critical, high-value business flows (e.g., login, checkout, payments).
- **Impact:** Serve as the final functional gate before release, ensuring the system behaves correctly from a user perspective.
- **Behaviour:** Often executed alongside other late-stage gates such as performance testing, security checks, or manual approvals.
- **Value:** Provides the highest level of release confidence while being intentionally limited due to cost and fragility.

Together, these gates form a layered defence strategy, where fast, low-cost checks stop most issues early, and slower, high-confidence validations ensure the system is truly ready for release.

Benefits of Using the Pyramid in Gating

Using the test pyramid as a framework for CI/CD gating provides multiple benefits. Faster feedback is achieved by prioritizing lower layers, such as unit and integration tests, which run quickly and catch issues early. This approach also improves pipeline efficiency, reducing reliance on slower, more brittle end-to-end tests. By structuring tests in layers, teams gain improved stability, minimizing false positives and flaky tests, while each level contributes to layered confidence, validating different aspects of system quality. Finally, the pyramid helps lower costs, as unit tests are inexpensive to run and maintain, and limiting the number of end-to-end tests keeps infrastructure and maintenance overhead manageable.

- **Faster Feedback:** Lower layers run faster and catch issues early
- **Pipeline Efficiency:** Limits reliance on slow, brittle E2E tests
- **Improved Stability:** Reduces false positives and test flakiness
- **Layered Confidence:** Each level validates a different aspect of system quality
- **Lower Cost:** Unit tests are cheap to run and maintain, while fewer E2E tests keep infrastructure costs down

Anti-Patterns to Avoid

Several common testing anti-patterns can undermine the effectiveness of CI/CD quality gates. The E2E Ice Cream Cone, where pipelines rely excessively on UI tests, leads to slow, brittle, and unreliable pipelines. Missing integration layers result in tests that pass in isolation but fail when components interact, masking critical issues. Skipping unit tests pushes the cost of failure downstream, making bugs harder and more expensive to diagnose. Finally, having no test gate criteria, where failures do not block progression, renders tests largely ineffective, as issues slip through without triggering corrective action. Avoiding these anti-patterns ensures that testing provides reliable, actionable feedback and maintains pipeline integrity.

Anti-Pattern	Problem
E2E Ice Cream Cone	Too many UI tests, slow and flaky pipelines
Missing Integration Layer	Tests pass individually but fail when components interact
Skipping Unit Tests	Shifts cost of failure downstream, harder to debug
No Test Gate Criteria	Tests exist, but failures don't block progression

Best Practices

Below is a summary of best practices that can be implemented to get the best out of your quality gating at this level:

- **Make unit test success a pre-merge requirement** in every PR
- **Run integration tests in parallel** where possible
- **Keep E2E tests minimal but meaningful** (happy paths, critical flows)
- **Monitor test flakiness** and exclude flaky tests from gating until fixed
- **Tag tests by purpose** (e.g., smoke, regression, contract) and run based on context
- **Visualize your pyramid** in dashboards to maintain healthy test distribution

Test Pyramid in Action: Example Pipeline

Below is a sample pipeline written in YAML with quality gates for each testing phase built in:

```
# CI/CD Pipeline Example with Failing Quality Gates

stages:
  - name: build
    description: "Compile code, run linting and unit
tests"
    steps:
      - name: lint
        run: |
          npm run lint
          if [ $? -ne 0 ]; then
            echo "Lint failed: Quality gate not met!"
            exit 1
          fi

      - name: unit_tests
        run: |
          npm test
          if [ $? -ne 0 ]; then
            echo "Unit tests failed: Quality gate not
met!"
            exit 1
          fi

  - name: integration
    description: "Run service integration tests"
    steps:
      - name: service_integration_tests
        run: |
          npm run integration-tests
          # Example gate: critical contract tests
          FAILED=$(grep    -c    "FAIL"    contract-
results.txt || true)
          if [ $FAILED -gt 0 ]; then
            echo "Integration gate failed: Critical
contracts broken"
            exit 1
          fi

  - name: pre_deployment
    description: "Run  end-to-end  and  smoke  tests
before deployment"
    steps:
      - name: smoke_tests
        run: |
          npm run smoke-tests
          if [ $? -ne 0 ]; then
```

```
          echo "Smoke tests failed: SLA-critical workflows broken"
          exit 1
        fi

    - name: e2e_tests
      run: |
        npm run e2e-tests
        # Check specific critical flows
        FAILED=$(grep -c "FAIL" e2e-results.txt || true)
        if [ $FAILED -gt 0 ]; then
          echo "E2E gate failed: Critical user flows failed"
          exit 1
        fi

  - name: approval_and_deploy
    description: "Final stage before deployment, may require manual approval"
    steps:
      - name: manual_approval
        run: |
          echo "Waiting for stakeholder approval..."
          read -p "Approve deployment? (yes/no): " APPROVAL
          if [ "$APPROVAL" != "yes" ]; then
            echo "Deployment blocked: Stakeholder did not approve"
            exit 1
          fi

      - name: deploy
        run: |
          echo "Deploying application..."
          # Actual deploy command
          npm run deploy
```

This CI/CD pipeline is structured around the test pyramid and enforces quality gates at each stage to ensure only high-quality code progresses to production:

The **Build stage** runs linting and unit tests, failing the pipeline if any code style or low-level logic issues are detected.

The **Integration stage** executes service integration tests and verifies critical contract compliance, preventing the pipeline from advancing if key service agreements are broken.

In the **Pre-Deployment stage**, smoke and end-to-end (E2E) tests validate SLA-critical workflows, such as checkout or login flows, halting deployment if any essential functionality fails.

Finally, the Approval and Deploy stage introduces a manual gate (we will look at these in more detail later in the book) requiring explicit stakeholder approval before deployment, ensuring that business or regulatory requirements are met. At every layer, failures are immediately surfaced with clear error messages, enforcing a disciplined, gated approach to quality while allowing teams to catch issues early in the development lifecycle.

The Test Pyramid isn't just a testing philosophy, it's a strategic guide to how you automate gates in your CI/CD pipeline. By leaning into the pyramid structure, you ensure that your quality gates are fast, efficient, and meaningful, enabling high-quality software delivery without sacrificing speed.

Ensuring Fast and Reliable Feedback

In CI/CD pipelines, the value of feedback is directly proportional to how fast and reliable it is. Developers need to know, as quickly and confidently as possible, whether their changes are good to go, or if they broke something. Without fast, actionable feedback, teams slow down, bugs sneak in, and quality gates lose credibility.

This makes fast and reliable feedback a cornerstone of any quality-focused DevOps practice.

Why Feedback Speed and Reliability Matter

Fast feedback allows developers to detect and fix issues while the code is still fresh in their minds, reducing the cognitive load of switching between tasks and minimizing the time spent tracking down the source of a problem.

Reliable feedback ensures that the signals coming from automated tests, static analysis, or security scans can be trusted; when results are accurate and consistent, teams can confidently make decisions without second-guessing and avoid the temptation to bypass important quality gates. Together, fast and reliable feedback enable development teams to:

- **Reduce context-switching**, by addressing issues immediately instead of letting them accumulate.
- **Maintain flow and velocity**, allowing developers to remain productive and focused on delivering value.
- **Build trust in automation**, ensuring that the test suite and CI/CD processes are seen as dependable tools rather than obstacles.
- **Catch defects early**, preventing bugs from reaching production where they are more costly and disruptive.

In essence, a CI/CD pipeline that delivers fast, reliable feedback creates a virtuous cycle: developers fix issues quickly, confidence in the system grows, and the overall quality of software improves while enabling faster, safer delivery.

Strategies to Ensure Fast Feedback

Below are some steps that will speed up the value of early feedback and ensure that as a development team you will get the most value of failures in your pipeline as soon as possible.

Prioritize Fast Tests Early

- Run unit tests and linters on every commit or PR.
- Defer slower tasks (e.g., performance or full E2E tests) to later stages unless gating production.

Parallelize Test Execution

- Split tests across multiple runners or containers.
- Use test sharding for large test suites (especially in E2E).

Cache Dependencies and Build Artifacts

- Reduce redundant build time by caching:
    1. Docker layers
    2. Maven/npm/pip packages
    3. Test binaries

Optimize Your CI Infrastructure

- Use scalable runners and autoscaling workers.
- Keep pipeline steps lean, remove unnecessary scripts or dependencies.

Test Impact Analysis

- Only run tests affected by recent changes.

- Tools like Jest (for JS), GitHub Actions matrix builds, and Bazel can support this.

Strategies for Reliable Feedback

Now the below strategies are useful for ensuring that the quality gate results from the automated test runs are more reliable and teams are expending too much effort dealing with false negatives every time the pipeline fails. Paired with the strategies above and teams should be able to find the right combination of speed and effectiveness out of their quality gates.

Eliminate Flaky Tests

- Track flakiness using test history.
- Quarantine flaky tests until fixed; don't use them as gating checks.
- Use retry logic only as a temporary workaround, not a solution.

Fail Fast and Clearly

- Fail early in the pipeline (e.g., on linting or failing unit tests).
- Surface root cause clearly in logs or pull request comments.

Use Strong Quality Gates

- Make test, code scan, and build results mandatory checks.
- Block merges or deployments on critical issues or unknown results.

Provide Actionable Feedback

- Integrate feedback into PRs with inline comments or summary statuses.
- Link scan results or test failures to documentation or remediation steps.

Monitor Feedback Time

- Track pipeline duration over time.
- Set SLAs (e.g., "CI feedback in under 10 minutes") and optimize for them.

Feedback Optimization in Practice

Pipeline Stage	Feedback Type	Target Time	Must Be Reliable?
Pre-merge PR check	Lint, unit tests	< 5 mins	Critical
Post-merge build	Integration tests	< 10 mins	Critical
Pre-release stage	E2E, security scans	< 30 mins	Mandatory
Nightly build	Full regression suite	Hours OK	Nice to have

Without fast and reliable feedback, even the best test suites or scanners lose their impact. The goal isn't just to check code, it's to empower developers with immediate, trustworthy insights that help them improve quality in real-time.

In a well-architected pipeline, feedback loops are optimized for speed at the bottom of the test pyramid, and confidence at the top, enabling both rapid iteration and high assurance.

Flaky Test Detection and Mitigation

Flaky tests, tests that intermittently pass or fail without any changes to the code, are one of the biggest threats to a healthy CI/CD pipeline. They undermine developer trust in test results, slow down delivery, and can cause teams to ignore quality gates altogether, arguably creating the biggest reason why many teams and companies may choose to abandon them altogether.

Managing flaky tests is not just a testing concern; it's essential to maintaining the credibility of quality gates and the effectiveness of continuous delivery pipelines.

What Is a Flaky Test?

A flaky test is one that produces inconsistent results:

- Passes sometimes, fails at others
- No code or environment change between runs
- Often resolved by re-running the test without any fix

Flakiness can occur in unit, integration, or E2E tests, and is especially common in:

- UI tests (e.g., Selenium, Cypress)
- Tests with external dependencies (e.g., APIs, databases)
- Asynchronous or timing-sensitive tests

Common Causes of Flaky Tests

Flaky tests are typically caused by factors that introduce unpredictability into test execution, such as timing issues like race conditions or sleep-based waits, unstable environments affected by network latency or constrained resources, and shared or dirty state between tests. They are often exacerbated by reliance on external dependencies such as real APIs or third-party services, the use of randomness or time-based data, and inadequate setup or teardown that leaves residual data behind. Together, these issues lead to inconsistent test outcomes, undermining confidence in test results and the reliability of quality gates.

Cause	Example
Timing issues	Race conditions, sleep-based waits
Environment instability	Network latency, slow containers, memory constraints
Shared state	Tests relying on global or dirty state
External dependencies	Calling real APIs, third-party services
Randomness or nondeterminism	Random input values or timestamps
Improper teardown/setup	Data left over from previous tests

Why Flaky Tests Are Dangerous

As already mentioned, flaky tests are one of the core reason many companies choose to abandon automated test execution directly from the CI/CD pipelines with the below the key reasons as to why:

- **Waste developer time** chasing false failures
- **Break trust in the pipeline**, leading to gate bypasses
- **Slow down delivery** as teams rerun or retry pipelines
- **Hide real regressions** when failures are ignored or automatically retried

In short: flaky tests make your feedback loop unreliable, which defeats the point of automation.

Detecting Flaky Tests

Given their importance the ability to therefore identify flaky tests as quickly as possible, allows teams to remediate these tests quicker and restore trust in the test executions as quickly as possible. Below are some basic tips that can help to detect flaky tests in your pipeline and eliminate them to improve accuracy, along with ways of mitigating those issues in your flaky tests.

Run Tests Multiple Times

Flaky tests often become apparent only when they are executed repeatedly under the same conditions, as their failures tend to be intermittent rather than deterministic. By deliberately rerunning tests multiple times in succession - using tools such as pytest-repeat, controlled test retries, or looped CI jobs - teams can surface hidden instability that may not appear in a single execution. Observing inconsistent outcomes across reruns helps distinguish genuine defects from environmental or timing-related issues, making it easier to identify and stabilise flaky tests before they undermine confidence in automated test results and quality gates.

Track Historical Test Results

When using test reporting and observability tools, teams should go beyond simple pass/fail status and analyse test behaviour over time. Specifically, they should look for tests that exhibit high variance in execution outcomes, such as tests that frequently alternate between passing and failing, show inconsistent execution times, or fail only under certain environments or load conditions. These patterns are strong indicators of flakiness and unreliable automation, and identifying them early allows teams to prioritise stabilisation efforts before such tests erode trust in the pipeline or slow delivery.

Mark and Isolate Flaky Tests

Once flaky tests have been identified, they should be explicitly tagged using annotations such as @Flaky or @Quarantined to make their status visible to the entire team. This allows pipelines to treat these tests differently, such as excluding them from strict quality gates or reporting on them separately, so they do not block merges or deployments while remediation work is underway. By clearly marking and isolating flaky tests rather than ignoring them, teams maintain pipeline flow and developer confidence while still holding themselves accountable for stabilising or fixing the underlying issues.

- Tag flaky tests with annotations (@Flaky, @Quarantined, etc.)
- Prevent them from blocking merges while they're being fixed.

Mitigation Strategies

After the flaky tests have been identified, the below strategies will help in remediating them appropriately to prevent continued reoccurrence of the failures.

Fix the Root Cause

It's important to avoid making superficial or rushed changes simply to get tests passing as quickly as possible. Instead, teams should invest the time to understand the true root cause of failures and implement durable, long-term fixes that prevent the issues from recurring.

Below are some useful steps that can help in identifying the root causes of your failures:

- Add explicit waits for async events instead of using fixed sleeps.
- Use mocked dependencies instead of real services.
- Ensure clean setup/teardown for test environments.
- Eliminate shared state between tests.

Quarantine Flaky Tests

Unstable tests should be moved into a separate test suite that runs outside of the main quality gate, allowing the core pipeline to remain reliable and fast. While these tests should continue to be executed and monitored to track failure patterns and progress, their results should not block builds until the underlying instability has been resolved.

Clean Up or Delete Persistently Flaky Tests

If a test has remained flaky for an extended period and does not cover critical functionality, it may be better to remove it altogether. Flaky tests that are not actively addressed add noise to the pipeline, dilute the value of test results, and ultimately erode trust in the overall test suite.

Refactor Large E2E Tests

Large, slow-running tests should be refactored into smaller, more focused flows that are easier to understand, faster to execute, and more reliable. Where possible, tests that rely heavily on the user interface should be replaced with API or integration-level tests, which are typically more stable, faster, and better suited to validating core business logic.

Use Retries Wisely

Often when tests fail, retries are executed to ensure it wasn't simply a brittle test and that it can pass on the second or third execution before establishing if it is a real failure or not. However this can be dangerous, slowing down execution and breaking trust in your pipeline considerably. It is best to therefore to use them sparingly and ensure retries are logged to ensure test execution instability remains visible

- Retries are a band-aid, not a fix.
- Use them sparingly and only as a temporary workaround while fixing root causes.
- Always log and report retries to keep visibility.

Incorporating Flaky Test Detection into CI/CD

Along with the identification steps mentioned above – you can incorporate some of the below strategies directly into. Your CI/CD processes to further help identify and remediate your flaky tests:

- Run a nightly or scheduled job that loops through tests multiple times and logs instability.
- Use test result history and dashboards to surface flakiness trends.
- Make test stability a quality metric alongside coverage and pass rates.
- Add pipeline rules to block flaky tests from gating until they're resolved.

Sample Metrics to Track

Below are some basic metrics that you can use to identify and measure the flakiness of test executions across your different test execution runs.

Metric	What It Measures	Why It Matters
Flaky test rate (%)	Percentage of tests that fail intermittently without code changes	Indicates overall reliability of the test suite and trustworthiness of test results
Flaky test frequency	How often a specific test fails randomly across runs	Helps prioritize which flaky tests need investigation first
Time to quarantine	Time taken to isolate or disable a flaky test after detection	Reduces noise in the pipeline and prevents wasted developer time
Time to resolution	Duration required to diagnose and permanently fix a flaky test	Reflects the team's ability to maintain a stable and reliable test suite
Flaky test impact	Percentage of pipeline failures caused by flaky tests	Quantifies the cost of flakiness and supports investment in test stabilization

As mentioned, flaky tests erode confidence in your automation and slow everything down. By treating flaky test detection and mitigation as part of your quality gate hygiene, you ensure that feedback remains fast, reliable, and trustworthy, exactly what high-performing teams need in a CI/CD environment.

Next up, we can explore topics like test result dashboards, quality trends reporting, or testing in production with feature flags, if you'd like.

Parallelism and Performance Optimization in CI/CD Pipelines

As CI/CD pipelines evolve to support faster, more frequent releases, the ability to optimize performance becomes essential. One of the most effective ways to reduce build and feedback times is through parallelism, breaking down work into smaller, independent pieces that can run simultaneously across multiple compute resources.

Done correctly, parallelism can cut execution times from hours to minutes, improve developer productivity, and keep quality gates tight without becoming bottlenecks.

Why Performance Optimization Matters

Slow pipelines can severely impact development velocity and quality:

- Developers wait longer for feedback, increasing context switching.
- Delays lead to larger, riskier batches of changes.
- Teams are discouraged from adding new quality checks due to time costs.
- Flaky tests and timeouts become more common under constrained resources.

Optimizing performance ensures your pipeline scales with your team and codebase, without compromising quality gates or developer experience.

What Is Parallelism in CI/CD?

Parallelism is the ability to run multiple steps or tasks at the same time across different executors (machines, containers, threads). This includes:

- Running unit tests in parallel across modules.
- Running integration or E2E tests across different environments or datasets.
- Building artifacts or images in parallel (e.g., frontend / backend services).
- Executing jobs across a build matrix (e.g., different OSes or language versions).

Strategies for Implementing Parallelism

Running tests in parallel is a very good way of speeding up the execution and value you will get out of executing your automated tests, but also one of the most difficult things to get right. Below are some important steps to help implement these effectively:

Split Tests by Type or Scope

- Group and run unit, integration, and E2E tests in separate jobs.
- Prioritize fast-running tests early in the pipeline.

Use Test Sharding

- Divide large test suites into chunks and run them across multiple runners.
- Tools like Jest, PyTest-xdist, JUnit5 (with Maven Surefire / Failsafe), and Cypress support this natively or via plugins.

Leverage Build Matrices

- Run builds or tests across multiple environments simultaneously:
    - Node 16 / Node 18
    - Linux / Windows / Mac
    - Java 8 / Java 17
- Supported in tools like GitHub Actions (strategy.matrix), GitLab CI, and CircleCI.

Parallelize Across Services

- In a microservices architecture, test or deploy services independently if they don't share dependencies.
- Helps isolate failures and reduce scope of regressions.

Performance Optimization Techniques

CI/CD pipelines can be made faster and more efficient by reducing unnecessary work and reusing results wherever possible. Techniques such as caching build dependencies and Docker layers prevent repeated downloads and image rebuilds, while incremental builds ensure that only changed components are rebuilt or tested.

Optimizing Dockerfiles and short-circuiting pipeline stages when earlier quality gates fail further reduce wasted execution time. Together with avoiding redundant steps through conditional execution and tuning concurrency to prevent runner overload, these practices help keep pipelines fast, predictable, and responsive, enabling quicker feedback without sacrificing reliability.

Technique	Description
Dependency Caching	Cache build dependencies (e.g., Maven, npm, pip)
Docker Layer Caching	Cache intermediate layers to avoid rebuilding images
Incremental Builds	Only build/test components that have changed
Optimized Dockerfiles	Minimize image size and build time
Short-circuiting Steps	Skip downstream jobs if earlier gates fail
Avoid Redundant Work	Use conditionals to skip tests or rebuilds when unnecessary
Concurrency Limits	Avoid overloading runners; tune thread/process count per job

Monitoring & Bottleneck Detection

Modern CI/CD platforms generate a rich set of execution data that can be used to continuously improve pipeline performance and developer experience. By leveraging pipeline analytics tools, teams can move beyond anecdotal complaints about "slow pipelines" and instead make data-driven decisions about where time is actually being spent and which steps are introducing unnecessary friction.

Visualizations such as job duration heatmaps and stage-by-stage execution times quickly highlight bottlenecks and variability across runs. Heatmaps make it easy to spot jobs that are consistently slow or occasionally spike in duration, while stage-level metrics help teams understand whether delays are occurring during build, test, security scanning, or deployment phases. This level of insight allows teams to focus optimisation efforts where they will have the greatest impact.

Test execution graphs and idle or wait-time metrics are particularly valuable for identifying inefficiencies in test strategy and pipeline orchestration. Long-running or highly variable tests may indicate poor test isolation, lack of parallelisation, or excessive end-to-end coverage at the wrong stage of the pipeline. Similarly, significant idle time between stages often points to unnecessary manual approvals, resource contention, or suboptimal job dependencies that can be streamlined or automated.

Finally, tracking success versus retry rates provides insight into pipeline stability and reliability. High retry rates often signal flaky tests, unstable environments, or brittle quality gates that erode developer confidence and slow delivery.

When used consistently, pipeline analytics become a powerful feedback mechanism for reducing friction, improving throughput, and reinforcing trust in the CI/CD process.

Use pipeline analytics tools to identify and fix bottlenecks:

- Job duration heatmaps
- Stage-by-stage execution times
- Test execution graphs
- Idle/wait times between stages
- Success vs. retry rate

To assist with this, the below tools offer very good visualisation of data and integrate easily into a wide range of CI/CD tooling:

- GitHub Actions Insights
- GitLab CI Analytics
- CircleCI Insights
- Buildkite, Harness, or custom Grafana dashboards

Best Practices for Sustainable Speed

In order to ensure your pipelines can run at a sustainable speed, it's important to following these best practices:

- **Start with the slowest pipeline**: optimize what hurts most.
- **Run fast tests early**: use the test pyramid to drive parallel structure.
- **Isolate flaky or unstable jobs**: prevent retries from affecting others.
- **Use consistent, disposable environments** (e.g., Docker containers or ephemeral VMs) for reproducibility.
- **Balance between job fan-out and startup overhead**: too many parallel jobs can overwhelm infrastructure or increase cold start times.

Parallelism and performance optimization aren't just for large teams, they're foundational to delivering quality software at speed. The key is to design pipelines that are modular, scalable, and intelligent, giving you faster feedback without compromising the rigor of your quality gates.

A slow pipeline erodes confidence and delivery pace. A fast, optimized pipeline empowers teams to ship better software, faster.

Conclusion: Making your testing failures the whole teams responsibility

In this chapter, we examined how testing functions as one of the most critical and effective quality gates within CI/CD pipelines. By treating automated tests - notably unit, integration, and end-to-end tests - as enforceable gates rather than optional checks, teams can detect defects early, reduce rework, and maintain confidence as changes progress through the pipeline. We also explored strategies for balancing coverage, speed, and reliability, emphasizing the importance of fast feedback, stable test suites, and thoughtful placement of test gates to support both quality and delivery velocity.

Building on this foundation, the next chapter expands the concept of quality gating into the domain of security and compliance. We will explore how security checks, vulnerability scanning, and policy enforcement can be integrated directly into CI/CD pipelines, transforming security from a late-stage review into a continuous, automated control. This shift not only reduces risk and exposure but also enables teams to meet regulatory and organizational requirements without sacrificing speed or autonomy.

Security and Compliance Gates

> **Purpose of chapter:** In this chapter we will look at the importance of adding security checks into your delivery pipelines, along with how to make them more effective. We will also look at the importance of compliance and how to build effective measures for companies and teams where compliance is critical.

We've now looked at the static and dynamic gates that will derive most of the gating required to ensure the quality of the software. Security is an incredibly critical thing and needs to look at more specifically – both from a static and dynamic perspective.

And this strong focus on security is largely what has driven the modern day progression from DevOps principles to DevSecOps principles.

Introducing DevSecOps Principles

As software delivery accelerates through CI/CD and automation, security must evolve to keep pace. Traditional models, where security checks happen at the end of the development cycle, no longer work in fast-moving environments. DevSecOps is the answer: a mindset and practice that integrates security as a shared responsibility across the entire software lifecycle.

DevSecOps brings security into the heart of DevOps pipelines, enabling secure-by-default software delivery without slowing teams down.

What Is DevSecOps?

DevSecOps stands for Development, Security, and Operations, and emphasizes that security is everyone's job, not just the security team's. It aims to:

- Embed security checks early and often in the pipeline
- Automate as much of the security process as possible
- Shift security left (closer to development) and right (into production)
- Promote collaboration between developers, operations, and security teams

Instead of being a gate at the end, security becomes a continuous, integrated feedback loop.

Why DevSecOps Matters in CI/CD

When security is treated as a late-stage or external concern, vulnerabilities are often discovered only shortly before release or, worse, after software is already in production. At that point, fixes tend to be costly, disruptive, and time-consuming, frequently requiring urgent patches or rollbacks. Under this pressure, teams may be tempted to bypass security checks altogether to meet delivery timelines, causing compliance efforts to become reactive and focused on damage control rather than prevention.

By contrast, when security practices are built into the delivery lifecycle from the outset, risks are identified and addressed much earlier. Automated checks and clear standards help teams move faster with greater confidence, reducing last-minute surprises and rework. Compliance shifts from a manual, after-the-fact activity to an auditable and repeatable process, allowing teams to deliver software that is both secure and reliable while positioning security as a business enabler rather than a barrier to progress.

Without integrated security:

- Vulnerabilities are discovered late or post-release
- Fixes are costly and time-consuming
- Teams bypass security to avoid delays
- Compliance becomes reactive instead of proactive

With DevSecOps:

- Security risks are caught before they reach production
- Teams release software faster and more safely
- Compliance is automated and auditable
- Security becomes a business enabler, not a blocker

Core DevSecOps Principles

The following DevSecOps principles provide a framework for embedding security seamlessly into the software delivery lifecycle, ensuring that risk is managed continuously rather than addressed reactively. By integrating security practices directly into CI/CD pipelines and day-to-day development workflows, teams can reduce vulnerabilities, improve compliance, and maintain delivery velocity.

These principles emphasise early feedback, automation, shared ownership, and enforceable policies, enabling security to scale alongside modern engineering practices without becoming a bottleneck.

Principle	Description
Shift Left	Move security earlier in the SDLC (e.g., static code scanning in PRs)
Security as Code	Treat security controls and policies as versioned, testable code
Automate Security Checks	Use tools to scan code, dependencies, infrastructure as part of the pipeline
Continuous Monitoring	Monitor runtime behaviour and security drift post-deployment
Culture of Ownership	Empower developers to fix vulnerabilities and understand security impacts
Policy Enforcement	Integrate quality gates for security rules (e.g., no critical CVEs allowed)

DevSecOps in Practice: Pipeline Integration Points

In practice, DevSecOps comes to life through deliberate integration of security controls at each stage of the CI/CD pipeline. Rather than relying on a single security gate at the end of delivery, effective pipelines distribute security checks across the entire lifecycle, aligning the right controls with the right phases. This approach ensures that risks are detected as early as possible, feedback is fast and actionable, and security becomes a continuous, automated part of delivery rather than a manual handoff.

By mapping security principles to concrete pipeline integration points, teams can address different categories of risk at the most appropriate time. Early stages focus on preventing insecure code and secrets from ever entering the codebase, while later stages validate dependencies, infrastructure, and runtime behaviour in increasingly realistic environments.

Together, these layered controls create defence in depth within the pipeline, balancing developer productivity with robust security assurance and making security outcomes measurable, repeatable, and scalable across teams.

Stage	Security Focus Areas	Tools/Practices
Pre-commit/PR	Linting, secret detection, static code analysis	Git hooks, ESLint, Bandit, SonarQube
Build	Dependency and SCA scanning	Snyk, OWASP Dependency-Check, Trivy
Test	Security test coverage, input validation checks	Unit + integration tests, fuzz testing
Deploy	Infrastructure as code scanning, policy-as-code	Checkov, OPA (Open Policy Agent), tfsec
Post-deploy	Runtime protection, threat detection, log analysis	Falco, Wazuh, AWS GuardDuty, Datadog

Key Areas DevSecOps Covers

Security essentially covers every aspects of the development process – but from a quality gate enforcement perspective the following are key implementations that can track adherence to the necessary security principles:

- **Static Application Security Testing (SAST)**
    - Scans source code for vulnerabilities
    - Should run in pull requests as part of early quality gates
- **Software Composition Analysis (SCA)**
    - Scans dependencies (open-source libraries) for known vulnerabilities
    - Gate builds based on severity and policy
- **Infrastructure as Code (IaC) Scanning**
    - Identifies misconfigurations in Terraform, Kubernetes, CloudFormation, etc.
- **Secrets Detection**
    - Detects hardcoded secrets and API keys in codebases
- **Policy-as-Code**

  - o Enforces security and compliance policies as version-controlled rules
- **Runtime Security**
  - o Detects anomalies, exploits, or drift after deployment

Best Practices for Adopting DevSecOps

Below are some key best practices that will help to drive the adoption of various DevSecOps principles in a team or organisation:

- **Start small and scale**, integrate one tool at a time, begin with SCA or secrets scanning
- **Automate where possible** - manual checks don't scale
- **Fail smart** - use soft gates for non-critical issues, hard gates for high severity risks
- **Visualize security posture** - dashboards help teams see trends and respond faster
- **Educate developers** - give them training and tools to fix what they break
- **Collaborate early** - involve security in architecture and design, not just reviews

DevSecOps Quality Gate in Action

The DevSecOps flow starts the moment a developer opens a pull request. This PR becomes the first formal quality gate, where automated checks validate not only correctness, but also security and maintainability before any code is merged. By enforcing these gates early, teams prevent defects and vulnerabilities from propagating downstream, where they become significantly more expensive to fix.

Once the pull request is created, the CI pipeline is triggered automatically. Early pipeline stages typically run linters and unit tests, providing fast feedback on code style, basic correctness, and regressions. At the same time, static code analysis tools scan the codebase for security smells and common vulnerability patterns. In this example, the scanner flags an insecure regular expression that could lead to catastrophic backtracking and a potential denial-of-service vulnerability. In parallel, a dependency scan inspects third-party libraries and identifies an outdated dependency containing a high-severity CVE.

Because these checks are enforced as quality gates, the pipeline fails immediately. The pull request is blocked from merging, and the developer receives clear, actionable feedback directly in the PR. This feedback includes details of the findings, severity levels, and links to remediation guidance or internal secure-coding standards. Importantly, this failure is not punitive, it is a guardrail that ensures insecure code never reaches shared branches or environments.

The developer then fixes the issues by refactoring the insecure regex and upgrading or replacing the vulnerable dependency. When the PR is updated, the pipeline re-runs automatically. All checks now pass, the quality gates open, and the PR can be merged with confidence. At this point, downstream deployment stages can proceed knowing that a defined baseline of security and quality has already been met.

Example: DevSecOps Quality Gate in a CI Pipeline (GitHub Actions)

Below is a simplified example of how this might look in a GitHub Actions workflow:

```
name: DevSecOps Quality Gates

on:
  pull_request:
```

```
    branches: [ "main" ]

jobs:
  quality-gates:
    runs-on: ubuntu-latest

    steps:
      - name: Checkout code
        uses: actions/checkout@v4

      - name: Run linter
        run: npm run lint

      - name: Run unit tests
        run: npm test -- --coverage

      - name: Static code security scan
        uses: sonarsource/sonarqube-scan-action@v2
        env:
          SONAR_TOKEN: ${{ secrets.SONAR_TOKEN }}

      - name: Dependency vulnerability scan
        uses: snyk/actions/node@v1
        env:
          SNYK_TOKEN: ${{ secrets.SNYK_TOKEN }}
        with:
          args: --severity-threshold=high
```

In this example:

- Linting and unit tests enforce baseline code quality.
- Static analysis identifies insecure patterns in the source code.
- Dependency scanning fails the build if high-severity vulnerabilities are detected.
- Any failure blocks the PR, acting as a hard quality gate.

This flow demonstrates the core value of DevSecOps quality gates: fast feedback, automated enforcement, and shared ownership. Security is no longer a late-stage review or external approval, it is embedded directly into the developer workflow. By the time deployment occurs, teams are not hoping the software is secure; they have objective, repeatable evidence that it meets agreed quality and security standards.

Security Scanning in CI/CD

Security scanning in CI / CD pipelines is a fundamental DevSecOps practice that helps teams identify vulnerabilities and misconfigurations early, before code or infrastructure reaches production. By embedding automated security scans into the development workflow, organizations can enforce quality gates that not only protect the integrity of the software, but also maintain delivery speed.

Done right, security scanning becomes a continuous, fast-feedback mechanism that detects risks in real time and allows developers to fix issues while they're still easy and inexpensive to resolve.

What Is Security Scanning?

Security scanning refers to the use of automated tools to inspect:

- Application code
- Third-party dependencies
- Infrastructure configurations
- Container images
- Secrets and credentials
- Runtime behaviour

These scans run at different stages of the CI / CD pipeline and help surface vulnerabilities, weaknesses, policy violations, or insecure practices.

Types of Security Scanning in CI/CD Pipelines

Type	Focus Area	Example Tools
Static Application Security Testing (SAST)	Scans source code for insecure patterns or bugs	SonarQube, Semgrep, Bandit
Software Composition Analysis (SCA)	Scans open-source libraries and dependencies for known CVEs	Snyk, OWASP Dependency-Check
Secret Detection	Detects hardcoded credentials, tokens, keys	GitLeaks, TruffleHog, GitGuardian
Infrastructure as Code (IaC) Scanning	Checks for misconfigurations in Terraform, Kubernetes, etc.	Checkov, tfsec, KICS
Container Image Scanning	Finds vulnerabilities in Docker images and base layers	Trivy, Anchore, Clair
Runtime Threat Detection	Monitors live systems for suspicious behaviour (post-deploy)	Falco, Aqua Security, Sysdig

Integrating Security Scans into Quality Gates

Security scans only become meaningful quality gates when they are automated, consistently enforced, and capable of stopping risky changes from progressing through the pipeline. When embedded correctly, these gates ensure that insecure code, vulnerable dependencies, or misconfigured infrastructure never silently move closer to production. Instead of being a separate security review, scanning becomes a natural extension of the developer workflow.

The key principle is progressive enforcement: lightweight, fast checks run early, while deeper and more expensive scans are applied later, once confidence in the change has increased. Each stage tightens the security posture without unnecessarily slowing developers down.

Example CI/CD Workflow with Security Gates

1. Pre-commit: Local Security Checks

Security starts before code ever leaves a developer's machine. Pre-commit hooks are used to detect obvious risks early, such as hardcoded secrets or credentials. Catching these issues locally prevents accidental exposure and avoids unnecessary CI failures later.

Example using a secrets scanner:

```
# .pre-commit-config.yaml
repos:
  - repo: https://github.com/zricethezav/gitleaks
    rev: v8.18.0
    hooks:
      - id: gitleaks
```

This ensures commits containing API keys, passwords, or tokens are blocked immediately, reinforcing good security hygiene with minimal friction.

2. Pull Request (CI): Code and Dependency Security Gates

When a pull request is opened, the CI pipeline enforces the first hard security quality gate. Static Application Security Testing (SAST) scans the changed code for common vulnerability patterns, while Software Composition Analysis (SCA) inspects third-party dependencies for known CVEs.

If high-severity issues are detected, the PR fails automatically and cannot be merged.

Example GitHub Actions job:

```
jobs:
  security-pr-gates:
    runs-on: ubuntu-latest
    steps:
      - uses: actions/checkout@v4

      - name: Run SAST
        uses: sonarsource/sonarqube-scan-action@v2
        env:
          SONAR_TOKEN: ${{ secrets.SONAR_TOKEN }}

      - name: Dependency scan
        uses: snyk/actions/node@v1
        env:
          SNYK_TOKEN: ${{ secrets.SNYK_TOKEN }}
        with:
          args: --severity-threshold=high
```

At this stage, security feedback is delivered directly in the pull request, making it clear, actionable, and easy to fix while the code is still fresh in the developer's mind.

3. Build Stage: Artifact and Infrastructure Security

Once the code passes PR gates, the build stage introduces artifact-level security checks. Container images are scanned for known vulnerabilities, and Infrastructure-as-Code (IaC) definitions are recorded and validated against secure configuration standards.

Typical failures here include outdated base images, vulnerable system packages, or insecure cloud configurations such as public storage buckets or overly permissive IAM roles.

Example Docker and IaC scanning:

```
- name: Scan Docker image
  uses: aquasecurity/trivy-action@v0.20.0
  with:
    image-ref: my-app:latest
    severity: HIGH,CRITICAL
    exit-code: 1

- name: Scan Terraform configuration
  uses: bridgecrewio/checkov-action@v12
  with:
    directory: infrastructure/
```

Failing the pipeline at this stage prevents insecure artifacts from ever being deployed, even if the application code itself is sound.

4. Pre-Production Deployment: Policy and Advanced Testing

Before deploying to pre-production or staging environments, policy-as-code gates enforce organisational and regulatory standards. Tools like Open Policy Agent (OPA) ensure deployments comply with predefined rules - for example, blocking services without encryption or enforcing mandatory logging.

Optionally, deeper security testing such as fuzz testing or targeted penetration testing can be triggered here, as the cost and execution time are higher.

Example OPA policy enforcement:

```
- name: Emforce deployment policies
  run: |
    opa eval --fail-defined \
      --data policy.rego \
      --input deployment.json \
      "data.security.allow"
```

At this point, promotion is only allowed if the system meets both technical and governance requirements.

By embedding security scans as quality gates throughout the pipeline, security becomes continuous, contextual, and developer-centric. Early checks are fast and educational, later checks are stricter and more comprehensive, and every failure provides clear remediation guidance. This model shifts security left without overwhelming teams and ensures that by the time code reaches production, note only functional, but demonstrably secure.

In practice, this approach transforms security from a final hurdle into a shared engineering responsibility, one enforced automatically, consistently, and at scale.

Best Practices for CI/CD Security Scanning

Below are some important best practices to implement and get the best value out of your security quality gates.

Scan early, scan often

- Run lightweight SAST and SCA checks on every commit or PR
- Catch issues before they compound in later stages

Fail smart

- Block builds only for critical or high-severity issues
- Flag medium/low risks with warnings and remediation guidance

Use baseline reports

- For legacy codebases, apply gates only to *new or changed code*

- This avoids overwhelming teams while still improving over time

Enforce policies automatically

- Define rules as code (e.g., "no deploy if CVSS > 7.0") and integrate them into pipeline logic

Customize rule sets

- Align scans with your tech stack, threat model, and compliance requirements

Make results actionable

- Surface feedback in PRs, dashboards, and build logs
- Link directly to remediation guidance where possible

Challenges to Watch For

As security analysis becomes more deeply embedded into CI/CD pipelines, teams inevitably encounter challenges that can undermine both effectiveness and adoption if left unaddressed. While automated security gates are powerful, they must be implemented thoughtfully to avoid unnecessary friction, slow delivery, or overwhelm engineers with low-value findings.

The following challenges are commonly seen when introducing or scaling security analysis in pipelines, along with practical strategies to mitigate them and ensure that security gates remain accurate, actionable, and supportive of developer productivity rather than an obstacle to it.

Challenge	Mitigation Strategy
Too many false positives	Tune scanning tools to better match the application context and technology stack Apply rulesets, baselines, or suppressions for known low-risk findings Regularly review and refine filters to keep results relevant and actionable
Developer fatigue	Block the pipeline only for high-severity or high-confidence issues Surface lower-severity findings as warnings or backlog items instead of hard failures Align severity thresholds with risk tolerance and business impact
Scan times slowing pipelines	Use caching and incremental scans to analyse only changed code or dependencies Run heavier scans asynchronously or outside the critical deployment path Separate fast "gate" scans from deeper scheduled or nightly scans
Poor visibility	Centralize results in dashboards that show trends, risk levels, and ownership Integrate findings with ticketing or work-tracking tools for clear follow-up Provide teams with clear feedback loops and reporting on remediation progress

Key Metrics to Track

And in reporting on the effectiveness of teams in addressing and improving their security practices, the below metrics are important to track.

Metric	What It Measures	Why It Matters
Number of vulnerabilities by severity	Tracks how many security findings exist at each severity level (critical, high, medium, low)	Helps teams understand overall risk exposure and prioritize remediation efforts based on impact

Time to remediation	Measures how long it takes to fix a vulnerability from detection	Provides insight into team responsiveness and how well security is integrated into delivery workflows
% of builds blocked due to security issues	Indicates how often security gates prevent builds or deployments from progressing	Highlights gate effectiveness and whether thresholds are appropriately tuned
False positive rate	Proportion of reported security findings that are ultimately non-issues	Assesses the accuracy of scanning tools and identifies need for better configuration or rule tuning
Coverage of code and infrastructure scanned	Shows the extent to which application code, dependencies, and infrastructure are analysed by security tools	Ensures security gates provide comprehensive and consistent protection across the pipeline

Security scanning in CI/CD is not just a safety net, it's a proactive defence mechanism that empowers developers to build secure software by default. When integrated thoughtfully into your quality gates, it supports rapid delivery without sacrificing security, turning DevSecOps from a buzzword into an everyday practice.

Licensing and Compliance Enforcement in CI/CD

Security is more than just looking for vulnerabilities in your solution. As modern software relies increasingly on open-source libraries, third-party services, and cloud infrastructure, ensuring legal and regulatory compliance is no longer just a legal team concern, it's a key part of engineering responsibility.

By integrating licensing and compliance enforcement into CI/CD pipelines, organizations can prevent unintentional license violations, meet industry standards, and avoid expensive remediation or legal exposure.

Done right, compliance becomes automated, traceable, and scalable, without becoming a bottleneck to delivery speed.

What Is Licensing and Compliance Enforcement?

Licensing and compliance enforcement ensures that all components of your software - code, dependencies, infrastructure, and deployment configurations - adhere to:

- Open-source license obligations
- Internal usage policies
- Regulatory frameworks (e.g., GDPR, SOC 2, HIPAA, PCI-DSS)
- Security and auditability standards

This is achieved through automated checks built into your CI/CD pipeline that act as quality gates to block non-compliant changes before they go live.

Why It Matters

- Avoid legal risk from using incompatible or restrictive licenses (e.g., GPL, AGPL)
- Maintain audit trails for regulatory compliance and certification

- Detect and stop use of prohibited packages, services, or configurations
- Build customer trust through transparency and adherence to security/privacy standards
- Scale governance across large teams and multiple pipelines

Types of Compliance Checks in CI/CD

As software delivery pipelines become more automated and reliant on third-party components and cloud infrastructure, compliance can no longer be treated as a periodic, manual exercise. Licensing, data protection, infrastructure standards, and auditability all introduce real legal, financial, and reputational risk if they are not enforced consistently.

By embedding compliance checks directly into CI/CD quality gates, teams can continuously validate that their software adheres to organisational policies and regulatory requirements, while still moving at speed.

The following areas highlight the most common compliance concerns addressed by modern pipelines, along with the tools and approaches typically used to enforce them automatically.

Area	What's Checked	Tools & Approaches
Open-source license checks	Flagging incompatible or risky licenses (e.g., GPL, SSPL)	Snyk, FOSSA, OWASP Dependency-Track, ScanCode
Dependency policy checks	Banning specific packages or versions (e.g., log4j, crypto libs)	Renovate, LicenseFinder, custom gate scripts

Data handling validation	GDPR/PII exposure in logs, configs, test data	Static checks, secrets scanners, regex tooling
Infrastructure compliance	Cloud configs, encryption standards, access controls	tfsec, Checkov, OPA, HashiCorp Sentinel
Audit trail enforcement	Verifying traceability of changes, approvals, and signatures	Git commit signing, PR templates, CI logs
Policy-as-Code	Enforcing security/privacy/compliance as code rules	OPA, Rego policies, Conftest, Sentinel

Integrating Licensing & Compliance Gates in the Pipeline

As organisations scale their use of open-source software and cloud-native platforms, licensing and compliance risks increasingly surface directly within the delivery pipeline rather than after release. Integrating licensing and compliance checks as first-class quality gates ensures that legal, regulatory, and governance requirements are enforced automatically and consistently, without relying on manual reviews or late-stage audits.

When implemented correctly, these gates provide early feedback to developers, reduce the risk of non-compliant releases, and create a verifiable trail of evidence that satisfies both internal governance teams and external regulators.

In practice, licensing and compliance gates span multiple stages of the CI/CD pipeline and address different layers of the system. Dependency licensing gates analyse all third-party packages during the build to ensure their licenses align with organisational policy, immediately failing the build if prohibited licenses are detected. Infrastructure compliance gates scan infrastructure-as-code definitions - such as Terraform or Kubernetes manifests - to prevent insecure or non-compliant configurations from being deployed.

Secrets and data protection checks stop hardcoded credentials or sensitive information from entering the codebase, while governance enforcement gates ensure the correct approvals, reviews, and signatures are in place for regulated components.

Finally, audit and artifact verification gates confirm that every release is fully traceable, with complete metadata, manifests, and changelogs, enabling teams to prove compliance long after the software has been deployed.

In summary

- **Dependency Licensing Gate**
  - Automatically scan all packages used in build
  - Fail build if license policy is violated (e.g., use of GPL in a commercial product)
- **Infrastructure Compliance Gate**
  - Run IaC scanning tools on Terraform, Kubernetes, etc.
  - Block deployments with unencrypted buckets or public databases
- **Secrets & Data Protection**
  - Prevent hardcoded secrets or sensitive info (e.g., PII) from entering the codebase

- **Governance Enforcement**
    - Require PR approvals, code owner reviews, or commit signing for regulated components
- **Audit & Artifact Verification**
    - Ensure all releases are traceable and compliant with changelog, license, and manifest requirements

Best Practices

Below are some best practices to help ensure your quality gates can best protect your software against licensing and compliance issues.

- **Automate Early**: Add license and compliance checks before merge, not just before deployment.
- **Use Allow/Deny Lists**: Create a curated list of approved licenses and packages for use across teams.
- **Treat Violations as Gates**: Block builds on high-risk violations; warn (but log) on low/medium issues.
- **Maintain SBOMs (Software Bill of Materials)**: Automatically generate and store SBOMs for every build to support traceability and audits.
- **Keep Policies in Code**: Version-control compliance rules with your codebase (Policy-as-Code) to support evolution and transparency.

Key Metrics to Monitor

And as with other scans, it's important to track key metrics to assess compliance across teams. These are especially effective for large organisations that need to track this risk against a wide number of code basis.

Metric	What It Measures	Why It Matters
Number of license violations per build	Tracks how many third-party components in a build violate the organisation's approved licensing policies	Helps ensure legal and contractual compliance and reduces legal risk
Time to resolve non-compliance issues	Measures how long it takes teams to fix licensing or compliance problems once detected	Indicates responsiveness and efficiency in addressing compliance issues
% of builds blocked by compliance gates	Shows how often builds fail due to licensing or regulatory non-compliance	Highlights risk exposure and the effectiveness of compliance policies
Audit readiness (e.g., % of components with SBOM and license metadata)	Reflects the completeness and accuracy of compliance evidence for released software	Enables faster, smoother audits and demonstrates regulatory readiness
Compliance gate coverage across teams/projects	Measures how widely compliance gates are implemented in pipelines	Ensures consistent enforcement of policies across the organisation

Incorporating licensing and compliance enforcement into CI/CD pipelines isn't about slowing things down, it's about shifting governance left to ensure secure, legal, and auditable delivery at scale. Just like tests and security scans, compliance gates protect your business, your customers, and your developers from downstream surprises.

They help turn compliance from a stressful checkpoint into a proactive, automated, and developer-friendly process.

Handling Vulnerabilities and CVEs Automatically in CI/CD

As modern applications increasingly depend on open-source libraries and complex infrastructure, security vulnerabilities, especially Common Vulnerabilities and Exposures (CVEs), have become a persistent challenge. Manually tracking and managing these threats is no longer scalable. To stay secure without slowing down delivery, teams must integrate automated vulnerability detection, prioritization, and remediation into their CI/CD pipelines.

Automating the handling of CVEs ensures that your software stays secure, your teams stay productive, and your pipeline enforces meaningful quality gates without creating friction.

What Are CVEs?

CVEs (Common Vulnerabilities and Exposures) are publicly disclosed security flaws in software components. Each CVE includes:

- A unique identifier (e.g., CVE-2024-12345)
- A severity score (CVSS)
- A description of the issue
- References to patches or mitigations

They can affect:

- Third-party libraries and dependencies
- Docker base images

- Operating system packages
- Infrastructure and cloud configurations

Why CVEs Matter in CI/CD

When CVEs are not identified and addressed promptly, they can lead to serious consequences such as data breaches, system exploits, and regulatory or compliance violations. Discovering these issues late in the delivery lifecycle often results in rushed fixes, increased operational risk, and costly remediation efforts. In complex environments with multiple services and frequent releases, manual tracking of vulnerabilities across hundreds of dependencies quickly becomes impractical.

Integrating CVE detection into CI/CD pipelines provides the automation and visibility needed to manage this risk at scale. By surfacing vulnerable dependencies early, ideally before code is merged or deployed, developers can fix issues while changes are still small and context is fresh.

This early feedback not only improves security outcomes but also supports faster, more confident delivery by preventing known risks from reaching production.

Automating CVE Detection and Remediation

To effectively manage CVEs, vulnerability scanning should be embedded at multiple stages of the CI/CD pipeline, with each stage focusing on a different risk surface. Running scanners early and often ensures that vulnerabilities are detected as close as possible to the point where they are introduced, reducing both remediation effort and overall risk.

At the pull request stage, scanners focus on source code dependencies and secrets. Software Composition Analysis (SCA) tools identify known vulnerabilities in third-party libraries before changes are merged, while secret scanning helps prevent credentials from being committed to source control. Catching issues at this stage allows developers to address them immediately, often by updating or replacing a dependency.

During the build stage, scanning expands to include containers, operating system packages, and language-specific dependencies. These checks validate the full artifact that will be deployed, ensuring that vulnerabilities are not introduced through base images or transitive dependencies. Infrastructure-as-Code and configuration scans further validate Terraform, Kubernetes manifests, and Dockerfiles, helping teams detect insecure configurations before they reach runtime.

Finally, post-deployment scanning and monitoring focus on runtime behaviour and emerging threats. These tools detect vulnerabilities, misconfigurations, or suspicious activity in running environments, providing an additional safety net after release. Across all stages, scanner results can be used to enforce severity-based quality gates, automatically failing the pipeline when critical risks are detected and ensuring consistent, auditable security controls.

Stage	What to Scan	Tools
Pull Request	Source code dependencies (SCA), secrets	Snyk, Dependabot, Mend, OWASP DC
Build	Successful code building	Trivy, Grype, Anchore, Clair
IaC/Configs	Terraform, Kubernetes, and Dockerfiles setups	tfsec, Checkov, kube-bench

Post-deploy	Runtime vulnerabilities, threat monitoring	Falco, Aqua Security, Sysdig, Wiz

These scanners generate reports and can fail the pipeline based on severity thresholds.

Set Severity Thresholds for Gates

By defining clear rules around severity thresholds, exceptions, and enforcement levels, teams can ensure that the most critical risks are addressed immediately while lower-risk issues are handled pragmatically. This approach creates a balance between maintaining strong security controls and preserving the speed and autonomy that modern development teams require.

- Fail the build on High / Critical vulnerabilities (e.g., CVSS > 7.0)
- Warn only for Medium / Low severity issues
- Allow exceptions with documented justification

This balances security rigor with development velocity.

Automated Pull Requests for Fixes

Automating dependency updates is a practical way to reduce the operational burden of managing CVEs while improving overall security posture. Tools that automatically detect vulnerable dependencies and open pull requests with recommended upgrades allow teams to address issues as part of their normal development workflow. Instead of relying on manual reviews or ad hoc updates, vulnerabilities are surfaced promptly and accompanied by concrete, actionable fixes.

By integrating these tools into source control platforms, teams can continuously keep their codebases up to date across multiple languages and frameworks. Automated pull requests make remediation visible, reviewable, and auditable, while significantly reducing manual effort.

This approach not only shortens the time between vulnerability disclosure and remediation but also helps maintain long-term code health without disrupting delivery velocity.

Tool	What It Does
Dependabot	Opens PRs to upgrade vulnerable dependencies (GitHub)
Renovate	Automates updates across language ecosystems
Snyk Fix	Suggests fixes and opens PRs directly

Automated updates reduce manual toil and help keep codebases current.

Track SBOMs (Software Bill of Materials)

Generating and tracking Software Bills of Materials (SBOMs) as part of the CI/CD build process provides teams with clear visibility into the components that make up their applications. An SBOM acts as an authoritative inventory of libraries, frameworks, and dependencies, making it easier to understand what is running in each build and where potential risk may exist. This level of transparency is increasingly important in complex, dependency-heavy software ecosystems.

By having SBOMs readily available, teams can respond quickly and confidently when new CVEs are disclosed, identifying affected components without manual investigation or guesswork. SBOMs also support regulatory and compliance requirements by providing auditable evidence of software composition.

Tools such as CycloneDX and Syft can generate SBOMs automatically during CI jobs, ensuring this information is always current and aligned with each released artifact.

Generate and track SBOMs as part of your build process to:

- Know exactly what components you use
- Respond quickly when a CVE affects your stack
- Meet compliance requirements (e.g., US Executive Order 14028)

Best Practices for Automated Vulnerability Management

Below is a summary of best practices that can be implemented to ensure your automated vulnerability measures are successful:

- Scan on every code change, not just scheduled jobs
- Treat new vulnerabilities as blocking gates, not just alerts
- Prioritize by exploitability, not just severity (e.g., fix known exploited CVEs first)
- Whitelist/ignore only with review and expiration date
- Integrate security feedback into PRs where developers work
- Track time-to-remediation as a key performance metric.

Metrics to Monitor

Below is a set of metrics that should be measured to get valuable feedback from your automation processes:

Metric	What It Measures	Why It Matters
Vulnerabilities by severity	Number of security issues in the code or dependencies, categorized by severity	Helps assess overall risk exposure
Time to detect and fix CVEs	How long it takes to identify and remediate known vulnerabilities	Indicates responsiveness to security threats
Number of blocking gates triggered	How often security or quality gates prevent a build from proceeding	Reflects pipeline effectiveness in enforcing standards
% of dependencies with known CVEs	Proportion of libraries or packages with reported vulnerabilities	Indicates codebase hygiene and potential risk
Number of outdated packages	Dependencies that are not up-to-date	Informs upgrade readiness and helps prevent security or compatibility issues

Real-World Scenario

Below is a brief world scenario of how this could look in action:

1. A developer submits a pull request (PR) to add a new Python library to the project. The CI/CD pipeline automatically kicks in to ensure that new code changes meet both functional and security standards.

2. **Dependency Scanning (SCA):** The pipeline runs a Software Composition Analysis (SCA) tool, such as Snyk, against the updated codebase. It detects that a transitive dependency of the new library contains a known vulnerability, CVE-2023-56789, with a critical CVSS score of 9.8.
3. **Automatic Build Failure:** Given the severity of the vulnerability, the pipeline fails the build immediately. This prevents insecure code from being merged into the main branch and ultimately deployed to production.
4. **Developer Feedback:** The pipeline automatically posts a detailed comment on the PR. The comment specifies the exact vulnerable dependency, its version, and a recommended remediation, typically an updated version that resolves the CVE.
5. **Automated Remediation:** To streamline the process, the pipeline also opens an automatic PR that updates the vulnerable dependency to the safe version. This reduces manual effort for the developer and accelerates resolution.
6. **Developer Action & Verification:** The developer reviews the suggested fix, merges the automatic PR, and the pipeline runs again. This time, all security checks pass, allowing the main PR to be merged safely.
7. **Outcome:** The organization maintains a secure codebase without slowing development. Security issues are caught and remediated before they reach production, exemplifying how DevSecOps integrates security into the software delivery lifecycle.

Automating the handling of vulnerabilities and CVEs ensures that security doesn't get left behind in fast-moving delivery pipelines. With the right tools and gates in place, your team can move quickly and confidently, knowing that critical risks are identified and addressed long before they reach your users.

Conclusion: Security is a vital part of the development process

Incorporating DevSecOps into the quality gating process ensures that security is no longer an afterthought but an integral part of the software delivery lifecycle. By embedding automated security checks, such as static analysis, dependency scanning, and compliance gates, directly into CI/CD pipelines, teams can catch vulnerabilities, licensing issues, and configuration risks early, before they reach production. This proactive approach not only reduces potential business and operational risk but also fosters a culture of shared responsibility for security across developers, testers, and operations teams.

Moreover, DevSecOps-driven quality gates create a feedback loop that accelerates remediation, provides actionable insights, and ensures consistent enforcement of organizational standards. Developers are empowered to fix issues as part of their workflow, while automated tools maintain visibility and traceability for auditing and compliance purposes. By aligning security, quality, and delivery objectives, organizations can achieve faster release cycles without compromising safety or reliability, demonstrating that secure software delivery is not a bottleneck but a strategic enabler of high-quality, resilient applications.

Building on the principles of DevSecOps and security-focused quality gates, the next step in ensuring robust software delivery is to extend these gates to performance and reliability. While security gates protect against vulnerabilities and compliance risks, performance and reliability gates ensure that applications not only function correctly but also meet user expectations under real-world conditions.

Performance and Reliability Gates

Purpose of chapter: In this chapter we look at the importance of assessing the non-functional aspects of software in the delivery process – especially its performance and reliability. We will explore why these are importance to track and build into your quality gates, how these can be measured and best practices that can allow then to be tracked directly in pipelines without affecting delivery times.

While functional correctness ensures your application *works*, performance and reliability testing ensure it works well under real-world conditions. In modern software delivery, where user experience and scalability are non-negotiable, integrating performance testing into CI/CD pipelines is essential to detecting regressions early and enforcing SLAs.

To be effective, performance testing must be strategic, automated, and lightweight enough to provide fast feedback, without sacrificing coverage or realism.

Why Performance Testing Belongs in CI/CD

Performance testing is a critical component of CI/CD because functional correctness alone does not guarantee a high-quality user experience. An application can behave correctly from a functional perspective while still being slow, unstable, or inefficient under load. By integrating performance testing into the delivery pipeline, teams can continuously validate that changes do not degrade speed, scalability, or resource consumption as the system evolves.

Including performance checks in CI/CD also enables teams to validate service-level objectives such as latency, throughput, and error rates before changes reach production. This early visibility helps identify bottlenecks and capacity issues when fixes are still relatively inexpensive and low risk. As codebases grow and user traffic scales, ongoing performance validation protects business-critical metrics like time-to-interaction and overall system reliability, ensuring that performance remains a first-class quality concern rather than an afterthought.

- Prevents regressions in speed, scalability, and resource usage
- Validates SLAs/SLOs (e.g., latency, throughput, error rates)
- Catches bottlenecks before production, when fixes are cheaper
- Supports business-critical metrics like time-to-interaction and system reliability
- Protects user experience as the codebase grows and traffic scales

Functional correctness ≠ acceptable performance. Teams need to test both to ensure quality.

When to Include Performance Testing in the Pipeline

Performance testing is most effective when it is distributed across the CI/CD pipeline rather than concentrated in a single, late-stage activity. By aligning different types of performance tests to specific stages, teams can detect regressions early while reserving more resource-intensive testing for points where it adds the most value. This tiered approach helps maintain fast feedback cycles without sacrificing confidence in production readiness.

Early in the pipeline, such as during pre-merge or post-merge CI builds, lightweight benchmarks and basic latency checks provide quick sanity validation and catch obvious regressions before they spread. Closer to release, more comprehensive load, stress, and soak tests are used to validate service-level objectives and ensure the system behaves as expected under realistic conditions. Scheduled or nightly tests establish performance baselines and detect long-term degradation, while post-deployment checks like canary analysis and real-user monitoring confirm that performance in production matches expectations.

Stage	Purpose	Type of Test
Pre-merge (optional)	Quick performance sanity checks	Lightweight benchmarks (e.g., function timing)
Post-merge CI build	Detect early regressions	Micro-benchmarks, API latency checks
Pre-release pipeline	Validate SLAs before deploy	Load, stress, or soak testing
Scheduled/Nightly job	Baseline trends, long-haul regression	Full load tests, endurance tests
Post-deploy	Validate production performance	Canary analysis, real-user

		monitoring (RUM)

Performance testing can be tiered, fast, focused checks early, and heavier simulations later or on schedule.

Types of Performance Testing in CI/CD

The following table outlines common types of performance tests that can be incorporated into CI/CD pipelines to ensure applications meet both functional and non-functional requirements. Each test type serves a specific purpose, from quick sanity checks to long-duration evaluations, and can be executed using a variety of tools tailored to the team's technology stack. Together, these tests provide a comprehensive view of system performance, helping teams identify bottlenecks, optimize resource usage, and maintain reliability under real-world conditions.

Type	Purpose	Tool Examples
Smoke Performance Tests	Quick sanity check on performance	Custom scripts, K6, JMeter
Load Testing	Validate system behaviour under expected traffic	Locust, Gatling, K6
Stress Testing	Assess performance under extreme load	Artillery, Taurus
Soak Testing	Detect degradation over time	Long-duration JMeter runs
Latency Testing	Track response time of key APIs or services	Postman monitors, K6, curl + metrics
Resource Profiling	Evaluate CPU, memory, DB usage	Prometheus, Grafana, Datadog

Including Performance Gates in CI/CD

Integrating performance testing into CI/CD starts with clearly defining what "good" performance looks like.

Teams should establish measurable thresholds for key indicators such as API response times, throughput, and resource utilization, using historical data or agreed business SLAs as a baseline. These benchmarks provide an objective standard against which every change can be evaluated, removing ambiguity and subjective decision-making from performance discussions.

Once expectations are defined, lightweight performance tests can be added to critical points in the pipeline. Short K6 or JMeter scripts targeting high-impact endpoints can run after builds to detect early regressions. These fast checks provide immediate feedback and can fail builds when performance drops beyond an acceptable threshold, preventing issues from progressing further down the pipeline.

More comprehensive performance testing should be handled through separate, scheduled jobs, such as nightly runs or pre-release validations. Results from these tests can be published to dashboards or surfaced directly in pull requests to improve visibility and accountability. By automating comparisons against previous baselines and integrating observability tools like APM and metrics platforms, teams gain a complete view of both synthetic test results and real-world behaviour, enabling data-driven release decisions and continuous performance improvement.

Below is a summary of what this looks like:

Define What "Good" Performance Means

- Set measurable thresholds for key indicators:
    - API response times < 300ms
    - Throughput > 1000 req/sec
    - CPU utilization < 70% under load
- Use historical data or business SLAs as a baseline.

Add Lightweight Tests to Critical Flows

- Run short K6 or JMeter scripts against critical endpoints after build.
- Use these to fail builds if regressions > threshold.

Run Full Performance Tests as Separate Jobs

- Schedule more intensive tests nightly or before releases.
- Publish results to dashboards or log them in PRs for visibility.

Automate Result Comparison

- Compare current test results to previous baselines.
- Gate releases if performance drops more than X% in key metrics.

Integrate Observability Tools

- Combine synthetic tests with real-time APM tools (e.g., New Relic, Datadog, Prometheus).
- Surface real-world degradation alongside synthetic test data.

Pitfalls to Avoid

While performance testing is critical for delivering reliable applications, teams often encounter common pitfalls that can reduce effectiveness or slow down delivery. The table below highlights key challenges in implementing performance gates and provides practical solutions to address them, ensuring that performance feedback remains actionable, consistent, and integrated seamlessly into the CI/CD pipeline.

Pitfall	Solution
Long test runs blocking pipelines	Run heavy tests asynchronously or on merge only
Flaky or environment-sensitive results	Use consistent test environments and warm-up periods
Lack of meaningful thresholds	Define realistic SLAs based on usage patterns and history
Ignored performance warnings	Treat performance feedback as seriously as test failures

Key Metrics to Monitor

Below are some key metrics that should be monitored to get the best out of your performance tests in your CI/CD pipelines:

Metric	What It Measures	Why It Matters
P95 / P99 Response Times	Response time for the slowest 5% or 1% of requests	Captures real user experience and exposes latency spikes that averages hide
Error Rate Under Load	Percentage of failed requests during performance tests	Indicates system instability or capacity limits before they impact users
Resource Consumption (CPU, Memory, I/O)	Infrastructure usage while under load	Helps identify inefficient code, memory leaks, or scaling bottlenecks
Requests Per Second (RPS)	Number of requests the system can handle per second	Validates throughput expectations and scalability targets
Duration & Throughput Trends Across Builds	Performance changes over time between builds	Reveals gradual degradation that might not fail a single test
Regression % vs Last Known Good Baseline	Performance change compared to a stable reference point	Enables objective gating decisions and prevents unnoticed performance decay

Performance testing is not just for late-stage QA or production, it belongs in your shift-left quality strategy. When integrated thoughtfully into CI/CD, it provides early, repeatable assurance that your application can meet real-world demands, protecting both your users and your business.

Using SLAs and SLOs in Gating Logic

As software delivery becomes faster and more continuous, maintaining system reliability and user experience requires more than just passing tests. It requires teams to define, measure, and enforce Service-Level Objectives (SLOs) and Agreements (SLAs) as part of their quality assurance strategy.

By integrating SLAs and SLOs into CI/CD gating logic, organizations can ensure that releases not only function as intended, but also perform reliably, at scale, and under expected conditions, before they reach production.

What Are SLAs and SLOs?

The below table describes these different terms in more detail:

Term	Description
SLA (Service-Level Agreement)	A **formal agreement** between a service provider and a customer, defining expected levels of service (e.g., "99.9% uptime per month").
SLO (Service-Level Objective)	A **measurable internal goal** for reliability or performance (e.g., "p95 response time < 500ms"). SLOs are how you **meet SLAs**.
SLI (Service-Level Indicator)	The actual **metric or measurement** used to assess service quality (e.g., latency, error rate, uptime).

SLOs are the engineering-facing targets that drive operational excellence and product health, while SLAs are the business-facing commitments that can carry legal or financial implications.

Why Use SLOs in CI/CD Quality Gates?

Below are some key reasons why you would want to considering implementing an SLO within your quality gate process:

- Enforces non-functional quality standards (like speed and uptime) before production.
- Shifts performance and reliability concerns left, catching regressions earlier.
- Prevents degradation over time by requiring concrete thresholds for metrics.
- Reduces firefighting by blocking bad releases that could breach SLAs.
- Empowers teams to release confidently, knowing they're meeting defined targets.

Example SLOs You Can Gate On

Below is a table of SLOs and how the gate logic could apply to enforce specific quality measures:

SLI Type	Example SLO	Gate Logic Example
Latency	95% of API calls respond in < 300ms	Fail pipeline if p95_latency > 300ms
Error Rate	< 0.1% request errors in a test run	Fail if error_rate > 0.001
Availability	99.95% uptime for the past 7 days (production)	Block release if recent uptime < target
Resource Usage	CPU stays below 80% during load test	Fail if CPU_util > 80% for > 10% of test time
Throughput	Handle 1,000+ RPS under expected load	Fail if RPS < 1000

These metrics can be collected via load tests, synthetic monitoring, or APM tools and used to automatically evaluate release readiness.

How to Integrate SLOs into CI/CD Gating

Establishing effective performance-based quality gates begins with collaboratively defining Service Level Objectives (SLOs). Product owners, developers, and SREs should work together to agree on objectives that are meaningful, measurable, and directly tied to user experience. Well-defined SLOs ensure that performance expectations are clear and shared, turning abstract ideas of "fast" or "reliable" into concrete targets that teams can design and test against.

Once SLOs are in place, Service Level Indicators (SLIs) should be collected automatically throughout the pipeline and runtime. Synthetic testing tools can generate latency, throughput, and error-rate data during CI runs, while observability platforms provide real-time insight before and after deployment. Pipeline logic can then compare these metrics against defined SLO thresholds, failing builds or blocking deployments when breaches occur. In more advanced setups, teams can even gate releases based on live system health, preventing new changes from being deployed when the system is already operating close to its limits.

Below is a brief summary of how this works:

Define SLOs Collaboratively

- Work with product, SREs, and developers to define meaningful objectives.
- Keep SLOs measurable, actionable, and aligned with user impact.

Collect SLI Metrics Automatically

Integrate tools like:

- K6 or JMeter for synthetic latency/RPS/error metrics
- Prometheus + Grafana for pre/post-deployment observability
- Datadog, New Relic, or Dynatrace for real-time analysis

Compare Against SLO Thresholds in Pipeline

Use scripts or tools to:

- Parse performance results
- Compare metrics to defined thresholds
- Fail the build or deployment if SLOs are breached

Gate Based on Recent Observability Data (Optional)

- Query real-time metrics (e.g., via Prometheus APIs) before allowing a new deployment.
- Block releases if system is already near a breach.

Example Gating Flow with SLO Enforcement

Below is an example of how gating flow will work in a pipeline:

1. Post-merge pipeline runs load test
2. Generates latency and error rate report
3. Parses metrics via custom script or performance tool
4. Compares:
    - p95_latency <= 400ms
    - error_rate <= 0.1%

5. If thresholds are exceeded → pipeline fails, blocking release
6. If thresholds are met → pipeline continues to deploy stage

Example pipeline script

Along with the above flow, it's important to understand how this looks in an actual pipeline script. The following YAML pipeline demonstrates how to enforce performance-based quality gates directly within a CI/CD workflow. By integrating synthetic load testing and automated evaluation of key metrics such as latency and error rate, the pipeline can compare actual results against predefined Service Level Objectives (SLOs). If any threshold is breached, the pipeline fails, preventing the deployment of code that does not meet performance expectations. This approach ensures that performance validation is fully automated, repeatable, and tightly coupled with the software delivery process.

```
name: Performance Gate Pipeline
on:
  push:
    branches:
      - main

jobs:
  performance_test:
    runs-on: ubuntu-latest
    steps:
      - name: Checkout code
        uses: actions/checkout@v3

      - name: Install dependencies
        run: |
          pip install -r requirements.txt

      - name: Run load test
        # Example using K6; output JSON report
        run: |
          k6 run --out json=performance_report.json
tests/load_test.js
```

```
    - name: Evaluate performance gate
      run: |
        python - <<'EOF'
        import json
        import sys

        # Load performance report
        with open("performance_report.json") as f:
            metrics = json.load(f)

        # Extract SLIs
        p95_latency = metrics["http"]["p95"]  # ms
        error_rate = metrics["http"]["error_rate"]
# %

        # Define SLOs
        SLO_LATENCY_MS = 400
        SLO_ERROR_RATE = 0.1

        # Compare against thresholds
        if p95_latency > SLO_LATENCY_MS or
error_rate > SLO_ERROR_RATE:
            print(f" Performance gate failed:
p95_latency={p95_latency}ms,
error_rate={error_rate}%")
            sys.exit(1)  # Fail pipeline
        else:
            print(f" Performance gate passed:
p95_latency={p95_latency}ms,
error_rate={error_rate}%")
        EOF
```

Explanation of above code:
Pipeline Trigger: Runs whenever changes are pushed to the main branch.

Load Testing Step: Executes a synthetic load test using a tool like K6, generating a JSON report containing key metrics.

Performance Gate Step:

- A small Python snippet reads the report and extracts the Service Level Indicators (SLIs) like latency and error rate.

- It compares the SLIs against predefined Service Level Objectives (SLOs).

- If the thresholds are exceeded, the script exits with a non-zero code, causing the pipeline to fail and block deployment.

- Otherwise, the pipeline continues to the next stage.

This YAML approach makes performance validation an automated gate in your CI/CD workflow, ensuring that code meets measurable performance standards before it is deployed.

Best Practices

Below are some best practices that can be implemented to get the most of your SLO enforcement:

- **Treat SLOs as code**: version-control them alongside infrastructure and application code
- **Visualize SLO compliance**: dashboards help teams understand trends over time
- **Gate only on critical indicators**: avoid noisy or low-value metrics
- **Set thresholds based on real usage,** not arbitrary targets
- **Combine automated checks with team alerts** to raise visibility without slowing velocity unnecessarily

Using SLAs and SLOs in gating logic brings real-world expectations into the pipeline. It bridges the gap between code that works in isolation and code that performs reliably under pressure, protecting both your users and your business.

With clear objectives, automated enforcement, and continuous feedback, SLO-based gating helps ensure that quality includes not just correctness, but also resilience, speed, and user satisfaction.

Load Testing in Pre-Prod Environments

As systems grow more complex and user expectations for speed and reliability increase, it becomes critical to test how applications behave under realistic load conditions, *before* deploying to production. This is where load testing in pre-production environments plays a vital role.

By running load tests in pre-prod, teams can detect performance bottlenecks, scalability limits, and breaking points early, preventing costly outages and SLA breaches in production. It's a powerful quality gate that ensures software not only works, but works well at scale.

Why Load Testing in Pre-Prod Matters

- Validates application behaviour under expected or peak load
- Exposes performance regressions before production rollout
- Ensures infrastructure scalability and auto-scaling readiness
- Reveals bottlenecks in backend services, APIs, databases, and caches
- Protects production uptime and customer experience
- Supports data-driven capacity planning

Relying solely on production monitoring to identify load issues is reactive, pre-prod load testing enables a proactive performance strategy.

What to Test in Pre-Prod Load Scenarios

Trying to performance test everything through your CI?CD pipelines can prove wasteful as not only would it prove expensive in your infrastructure, but the slowdown in execution would reduce any speed benefits that would be gotten from having a pipeline. Below are the key things that should be tested – and even then – only on specific

Area	What to Validate
API Endpoints	Latency, throughput, error rate, concurrency limits
Database Performance	Query execution time, connection pooling behaviour
Caching Layers	Cache hit/miss ratio, eviction performance
Message Queues / Streams	Processing lag, backpressure behaviour
Web UI	Load time under concurrent users (optional)
Autoscaling & Failover	System elasticity and recovery under stress

Load testing in pre-prod is also the ideal place to simulate edge cases, such as:

- Sudden traffic spikes
- Long-running sessions
- Traffic skew to specific endpoints

Types of Load Testing in Pre-Prod

Pre-production load testing is essential for ensuring that applications perform reliably under varying conditions before reaching end users. The table below summarizes common types of load tests, their purpose, and typical use cases. Each test type targets a specific aspect of system performance, from validating expected user load to uncovering potential bottlenecks, helping teams proactively identify and address issues that could impact scalability, stability, and user experience.

Type	Description	Use Case
Baseline Load Test	Verifies system handles expected user load	Routine release check
Stress Test	Pushes system beyond capacity to find failure point	Scalability limits, chaos testing prep
Spike Test	Tests response to sudden, sharp increases in load	Black Friday-style event readiness
Soak Test	Runs steady load for an extended time	Memory leaks, performance degradation over time
Component Isolation	Tests subsystems (e.g., DB, cache) under load	Bottleneck identification

Tools Commonly Used for Load Testing

A variety of tools are available to support performance and load testing, each offering different features and strengths depending on the application and testing requirements. The table below highlights some of the most commonly used tools, ranging from lightweight, developer-friendly options to mature, extensible frameworks capable of simulating complex user behaviour. Selecting the right tool helps teams efficiently design, execute, and analyse performance tests to ensure systems meet defined reliability and scalability objectives.

Tool	Highlights
K6	Modern, developer-friendly, scriptable
JMeter	Mature, GUI + CLI support, extensible
Locust	Python-based, user behaviour simulation
Artillery	Lightweight, YAML-based, good for APIs
Gatling	Scala-based, detailed scenario scripting

Taurus	Wrapper to run multiple load tools

Many of these tools integrate with CI/CD pipelines, allowing automated execution and result validation.

Integrating Load Testing into CI/CD Pipelines

To implement effective performance and reliability gates in pre-production, teams should follow a structured approach that ensures tests are both realistic and actionable. This includes triggering tests on pre-production deployments, parameterizing them to reflect real-world usage, defining clear pass/fail thresholds, and reporting results in a way that is easily accessible to developers and SREs. Together, these practices provide actionable insights, enforce quality gates, and help ensure that applications meet performance expectations before reaching end users.

1. **Trigger on Pre-Production Deployment**
   - Run tests post-deployment, but before go-live
   - Use same infrastructure as production (e.g., staging or blue/green)
2. **Parameterize Tests**
   - Use real-world traffic patterns, data sizes, and authentication
   - Adjust concurrency levels to simulate realistic usage
3. **Set Pass/Fail Thresholds**
   - Define quality gates for:
     - p95 latency < X ms
     - error rate < Y%
     - CPU usage < Z%
   - Use automation to parse results and gate further promotion
4. **Report and Visualize**
   - Push results to Grafana, Prometheus, or CI dashboards

  - Enable developers and SREs to quickly analyse trends and anomalies

We won't look further into any specific yaml files here, as the one from the preceding section above on performance testing, should apply here as well.

Best Practices for Effective Load Testing in Pre-Prod

Below are some best practices worth considering to get the most out of load testing in your pre-production environments:

- **Use production-like environments**: Mirror configurations, services, and data volume (anonymized if needed)
- **Run tests with clean rollback support**: Don't risk test failures blocking recovery: use blue/green or ephemeral setups
- **Schedule tests regularly**; Nightly or post-merge tests help detect regressions incrementally
- **Correlate with observability tools**: Monitor logs, traces, and resource usage during tests for deeper insights
- **Involve cross-functional teams**: Developers, QA, and SREs should jointly define test scenarios and thresholds

What to Measure

The table below summarizes key performance metrics commonly monitored during load and reliability testing, explaining what each metric measures and why it is important for ensuring scalable, responsive, and resilient systems.

Performance and Reliability Gates

Metric	What It Measures	Why It Matters
Requests per second	Number of requests the system can handle per second	Indicates throughput and overall service efficiency under load
Latency (p50/p95/p99)	Time taken to respond to requests at different percentiles	Reflects user-perceived responsiveness and identifies slow requests
Error rate	Percentage of requests that fail or return errors	Shows the frequency of API or service failures under load
CPU/Memory usage	Utilization of compute and memory resources	Detects resource saturation and helps assess scalability limits
Queue depth / lag	Number of requests waiting to be processed	Identifies throughput bottlenecks and potential system congestion
System recovery time	Time taken to return to normal operation after a load spike	Measures post-load resilience and availability recovery

Load testing in pre-production is a safety net and a performance guarantee, not a luxury. When included as a CI/CD quality gate, it ensures that your application can handle what's coming, whether it's expected traffic or an unexpected surge. It's the difference between shipping software and shipping software that scales confidently.

Let me know if you'd like to follow this up with guidance on automated baselining, performance regression dashboards, or testing under production mirroring.

Chaos and Fault-Injection Testing

With companies relying on a complexity of microservices, distributed systems, and complex cloud infrastructure, failures are not just possible, they're inevitable. The question is not if things will fail, but how gracefully your system will recover when they do.

That's where chaos and fault-injection testing come in. These advanced techniques go beyond traditional testing by deliberately introducing failures into your system to verify its resilience, ensure fault tolerance, and identify weaknesses before your users do.

What Is Chaos Testing?

Chaos testing is the intentional disruption of system components, services, infrastructure, networks, or dependencies - to simulate unpredictable, real-world failure conditions. The goal is to observe how the system behaves, recoveries trigger, alerts fire, and whether user-facing SLAs are still met.

It's not about breaking things randomly, it's a controlled and strategic exercise to build confidence in system reliability.

What Is Fault-Injection Testing?

Fault injection is a more targeted form of chaos testing, where specific errors or anomalies are introduced (e.g., latency spikes, dropped packets, corrupted messages) to validate how the system or service responds to known failure modes.

Together, they form the backbone of resilience engineering.

Why Include Chaos Testing in Your Quality Gates?

- Validates system resilience and failover mechanisms
- Ensures high availability targets (e.g., 99.99% uptime) can be realistically achieved
- Uncovers cascading failures, hidden coupling, and poor retry strategies
- Reduces mean time to recovery (MTTR) by proactively testing recovery paths
- Builds confidence to release quickly, even in volatile environments

Where Chaos Testing Fits in the Pipeline

The table below outlines where chaos testing can be integrated within the CI/CD pipeline, highlighting the environments and use cases where controlled disruption helps validate system resilience and reliability.

Stage	**Use Case**
Pre-prod (safe)	Run chaos experiments before production rollout
Staging/Blue-Green	Validate system behaviour in isolated replica environments
Production (optional)	Controlled chaos with strong safeguards (e.g., during off-peak)

Chaos testing is not for every build, it's typically used as a scheduled job, during critical releases, or as part of release hardening workflows.

Common Faults to Inject

Chaos testing relies on simulating a variety of fault types to evaluate how systems behave under adverse conditions. The table below highlights common fault scenarios, ranging from service crashes and network disruptions to resource exhaustion and dependency failures. By deliberately introducing these faults in a controlled manner, teams can identify weaknesses, validate recovery mechanisms, and improve overall system resilience.

Fault Type	Example Scenarios
Service failure	Kill pod/service unexpectedly
Network latency	Inject 300ms delay between services
Packet loss	Drop 5% of outgoing traffic
Dependency timeout	Simulate unresponsive external API
Resource exhaustion	Fill disk or max out memory on a node
DNS failures	Corrupt or delay DNS resolution

These tests help validate retry logic, circuit breakers, timeouts, autoscaling, and observability tooling.

Tools for Chaos and Fault-Injection Testing

A variety of tools are available to support chaos and fault-injection testing, each offering different capabilities for simulating failures and evaluating system resilience. The table below highlights popular options, from Kubernetes-native orchestrators to network simulation utilities and SaaS platforms, enabling teams to safely introduce controlled disruptions and assess how their applications respond under stress.

Tool	Features
Chaos Mesh	Kubernetes-native chaos orchestration
LitmusChaos	CNCF project for chaos workflows in K8s
Gremlin	SaaS platform with safe fault injection
Toxiproxy	Network condition simulation for services

Istio + Envoy filters	Inject latency/errors at service mesh level
Netflix Chaos Monkey	Random instance termination in prod (legacy)

Many of these tools support automated validation and rollback, making them ideal for safe integration into CI/CD workflows.

How to Integrate Chaos Testing into Pipelines

Integrating chaos testing into CI/CD pipelines helps teams proactively validate system resilience and recovery mechanisms before failures impact end users. The following steps outline a structured approach, from defining expected behaviour and running controlled fault scenarios to automatically validating outcomes, tagging experiments to releases, and capturing detailed observability data. This ensures that chaos experiments are repeatable, actionable, and closely tied to the software delivery process.

1. **Define Expected Behaviour**
    - What should the system do during a fault? (e.g., degrade gracefully, retry, failover)
2. **Run Controlled Fault Scenarios**
    - Execute chaos experiments in pre-prod or shadow environments
3. **Validate Outcomes Automatically**
    - Compare real system metrics (SLOs, alerts) against expectations
    - Fail the pipeline if the system doesn't meet recovery objectives
4. **Tag Experiments to Releases**
    - Associate chaos experiments with specific builds or infrastructure changes
5. **Observe and Log Everything**
    - Use tracing, metrics, and logs to understand how failures propagate

What to Measure

Chaos testing generates valuable insights into system resilience by measuring how applications respond to faults and failures. The table below summarizes key metrics commonly monitored during chaos experiments, what each metric measures, and why it matters for ensuring recoverability, containment, and end-user experience.

Metric	What It Measures	Why It Matters
Recovery time (MTTR)	Time taken for the system to recover after a fault	Indicates how quickly services return to normal, minimizing downtime and impact on users
Error rate under chaos	Frequency of errors while faults are injected	Measures the resilience of retry logic, failovers, and fallback mechanisms
SLO compliance during fault	Percentage of SLOs met during fault scenarios	Reflects whether end-user experience remains acceptable under adverse conditions
Alerting coverage	Whether the appropriate monitoring alerts were triggered	Ensures observability and timely detection of issues during failures
Blast radius	Scope of impact caused by the fault	Evaluates whether failures are contained or propagate, guiding design improvements for system isolation

Best Practices

Below is a list of best practices to help you introduce chaos testing successfully into any teams or organisation.

- **Start small**: Inject basic failures (e.g., service restarts) before escalating
- **Test in production only with guardrails**: Use canary releases and user segmentation
- **Use hypotheses**: Define what you expect to happen during the fault
- **Automate rollback**: Design pipelines that can revert to safe state quickly
- **Make it regular**: Schedule chaos drills as part of your release lifecycle

Chaos and fault-injection testing shift quality gates from *"Does it work?"* to *"Does it survive real-world failure?"* It's a sign of a mature engineering culture, one that treats resilience as a feature and proactively engineers for failure.

When integrated safely into CI/CD, chaos testing doesn't slow down delivery, it builds the confidence to move faster.

Conclusion: Stability is key to software success

Performance and resilience gating in CI/CD pipelines ensures that applications not only function correctly but also meet defined expectations for speed, stability, and fault tolerance. By integrating load testing, monitoring key performance metrics, and leveraging chaos testing, teams can detect bottlenecks, validate recovery mechanisms, and enforce automated quality gates that prevent substandard code from reaching production. These practices embed reliability and scalability into the delivery process, enabling faster, safer releases and stronger alignment with user expectations.

Building on this foundation, the next chapter explores custom and context-driven quality gates, which allow teams to define pipeline checks tailored to specific business requirements, technology stacks, or operational contexts. This approach ensures that every release is evaluated not just against generic standards, but against metrics and thresholds that matter most to the organization and its end users.

Custom and Contextual Quality Gates

Purpose of chapter: The chapter explores how teams can go beyond standard checks to implement pipeline validations tailored to their unique applications, business requirements, and operational environments. It covers defining meaningful, context-specific metrics, integrating business and technical rules into automated gates, and using dynamic thresholds that adapt to evolving workloads or user behaviour.

It's impossible to measure everything – especially when trying to move fast at the same time. This is where contextualisation of quality gates becomes important, as it allows teams to configure rules to apply in certain situations ensuring that strictness in certain checks is only applied when necessary and doesn't create an unnecessary slowdown in delivery when certain checks may not apply.

Setting up a variety of custom quality gates within a team or organization is important because not all applications, services, or workflows have the same priorities or risk profiles. While standard gates like security, performance, and compliance cover broad concerns, custom gates allow teams to enforce rules that are specific to their business context, technology stack, or operational requirements. For example, a payment service may need stricter latency and error thresholds than a content management system, while a machine learning pipeline might require model accuracy or data quality gates before deployment.

Additionally, custom quality gates promote consistency and accountability across teams. They provide clear, enforceable standards that reflect organizational priorities and best practices, ensuring that all releases meet agreed-upon expectations. By defining gates that are relevant to each project or environment, teams can catch issues earlier, reduce rework, and make pipeline feedback more actionable. Ultimately, a well-designed set of custom quality gates empowers teams to balance agility with reliability, delivering software that is both high-quality and aligned with the organization's goals.

Feature Flag Gating

As modern development embraces continuous integration and delivery, the ability to control the release of features independently from deployment has become essential. This is made possible by feature flags, a powerful technique that decouples code changes from feature exposure, and when used strategically, serves as an effective quality gate within CI/CD pipelines.

Feature flag gating enables teams to ship code quickly while controlling risk, improving testability, and gathering real-time feedback from production environments, all without sacrificing stability or user experience.

What Is Feature Flag Gating?

Feature flag gating is the practice of using feature flags (also called toggles) to:

- Gate access to features based on conditions (e.g., environment, user group, region)
- Allow or block feature activation dynamically
- Integrate gating decisions into CI/CD pipelines for controlled rollout

It effectively turns feature release into a runtime decision, not just a deployment one.

Why Use Feature Flags as Quality Gates?

Feature flags and progressive delivery techniques provide teams with powerful tools to manage how and when new functionality reaches users, enabling controlled rollouts, experimentation, and rapid feedback while reducing risk in production environments.

- **Decouple deployment from release**: Ship features hidden behind flags and activate them later
- **Enable progressive delivery**: Roll out gradually (e.g., 1% → 10% → 100%)
- **Minimize blast radius**: Quickly disable faulty features in production without redeploying
- **Facilitate A/B testing and experimentation**
- **Control access during testing**: Enable features only for QA, internal teams, or beta users
- **Accelerate feedback**: Test features in production-like conditions with real data

Use Cases for Feature Flag Gating in CI/CD

Feature flag gating in CI/CD pipelines provides teams with a flexible mechanism to control how and when new functionality is exposed to users, helping balance speed of delivery with risk management. By gating risky features behind flags, organizations can validate functionality in production without impacting all users, enabling safer rollouts and more targeted testing. Canary deployments allow features to be enabled for a small subset of users, collecting feedback and monitoring system behaviour before a full-scale release.

Feature flags also support hotfixes or workarounds by temporarily disabling problematic functionality, serve customer-specific features for different accounts or tenants, and facilitate automated testing by triggering gated flows in a controlled manner.

Additionally, kill switches allow teams to instantly disable features if unexpected issues arise, eliminating the need for costly rollbacks. Collectively, these capabilities make feature flags a powerful tool for delivering software more safely, iteratively, and with greater confidence in production environments.

Scenario	**How Feature Flags Help**
Risky feature rollout	Gate behind a flag until it's validated in production
Canary deployments	Enable features for a small subset of users
Hotfixes or workarounds	Temporarily disable or route around a broken feature
Customer-specific features	Serve or hide features based on account or tenant
Test gating	Enable test automation to trigger gated flows explicitly
Kill switches	Instantly disable features without rollback

Where Feature Flags Fit in the Pipeline

Feature flags integrate throughout the CI/CD pipeline to provide controlled, flexible release management from development to production. During development, developers build new functionality behind flags, ensuring that both gated and non-gated logic coexist in the codebase. In the build stage, this allows features to be compiled and packaged safely without exposing them prematurely. Test automation can explicitly toggle flags to verify new behaviour under controlled conditions, while staging or pre-production environments enable features in a realistic setting to validate functionality and performance.

When deploying to production, code can be released safely with new features disabled by default, and the actual release is managed dynamically, often through a UI or API, allowing teams to enable features selectively, progressively, or for targeted user segments. This integration ensures that feature flags support safer, more flexible, and iterative delivery throughout the software lifecycle.

Pipeline Stage	Role of Feature Flags
Development	Developers commit with flags already in place
Build	Code includes both gated and non-gated logic
Test Automation	Tests explicitly toggle flags to test new functionality
Staging/Pre-prod	Features activated in test environments
Production Deploy	Code deploys safely with features disabled by default
Release	Features are turned on dynamically, often via UI or API

This allows safe experimentation while maintaining a consistent deployment pipeline.

Tools That Support Feature Flag Gating

A variety of tools are available to implement and manage feature flags, ranging from full-featured commercial platforms to lightweight open-source solutions, enabling teams to control feature exposure, experiment safely, and tailor releases to specific users or environments.

Tool	Highlights
LaunchDarkly	Full-featured feature management and targeting engine
Unleash	Open-source, customizable strategy-based flags
Flagsmith	Open-source with API control and remote config
Split.io	A/B testing and analytics-driven gating
ConfigCat, Flipt	Lightweight and developer-friendly
Roll your own	Custom toggles backed by config files or DB

Most platforms support:

- Targeting rules
- Auditing and logging
- Real-time flag toggling
- SDKs for many languages

Best Practices for Feature Flag Gating

Below are a list of best practices to consider when introducing feature flag gating into your software delivery process:

- **Treat flags as temporary**: Clean them up after rollout to avoid technical debt.
- **Use naming conventions**: E.g., feature_checkout_redesign
- **Avoid flag sprawl**: Limit the number of concurrent active flags per service
- **Gate with intent**: Use flags to control rollout, not to avoid proper testing
- **Test both flag states**: Ensure that both "on" and "off" conditions are covered in CI

- **Restrict who can toggle flags**: Use RBAC and audit trails to avoid accidental exposure

Security and Compliance Considerations

Along with these best practices – it's important to also consider the following security and compliance rules are implemented to ensure your different feature flag rules continue to enforce the correct compliance measures:

- **Secure the control plane**: Ensure only authorized users or services can toggle flags
- **Log all changes**: Maintain an audit trail of flag state changes
- **Treat flags as code**: Version-control rules and rollout plans alongside application code

Key Metrics to Track

The table below highlights key metrics for monitoring feature flag usage, measuring both their operational impact and potential risks, and ensuring that feature flags remain effective, safe, and maintainable throughout the software lifecycle.

Metric	What It Measures	Why It Matters
% of users exposed to a new feature	Proportion of users who see a gated feature	Tracks adoption while managing risk exposure during rollouts
Flag-related errors or exceptions	Errors or failures occurring in feature-flagged code	Indicates runtime bugs or instability introduced by gated logic
Time to disable after issue detection	How quickly a feature flag can be toggled off	Measures responsiveness to production incidents and limits user impact

	after a problem is found	
Number of stale flags	Count of unused or outdated feature flags in the codebase	Highlights technical debt and the need for cleanup to maintain maintainable code

Feature flag gating enables a more controlled, flexible, and resilient approach to releasing software. It empowers teams to move fast without breaking things, by allowing safe exposure, faster rollback, and smarter experimentation.

Used as a quality gate in CI/CD, it transforms the pipeline into a progressive delivery engine, where shipping faster doesn't mean taking on more risk, it means managing it more intelligently.

Environment-Specific Gates in CI/CD Pipelines

As software moves through development, testing, staging, and production environments, it encounters increasingly complex requirements, risks, and quality expectations. This is where environment-specific gates come into play, allowing teams to apply context-aware quality checks at each stage of the pipeline.

Environment-specific gates ensure that the right validations, policies, and controls are enforced based on where the code is and what it's about to impact, helping to balance speed with safety and reliability.

What Are Environment-Specific Gates?

Environment-specific gates are conditional quality controls tailored to specific stages or environments in your CI/CD pipeline. They ensure that:

- Each environment (dev, test, staging, prod, etc.) applies only the checks relevant to its purpose
- The progression of a build or release is gated by environment-critical criteria
- Risk increases are matched with stricter validation as code moves closer to users

They provide granular control and help avoid "one-size-fits-all" pipeline logic.

Common Environments and Their Purpose

The table below outlines common software environments used in CI/CD pipelines, describing their primary purpose and role in ensuring quality, reliability, and safe delivery throughout the development lifecycle.

There can be many different variation of these utilised in different teams – sometimes in a more streamlined approach and sometimes delivery processes may require more environments to cater for a wider range of different configurations and integrations. Many of these other environments though will likely fall into one of these 4 categories and dealt with accordingly in the respective gating measures.

Environment	Purpose
Development	Fast iteration, local validation, pre-commit tests
Testing	Run automated tests (unit, integration, E2E)
Staging/UAT	Production-like validation, manual QA, perf tests
Production	Live user traffic, highest risk, final deployment

Each environment has different risk tolerance and requires different quality signals.

Examples of Environment-Specific Gates

Environment-specific quality gates enforce checks tailored to each stage of the CI/CD pipeline, ensuring that code meets progressively stricter standards as it moves closer to production. The table below illustrates typical gates applied at different environments, from development through production, helping teams catch issues early, maintain code quality, and reduce risk during deployment.

Environment	Typical Quality Gates Enforced
Development	Code formatting, linting, unit tests, pre-commit hooks
Test/CI	Build success, test coverage threshold, dependency scan
Staging	Integration test pass, load test results, feature flag configuration, manual approval
Production	SLO checks, change approval, security sign-off, artifact promotion, rollback readiness

These gates progressively raise the bar, reducing the likelihood of issues reaching production.

How to Implement Environment-Specific Gates

Implementing environment-specific gates in a CI/CD pipeline ensures that code meets progressively stricter criteria as it moves through development, testing, staging, and production. By defining clear objectives for each environment, segmenting the pipeline into stages, applying appropriate tooling conditionally, and automating promotion only after all gates pass, teams can enforce quality, security, and reliability standards in a structured and repeatable way.

1. **Define per-environment objectives**
   - What must be true before promoting to the next stage?

   - Align with risk level and purpose of each environment
2. **Segment your pipeline**
   - Break your pipeline into **stages mapped to environments**
   - Use environment conditions to control what checks run and when
3. **Apply tooling conditionally**
   - Use CI/CD features (e.g., GitHub Actions environments, GitLab stages, Azure DevOps approvals) to gate execution
   - Integrate external tools for approvals, test reports, or metrics
4. **Automate promotion only after passing gates**
   - Ensure promotion from one environment to the next (e.g., test → staging) only happens if all relevant gates pass

Here's a simple example using a YAML pipeline (GitHub Actions style) to illustrate environment-specific gates:

```
name: Environment-Specific Gates Pipeline
on:
  push:
    branches:
      - main

jobs:
  build:
    runs-on: ubuntu-latest
    steps:
      - name: Checkout code
        uses: actions/checkout@v3
      - name: Run unit tests
        run: pytest

  test:
    needs: build
    runs-on: ubuntu-latest
    steps:
      - name: Run integration tests
        run: pytest tests/integration
```

```
  staging:
    needs: test
    runs-on: ubuntu-latest
    environment: staging
    steps:
      - name: Run load tests
        run: k6 run --out json=staging_perf.json
tests/load_test.js
      - name: Manual approval
        uses: hmarr/auto-approve-action@v2

  production:
    needs: staging
    runs-on: ubuntu-latest
    environment: production
    steps:
      - name: Check SLOs
        run: |
          python check_slo.py
performance_report.json
      - name: Deploy
        run: ./deploy_prod.sh
```

Explanation:

- **Define per-environment objectives:** Each job corresponds to an environment, with checks appropriate for its risk level (e.g., unit tests in development, load tests in staging, SLO checks in production).
- **Segment the pipeline:** needs: ensures that jobs run in sequence, reflecting the promotion flow between environments.
- **Apply tooling conditionally:** The environment field maps jobs to specific environments, enabling features like approvals, secrets, or policies that vary by environment. External tools, such as K6 or custom SLO scripts, enforce environment-specific gates.
- **Automate promotion:** The next stage only runs if all prior jobs pass, ensuring that promotion from one environment to the next is fully gated.

This structure provides a repeatable, automated approach to enforcing quality gates tailored to each stage of the CI/CD pipeline.

Tools Supporting Environment-Specific Gates

Different CI/CD platforms provide built-in features to implement environment-specific gates, enabling teams to control promotions, approvals, and environment-specific configurations throughout the pipeline.

CI/CD Platform	Feature
GitHub Actions	environments, required reviewers, secrets by env
GitLab CI	environments, only/except, manual approvals
Azure DevOps	Stage approvals, environment checks, release gates
Jenkins	Pipeline stages + conditional logic per env
Spinnaker/Argo	Multi-environment promotion with gates

Benefits of Environment-Specific Gating

Environment-specific gating provides multiple benefits by aligning quality checks with the risk and purpose of each stage, helping teams manage risk, accelerate development, enforce compliance, and progressively harden code before it reaches production.

- **Improves risk management**: Critical checks only happen where they're most needed
- **Accelerates lower-risk deployments**: Dev and test gates stay lightweight
- **Prevents accidental production exposure**: Manual gates and approvals add a human layer
- **Supports compliance**: Easily enforce policy-as-code, segregation of duties, and audit trails
- **Enables gradual hardening**: Code becomes more production-ready with each stage

Best Practices

Below are some best practices that you should consider implementing when introducing environment specific gating measures:

- **Make gates visible and transparent**: Developers should know what's blocking and why
- **Fail fast in lower environments**: Catch issues early with lighter, faster checks
- **Treat production differently**: Never deploy automatically unless all gates are passed and monitored
- **Automate where possible**: Manual approval should be the exception, not the norm
- **Track gate outcomes over time**: Identify frequently failing gates and resolve root causes

What to Monitor Per Environment

The table below highlights key metrics for monitoring environment-specific quality gates, showing what each metric measures and why it is important for maintaining efficient, reliable, and safe pipeline progression.

Metric	What It Measures	Why It Matters
Gate failure rates by environment	Frequency at which gates fail in each environment	Helps identify bottlenecks, flaky tests, or unstable conditions that could delay pipeline progression
Time to pass each gate	Duration taken to complete each environment-specific gate	Detects slow validation steps that may impact pipeline efficiency and release velocity

Frequency of gate bypass	How often gates are skipped or overridden	Highlights risky practices or process shortcuts that could compromise quality or compliance
Manual vs. automated gate ratio	Proportion of gates that require human intervention versus automated checks	Identifies opportunities to increase automation and improve consistency, speed, and reliability

Environment-specific gates help teams balance speed with safety, enabling fast development while enforcing stricter checks as risk increases. They bring discipline, visibility, and flexibility to your CI/CD pipelines, ensuring that every environment enforces what matters most to it.

Business Rule Validation as a Quality Gate

While functional tests and technical checks validate that software "works," business rule validation ensures that it works correctly for the business. These rules are the logic that governs how systems should behave in line with business policies, compliance, and operational needs, and validating them is critical before software reaches production.

By treating business rule validation as a quality gate in the CI/CD pipeline, teams ensure that feature releases, workflows, or data changes do not violate core business logic or regulatory constraints, reducing the risk of costly production errors or compliance violations.

What Are Business Rules?

Business rules are specific, structured statements that define or constrain some aspect of business behaviour. They may include:

- Eligibility criteria (e.g., "only users over 18 can apply")
- Calculations (e.g., "apply a 15% discount if purchase > R1000")
- Approval workflows (e.g., "manager approval required for expense > R5000")
- Regulatory requirements (e.g., "transactions over R25,000 must trigger reporting")
- Data constraints (e.g., "customer ID must be unique")

Unlike general technical correctness, business rules embody what the business needs the system to do, and they often change as business policies evolve.

Why Use Business Rule Validation as a Gate?

Business rule validation as a quality gate ensures that the core logic and policies governing an application are enforced consistently throughout the CI/CD pipeline. By automatically checking business rules, teams can prevent regressions during feature enhancements or refactors, maintain regulatory and contractual compliance, and reduce the reliance on manual verification during UAT. These gates help safeguard against unintended consequences of technical changes, increase confidence when releasing business-critical features, and make business logic explicit, testable, and visible to all stakeholders, fostering both reliability and transparency.

- Prevents logic regression during feature enhancements or refactors
- Ensures regulatory and contractual compliance
- Reduces manual testing and verification time in UAT
- Guards against unintended consequences of technical changes
- Increases confidence when releasing business-critical features
- Makes logic explicit, testable, and visible to stakeholders

How to Validate Business Rules

Validating business rules within the CI/CD pipeline ensures that application logic behaves as intended and continues to meet organizational requirements as code evolves. This involves explicitly modelling business logic in a way that is understandable to both technical and non-technical stakeholders, automating tests to cover real-world scenarios and edge cases, and integrating these validations directly into pipeline stages. Optionally, runtime monitoring can be added to catch violations in production, providing continuous assurance that business-critical rules are consistently enforced and reducing the risk of costly errors.

- **Model business logic explicitly**
    - Use decision tables, rules engines, or code annotations
    - Make rules understandable to both technical and non-technical stakeholders
- **Automate business rule tests**
    - Build test cases that simulate real-world scenarios and edge cases

    - Use DSLs (domain-specific languages) or behaviour-driven frameworks (e.g., Cucumber)
- **Run validations as part of the pipeline**
    - Include business rule test suites in CI stages alongside unit/integration tests
    - Fail the pipeline if critical business logic is violated
- **Monitor for production violations (optional)**
    - Implement runtime checks or business observability dashboards to catch missed scenarios

Tools and Approaches

A variety of tools and approaches are available to model, simulate, and validate business rules, enabling teams to ensure correct logic execution across different scenarios, environments, and inputs.

Approach	Tools/Frameworks
Rule engines	Drools, Camunda, Business Rules Composer
BDD-style testing	Cucumber, SpecFlow, Behave
Custom rule validation	Python, JavaScript, Java test suites
Low-code rule builders	Decision modelling tools, BPMN
Policy-as-code (for compliance)	Open Policy Agent, Rego

These tools help model, simulate, and validate rule outcomes across different inputs and environments.

Examples of Business Rule Gates

The table below provides examples of business rule gates, illustrating how specific rules can be validated through automated tests, mocks, and scenario-based checks to ensure correct and consistent application behaviour. This is not an exhaustive list given the complexity of all rules here – but does help to provide context of how these rules will apply here.

Example Rule	Validation Strategy
"VAT should be applied only to users in EU"	Automated tests with varied geolocation inputs
"Loan applicants must pass credit score check"	Mock credit scores in test scenarios
"Workflow requires CFO approval over R1 million"	Verify workflow logic with business role mocks
"Email must be sent after user signs up"	Assert event flow and message delivery
"Discounts can't stack with promo codes"	Conflict scenario testing

Best Practices

Below are some best practices to consider when introducing business rules validation as a quality gate:

- Involve domain experts in rule definition and validation
- Keep business rules decoupled from application logic when possible
- Use clear, testable language to define rules (e.g., Gherkin)
- Version control your rules: track rule changes like code
- Automate validation: include in CI pipelines to enforce non-negotiable logic
- Document failed rules clearly to speed up debugging and stakeholder communication

What to Monitor

Monitoring metrics for business rule validation helps teams ensure that critical logic is consistently enforced, detect gaps in coverage, and measure the effectiveness of automated validations.

Metric	What It Measures	Why It Matters
% of test coverage for business rules	Proportion of business rules covered by automated tests	Detects untested scenarios and reduces the risk of logic regression
Frequency of rule changes	How often business rules are modified	Identifies volatile or frequently changing logic that may require closer monitoring
Rule-related production incidents	Number of incidents caused by failed or incorrect rules	Tracks missed or broken validations and highlights areas of risk
Manual overrides or exceptions	Occurrences where rules are bypassed manually	Signals complexity, gaps in automated rules, or potential process weaknesses

Business rule validation is often overlooked as a CI/CD quality gate, but it's one of the most impactful and risk-reducing practices you can adopt. It brings the voice of the business into the delivery pipeline, ensuring that code changes do more than just compile: they preserve the integrity, trust, and policies that your business relies on.

AI/ML-Based Anomaly Detection Gates

As CI/CD pipelines become more complex and fast-moving, traditional quality gates, relying on fixed thresholds or rule-based logic, can struggle to detect subtle issues, regressions, or outliers. This is where AI/ML-based anomaly detection steps in, adding intelligent, adaptive gating logic that evolves with your system over time.

Anomaly detection gates use machine learning to identify unexpected behaviour in metrics, logs, performance, and test outcomes, flagging regressions that would otherwise pass unnoticed in static quality checks.

What Is AI/ML-Based Anomaly Detection in CI/CD?

AI/ML-based anomaly detection uses statistical modelling and machine learning algorithms to:

- Learn normal behaviour over time from historical CI/CD data
- Flag unusual patterns, spikes, drifts, or inconsistencies during builds or deployments
- Trigger pipeline gates when anomalies are detected

It moves beyond static thresholds (e.g., "error rate > 2%") and instead asks:

"Is this behaviour statistically unusual compared to the system's recent history?"

Why Use AI/ML for Quality Gates?

AI and machine learning can enhance quality gates by identifying subtle, non-obvious issues, adapting to changing system behaviour, and providing intelligent insights that improve release confidence while reducing manual effort and alert fatigue.

- Detect subtle regressions before they escalate into production issues
- Adapt automatically to system changes, seasonality, or usage patterns
- Catch non-obvious issues that escape traditional test coverage
- Reduce alert fatigue by filtering false positives

- Improve release confidence through behavioural intelligence

AI technology continues to evolve rapidly through and the benefits that could be gained from these tools and how we need to govern them will likely rapidly evolve along with the technology. However this rapid growth only reinforces the importance of applying these in our gates to ensure that the gates evolve along with the technology. As long as we have the other functional and non-functional quality gates mentioned in this book in place – it ensures that companies are not overly exposed to potential AI failure.

What Can Be Monitored with Anomaly Detection?

Anomaly detection can be applied across a variety of data sources in CI/CD pipelines to automatically identify unusual patterns or deviations, helping teams catch issues that might be missed in high-change, high-volume environments.

Data Source	Examples of Anomalies Detected
Build/test metrics	Sudden increase in test failures or duration
Performance benchmarks	Latency regression in specific endpoints
Code analysis	Unusual code churn, commit size, or dependency spikes
Security scans	Unusual spike in vulnerabilities or CVEs
Infrastructure metrics	Memory leaks, CPU spikes, resource saturation
Service logs	Novel error messages or log volume anomalies

This works especially well in high-change, high-volume pipelines, where humans can't track everything.

Common Tools and Approaches

A variety of tools and approaches are available for anomaly detection in CI/CD pipelines, providing capabilities ranging from time-series analysis and ML-powered metric monitoring to event-based detection and custom predictive models.

Tool/Platform	Capabilities
Prometheus + Anomaly Detector	Time-series based anomaly rules
Datadog Watchdog	ML-powered anomaly detection on metrics/logs
New Relic Lookout	Baseline-aware anomaly alerts
Amazon Lookout for Metrics	Managed ML anomaly detection for KPIs
Sentry, Honeycomb, OpsGenie	Event or log-based anomaly detection
Custom models (Python)	Use SciKit-learn, Prophet, or AutoML pipelines

You can integrate these tools directly into CI/CD workflows as gating steps via APIs or CLI checks.

Example: Anomaly Gate in Action

Anomaly-based quality gates leverage AI and ML to detect deviations from normal behaviour that static thresholds might miss, enabling proactive prevention of performance regressions and operational issues. By analysing historical metrics, usage patterns, and system behaviour, these gates can dynamically identify anomalies and automatically enforce pipeline actions.

Technical Example: Anomaly Gate in Action

Consider a CI pipeline that runs load tests on a payment API, where the historical p95 latency typically ranges between 120–150ms. Using AI-based gating:

- **Model training and baseline creation:** An anomaly detection model (e.g., using time-series forecasting with Prophet or ML-based outlier detection) learns normal latency patterns, including daily / weekly variations and peak traffic behaviour.
- **Real-time evaluation:** During the pipeline, the current p95 latency of 250ms is compared against the model's predicted baseline. Although below the static threshold of 300ms, the model flags it as anomalous because it deviates significantly from expected behaviour.
- **Automated gating and alerting:** The pipeline halts promotion, triggers an alert to the team, and logs the anomaly for further analysis.
- **Adaptive learning:** Over time, the model updates its understanding of normal latency, reducing false positives while remaining sensitive to regressions.

Without AI-based gating, the spike to 250ms would have passed undetected, potentially degrading user experience in production. By integrating anomaly detection, teams can catch subtle regressions early and enforce more intelligent, context-aware quality gates.

Draft YAML script:

Below is a YAML pipeline script showing how this can be achieved:

```
name: Anomaly-Based Performance Gate
on:
  push:
    branches:
      - main

jobs:
```

```
  build:
    runs-on: ubuntu-latest
    steps:
      - name: Checkout code
        uses: actions/checkout@v3

      - name: Install dependencies
        run: |
          pip install -r requirements.txt
          pip install pandas prophet

  load_test:
    needs: build
    runs-on: ubuntu-latest
    steps:
      - name: Run load test
        run: |
          k6 run --out json=load_test_report.json
tests/load_test.js

  anomaly_gate:
    needs: load_test
    runs-on: ubuntu-latest
    steps:
      - name: Detect anomalies in latency
        run: |
          python - <<'EOF'
          import json
          import pandas as pd
          from prophet import Prophet
          import sys

          # Load historical and current metrics
          historical =
pd.read_csv("historical_latency.csv")  # columns:
ds, y
          current_report =
json.load(open("load_test_report.json"))
          current_latency =
current_report["http"]["p95"]

          # Fit model on historical latency
          model = Prophet(daily_seasonality=True)
          model.fit(historical)

          # Predict expected latency for now
          future = pd.DataFrame({'ds':
[pd.Timestamp.now()]})
          forecast = model.predict(future)
          predicted_latency =
forecast['yhat'].iloc[0]
```

```
          # Calculate deviation
          threshold_factor = 1.2  # 20% deviation
triggers anomaly
          if current_latency > predicted_latency *
threshold_factor:
              print(f"Anomaly detected! p95
latency={current_latency}ms,
expected={predicted_latency:.2f}ms")
              sys.exit(1)  # Fail pipeline
          else:
              print(f"Latency within expected range:
{current_latency}ms (predicted
{predicted_latency:.2f}ms)")
          EOF
```

How it works:

1. **Build stage:** Installs dependencies and sets up the Python environment.
2. **Load test stage:** Executes a synthetic load test (using K6 in this example) and outputs results as JSON.
3. **Anomaly gate stage:**
    - Loads historical latency data to train a predictive model (Prophet in this example).
    - Compares the current p95 latency against the model's predicted baseline.
    - Flags an anomaly and fails the pipeline if the observed latency exceeds a configurable deviation threshold.
4. **Adaptive behaviour:** Over time, the historical data can be updated, improving the model's accuracy and reducing false positives.

This pattern allows AI-driven anomaly detection to act as **a** dynamic quality gate, catching subtle regressions that static thresholds might miss.

How to Integrate AI/ML Anomaly Gates into CI/CD

Integrating AI / ML-based anomaly detection into your CI / CD pipelines allows teams to catch subtle regressions and unusual behaviours that traditional static thresholds might miss. A structured approach ensures that anomaly gates are both effective and maintainable:

Collect historical data: Start by gathering a rich set of historical metrics that reflect the normal behaviour of your systems. This can include build logs, performance benchmarks (latency, throughput, error rates), automated test outcomes, telemetry from production or pre-production environments, and infrastructure monitoring data. High-quality historical data is crucial for establishing accurate baselines and training predictive models.

Train or apply a model: Depending on the use case, select an appropriate detection technique. Statistical methods such as Z-score, moving averages, or Holt-Winters exponential smoothing can identify sudden deviations in key metrics. Machine learning models like Isolation Forest, Prophet, LSTM networks, or AutoML pipelines can detect complex, non-linear patterns, adapt to seasonality, and account for correlations across multiple signals. For new pipelines, pre-trained models can be applied, whereas evolving systems benefit from models trained on historical operational data.

Set up automated gating: Once models are trained, integrate anomaly detection directly into the CI / CD pipeline. This typically involves a script or tool (e.g., fail_if_anomaly_detected.py) that reads current metrics, compares them to expected behaviour from the model, and automatically fails the pipeline or blocks promotion if an anomaly is detected. By embedding this check in the pipeline, teams ensure that performance regressions or unusual failures are caught before code reaches production.

Visualize and log results: Anomaly detection outputs should be logged and visualized for transparency, investigation, and auditing. Push results to dashboards or observability platforms such as Grafana, Prometheus, Datadog, or Kibana. This allows teams to review anomalies in context, correlate them with recent changes, and maintain a historical record of system behaviour and gate decisions.

Tune and retrain periodically: Anomaly detection models can drift over time as systems evolve, usage patterns change, or infrastructure scales. Periodically retrain models with fresh data, adjust sensitivity thresholds, and refine detection rules to maintain accuracy. Regular tuning ensures that gates remain effective, reducing false positives and maintaining confidence in automated decisions.

By following these steps, AI/ML anomaly gates can become a dynamic, intelligent layer in your CI/CD pipeline: proactively protecting production quality while providing teams with actionable insights into system behaviour.

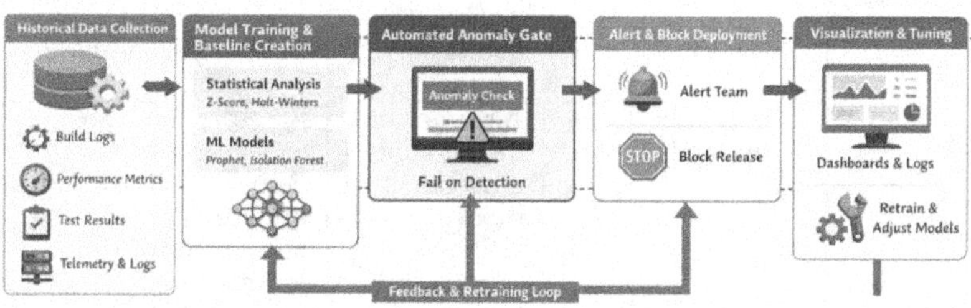

Best Practices

Below are some best practices to consider to ensure your usage of AI/ML are effective in your quality gates:

- **Start with hybrid gating**: Use AI checks alongside traditional ones to build trust
- **Avoid gating on noisy metrics**: Choose stable, high-signal indicators
- **Use explainable models**: Provide context on *why* something is flagged
- **Monitor model drift**: Ensure models continue to reflect reality over time
- **Correlate across multiple signals**: Anomalies are stronger when patterns emerge across dimensions

Metrics for Anomaly Gating Effectiveness

Monitoring metrics for AI/ML anomaly gates helps teams evaluate the effectiveness, accuracy, and operational impact of their automated detection, ensuring that gates remain reliable and actionable over time.

Metric	What It Measures	Why It Matters
Anomaly gate pass/fail ratio	Frequency at which AI/ML gates detect anomalies	Indicates how often the gates are catching actionable issues and enforcing quality
False positive/negative rate	Accuracy of the anomaly detection model	Assesses model trustworthiness and helps reduce unnecessary pipeline failures or missed regressions

Time to investigate anomaly	Duration taken to analyse flagged issues	Reflects the operational impact and effort required to respond to anomalies
Model retraining frequency	How often the detection model is updated	Ensures the anomaly detection adapts to system changes, maintaining relevance and effectiveness

AI/ML-based anomaly detection gates bring predictive intelligence to your CI/CD pipeline. They don't just check if something is broken, they watch for signals that something is *about to* break. As systems scale, this forward-looking approach becomes an essential layer of defence in delivering stable, high-quality software at speed.

Conclusion: It's all about context

This chapter on custom and contextual quality gates highlights the importance of tailoring CI/CD pipeline validations to the unique requirements of applications, business logic, and operational contexts.

By implementing gates that go beyond standard checks- such as feature flag controls, business rule validations, and AI/ML-based anomaly detection - teams can enforce policies that are meaningful, actionable, and aligned with organizational priorities.

Custom gates help manage risk, prevent logic regressions, ensure compliance, and provide early detection of subtle issues, all while enabling faster feedback and more confident releases. Contextual gates, meanwhile, allow rules to adapt to the environment, usage patterns, or target users, ensuring that checks are relevant and proportionate to the risk at each stage. Collectively, these gates strengthen pipeline resilience, promote consistent quality standards, and make the release process more intelligent and responsive.

Building on this foundation, the next chapter will focus on designing gate policies and thresholds. It will explore how to define meaningful criteria for passing or failing a gate, balance risk versus agility, and configure thresholds for metrics, tests, and rules. By understanding how to set and tune these policies, teams can ensure that gates are both protective and practical, providing clear guidance for automated promotion while avoiding unnecessary bottlenecks or false alarms.

Designing Gate Policies and Thresholds

Purpose of chapter: Provide guidance on translating quality objectives into clear, measurable criteria that determine whether a CI/CD pipeline stage passes or fails. It helps teams balance risk and delivery speed, enforce consistent standards, and ensure gates remain effective and actionable across environments.

Gate policies and thresholds form the backbone of an effective CI/CD quality gating strategy. While quality gates themselves define what checks are performed, gate policies determine how those checks are evaluated, specifying the criteria for success or failure. By translating high-level objectives: such as reliability, security, performance, and compliance, into measurable thresholds, teams can ensure that gates provide actionable feedback rather than arbitrary pass/fail results. This clarity helps prevent both false confidence and unnecessary pipeline failures, enabling development and operations teams to make informed decisions about promoting changes.

Setting thresholds is inherently a balance between risk mitigation and delivery speed. For example, overly strict thresholds may catch every minor deviation but can slow down the release process and frustrate teams, whereas overly lenient thresholds may allow regressions to slip into production. A well-designed policy considers the context of the check, the criticality of the environment, and historical system behaviour. By leveraging data from previous builds, test outcomes, and production metrics, teams can define realistic and meaningful thresholds that reflect actual operational risk.

Gate policies also support environment-specific enforcement. Different thresholds can be applied depending on the stage of the pipeline - development, test, staging, or production - ensuring that gates are proportionate to the potential impact of failures. For instance, a performance metric may have a lenient threshold in development but a strict Service Level Objective (SLO) in production. Similarly, business rule validation might enforce strict compliance in production while remaining more flexible in pre-production environments.

Finally, gate policies and thresholds should be monitored and refined over time. As systems evolve, user patterns change, and new technologies are adopted, thresholds may need adjustment to remain effective. By continuously evaluating gate outcomes, teams can fine-tune their policies, reducing false positives and negatives, improving release confidence, and ensuring that the CI/CD pipeline remains both safe and efficient.

This chapter will explore practical approaches for defining, implementing, and evolving gate policies and thresholds, providing teams with the tools and mindset needed to enforce quality intelligently and consistently across the software delivery lifecycle.

Progressive Thresholds (Green / Yellow / Red) in Quality Gates

Not all failures are equal, and not all warnings should block a release. In real-world CI/CD pipelines, binary pass/fail logic can be too rigid, leading to bottlenecks, unnecessary delays, or even skipped quality checks. This is where progressive thresholds, also known as traffic-light gating (green/yellow/red), provide a more flexible, risk-aware alternative.

By defining graduated gate policies, teams can prioritize critical failures, allow lower-severity warnings to pass conditionally, and enforce smarter decisions during promotion and deployment.

What Are Progressive Thresholds?

Progressive thresholds divide the results of a quality gate into three distinct levels:

Status	Meaning	Action
Green	Everything within safe limits	Proceed automatically
Yellow	Minor issues, elevated risk, or early warnings	Proceed with caution, manual approval may be required
Red	Critical failure or violation of non-negotiable policies	Block the pipeline or trigger rollback

This triage approach gives teams more situational awareness and enables nuanced decision-making based on impact, risk, and urgency.

Why Use Green/Yellow/Red Thresholds?

Using risk-based gate thresholds allows teams to respond proportionately to issues, ensuring that quality gates provide meaningful guidance without unnecessarily blocking delivery or overwhelming developers with low-impact failures.

- Prevents overreaction to low-priority issues
- Avoids gate fatigue where developers learn to ignore noisy failures
- Encourages continuous improvement without halting progress
- Enables conditional promotion: "Only let staging proceed if no red gates and <2 yellow"
- Aligns with risk-based release strategies (e.g., higher thresholds for prod than dev)

Example Use Cases

The table below illustrates how graduated (green–yellow–red) thresholds can be applied across different gate types to distinguish between healthy, warning, and critical states, enabling teams to make risk-aware promotion decisions rather than relying on blunt pass/fail rules.

Gate Type	**Green Threshold**	**Yellow Threshold**	**Red Threshold**
Test Coverage	≥ 85%	75–84%	< 75%
Performance (p95)	< 500ms	500–800ms	> 800ms
Security Scan	0 critical/high findings	1–2 high, or any medium	> 2 high or any critical CVEs
Error Rate	< 0.5%	0.5% – 1%	> 1%
Flaky Tests	< 1% test flakiness	1–5%	> 5%

The thresholds can be customized per service, team, or environment.

How to Implement Progressive Gates

Below are some key principles and steps on implementing progressive gates into an organisation and delivery process:

Define your signal-to-noise ratio

Not all metrics deserve equal weight. Start by identifying which signals represent real user or business risk versus those that indicate early warnings or technical debt.
For example, a critical security vulnerability or SLO breach is high-signal and should immediately block promotion, whereas a slight dip in test coverage or a small latency increase may be tolerable in the short term. Clearly classifying metrics up front prevents pipelines from becoming noisy and ensures teams focus on what truly matters.

Set clear thresholds collaboratively

Thresholds should never be arbitrary. Involve developers, QA, SREs, and security to define what constitutes *green* (safe), *yellow* (warning), and *red* (blocker).
These thresholds should be:

- Data-driven (based on historical baselines)
- Environment-aware (stricter in production than in dev)
- Explicitly documented so everyone understands the trade-offs being made

This shared ownership increases trust in the gates and reduces friction when failures occur.

Visualize thresholds clearly

A gate is only useful if its status is immediately visible. Use CI pipeline UIs, dashboards, badges, or pull request checks to surface gate outcomes clearly as green, yellow, or red. Visualization helps teams quickly understand whether they are dealing with a hard stop, a warning that needs attention, or a healthy build, without digging through logs or metrics.

Make yellow gates actionable, not blocking

Yellow gates should trigger action, not paralysis. Instead of blocking the pipeline, they can:

- Send Slack or Teams notifications
- Open a ticket automatically
- Require a lightweight sign-off or acknowledgment

This approach encourages continuous improvement while still allowing delivery to progress, especially when the risk is understood and accepted.

Enforce red gates strictly

Red gates represent unacceptable risk and should be enforced consistently. When a red threshold is breached:

- Builds or deployments should be blocked automatically
- Promotions to higher environments should be prevented
- Overrides should require explicit approval and justification

Strict enforcement protects production systems and reinforces the credibility of the gating process.

Audit gate decisions

Every bypass or override, especially for yellow or red gates, should be recorded. Capturing who approved it, why, and when provides traceability for audits, post-incident reviews, and compliance requirements. Over time, this data also helps teams identify patterns, such as thresholds that are too strict or areas of recurring technical debt.

Example: Green / Yellow / Red Gates in a CI/CD Pipeline (YAML)

Below is a simplified GitHub Actions-style example that evaluates performance metrics and applies graduated gating:

```
jobs:
  quality-gates:
    runs-on: ubuntu-latest
    steps:
      - name: Run performance tests
        run: |
          ./run_load_test.sh --output results.json

      - name: Evaluate performance gate
        run: |
          P95=$(jq '.p95_latency_ms' results.json)

          if [ "$P95" -gt 800 ]; then
            echo "RED gate: p95 latency too high
($P95 ms)"
            echo "GATE_STATUS=red" >> $GITHUB_ENV
            exit 1
          elif [ "$P95" -gt 500 ]; then
            echo "YELLOW gate: p95 latency warning
($P95 ms)"
            echo "GATE_STATUS=yellow" >> $GITHUB_ENV
          else
            echo "GREEN gate: p95 latency healthy
($P95 ms)"
            echo "GATE_STATUS=green" >> $GITHUB_ENV
          fi

      - name: Notify on yellow gate
```

```
        if: env.GATE_STATUS == 'yellow'
        run: |
          echo "Sending warning notification to
Slack"

      - name: Deploy to staging
        if: env.GATE_STATUS != 'red'
        run: |
          ./deploy.sh staging
```

How this works

- **Green**: Pipeline proceeds normally
- **Yellow**: Pipeline continues, but triggers notifications or follow-up actions
- **Red**: Pipeline fails immediately and blocks promotion
- Thresholds are explicit, visible, and enforced consistently

Graduated gate policies turn quality gates from blunt stop/go switches into risk-aware decision systems. By combining clear thresholds, strong visualization, strict enforcement where it matters, and auditable exceptions, teams can protect quality *and* maintain delivery velocity, without gate fatigue.

Integrating into CI/CD Tools

Most modern CI/CD tools support conditional gating logic via APIs or plugins:

Tool	**Support for Thresholds**
GitHub Actions	Custom workflow steps, conditional expressions
GitLab CI	rules, when: manual, custom status badges
Azure DevOps	Release gates with custom conditions

Jenkins	Declarative pipeline with scripted logic
Spinnaker/Argo	Manual judgments, canary analysis scoring

Custom scripts or policies-as-code tools (e.g., OPA) can help codify and enforce thresholds.

Best Practices

Below are some best practices that should be considered when introducing progressive gates into your delivery processes:

- **Tailor thresholds to context**: Don't apply the same standards across all environments or services
- **Review thresholds regularly**: Update them as your quality bar or system performance evolves
- **Use historical baselines**: Avoid hardcoding numbers, let data drive your thresholds
- **Educate teams**: Make sure everyone understands what the colours mean and how to act
- **Automate yellow follow-ups**: Open backlog tickets, schedule cleanups, or run delayed jobs

Metrics to Monitor

Tracking metrics for graduated (green–yellow–red) gates helps teams understand how effectively warnings and blockers are being used, ensuring thresholds remain meaningful, enforced, and aligned with real risk.

Metric	What It Measures	Why It Matters
Frequency of yellow gates	How often warning-level	Indicates recurring risk signals and early quality

	thresholds are reached	degradation before hard failures occur
% of yellow gates bypassed	Proportion of warnings that are overridden	Reflects organizational risk tolerance and whether yellow gates are being taken seriously
Red gate trigger rate	How often critical thresholds block pipelines	Measures how effectively severe issues are being caught early in the delivery process
Time to resolve yellow issues	Duration taken to address warning-level findings	Shows whether warnings drive corrective action or are ignored over time
Threshold drift	Changes to gate thresholds over time	Tracks how quality definitions evolve and helps identify threshold weakening or hardening trends

Progressive gating enables a more human-aware, business-aligned CI/CD pipeline, one that recognizes nuance, supports decision-making, and balances velocity with risk management. It transforms quality gates from blunt instruments into intelligent signals that guide teams toward better software without blocking them unnecessarily.

Tolerance and Risk-Based Gating

As engineering teams scale, not every code change needs to meet the same level of scrutiny. Some changes are low-impact and routine, while others pose significant risks to the system. Tolerance and risk-based gating is a strategy that adapts quality gate requirements based on the potential risk and blast radius of a given change, rather than applying the same rigid rules to every deployment.

This approach recognizes that one-size-fits-all gating can lead to wasted time, over-engineering, or worse, teams bypassing gates altogether. By aligning gate strictness with risk tolerance, pipelines become smarter, safer, and faster.

What Is Risk-Based Gating?

Risk-based gating tailors CI/CD quality gates based on:

- The **type of change** (e.g., config vs. core logic)
- The **environment** (e.g., test vs. production)
- The **service criticality**
- The **team's past reliability**
- Real-time signals (e.g., test flakiness, prior incidents)

It introduces a flexible gating model, where higher-risk changes undergo more rigorous validation and approval, while low-risk changes pass through lighter checks.

Why Use Risk-Based Gating?

Adopting risk-based quality gates allows teams to optimize their CI/CD pipelines by applying the right level of control to the right changes, improving delivery speed and confidence without sacrificing stability.

- Speeds up low-risk, high-frequency changes
- Focuses validation effort where it matters most
- Reduces manual approvals and gate fatigue
- Encourages trust and ownership across teams
- Improves release efficiency without compromising stability

Tolerance Levels and Gating Logic

Defining gate policies along a risk spectrum allows teams to proportionally increase validation, controls, and approvals based on the potential impact of a change, ensuring that higher-risk modifications receive deeper scrutiny without slowing down low-risk work:

Risk Level	Example Changes	Required Gates
Low	UI copy changes, internal dashboards	Linting, unit tests, basic code review
Medium	Config changes, minor feature updates	Full test suite, code review, performance check
High	Auth logic, pricing rules, DB schema changes	Security scan, business rule validation, multiple reviewers
Critical	Payment flow, PII handling, regulatory logic	Manual approval, observability checks, staged rollout

Gates escalate in breadth, depth, and approval requirements as the risk increases.

Inputs to Determine Risk

Risk classification for quality gating is driven by a combination of code, service, and historical context, allowing pipelines to dynamically assess the potential impact of a change before deciding how strictly it should be validated.

- Code diff metadata (lines changed, files affected)
- Git commit tags (e.g., #infra, #prod, #lowrisk)
- Service classification (tier-1, user-facing, revenue-impacting)
- Historical incident data (has this code broken prod before?)

- Change volume / frequency (larger changes tend to carry more risk)

You can use custom scripts, CI plugins, or policies-as-code (e.g., Open Policy Agent) to dynamically assign risk levels.

Tooling Support

Modern CI/CD platforms provide built-in and extensible tooling that enables risk-based gating by evaluating change context, metadata, and policies to dynamically adjust pipeline behaviour.

Tool/Platform	Feature
GitHub Actions	Branch protections, required reviewers based on labels
GitLab	rules: logic to define different paths for risk levels
Azure DevOps	Conditional approvals and environment checks
OPA/Rego	Fine-grained policies that evaluate change context
Jenkins	Custom scripted stages based on metadata

Risk classification can also integrate with incident management platforms, error tracking systems, or internal change approval workflows.

Best Practices

Below are some best practices worth considering when introducing risk based quality gates:

- **Define a clear risk model**: Use simple categories and examples to guide developers
- **Make risk self-declared but auditable**: Let developers tag risk level, but track misuse

- **Set soft and hard gates**: Allow yellow-level changes to proceed with alerts or time-delayed deployment
- **Incorporate past behaviour**: Use ML or heuristics to assess change patterns and outcomes
- **Don't block all risk, manage it**: Allow mitigations like feature flags or phased rollout

What to Measure

Measuring risk-based gating metrics helps teams validate whether their risk classification and thresholds are effective, ensuring that delivery speed and system stability are balanced appropriately.

Metric	What It Measures	Why It Matters
% of changes by risk level	Distribution of deployments across risk categories	Indicates how frequently each risk level is applied and whether risk classification is being used consistently
Failure rate by risk level	Frequency of pipeline or runtime failures per risk category	Helps validate whether gating thresholds are appropriately calibrated for each risk level
Time to deploy vs. risk level	Deployment lead time segmented by risk classification	Reveals bottlenecks or overly strict gates impacting higher- or lower-risk changes
Incident correlation by risk tag	Relationship between risk classification and production incidents	Enables continuous refinement of the risk model based on real operational outcomes

Risk-based gating moves CI/CD from rigid automation to intelligent decision-making. By scaling quality gates to match the potential impact of a change, you create a pipeline that is both agile and resilient, encouraging teams to deliver faster while respecting the realities of software risk.

Making Gates Configurable

As teams evolve, services grow, and risk profiles change, the ability to configure gates dynamically becomes essential to scale quality enforcement without blocking innovation.

Configurable quality gates empower teams to define, adapt, and control their gating policies without deep pipeline rewrites, enabling fine-tuned governance, service-specific criteria, and continuous improvement of the CI/CD workflow.

What Are Configurable Gates?

A configurable gate is a quality check in the CI/CD pipeline whose:

- Thresholds
- Conditions
- Applicability
- Enforcement levels

...are all defined through external configuration, rather than hardcoded into pipeline logic.

This may include YAML/JSON config files, environment variables, service-specific settings, or policy-as-code modules.

Why Make Gates Configurable?

Using modular and configurable gate policies allows organizations to balance centralized governance with team autonomy, making it easier to evolve quality standards, encourage experimentation, and reuse gating logic across services without rigid, one-size-fits-all pipelines.

- **Enables service-level autonomy**: Teams can tailor gating logic based on their maturity, risk, and context
- **Supports evolving standards**: Gates can be updated without reengineering entire pipelines
- **Simplifies governance**: Central teams can enforce baselines while allowing flexibility
- **Accelerates experimentation**: Easier to test new gate types, thresholds, or enforcement models
- **Improves reuse**: Shared gate templates can be applied across projects with configuration overrides

What Can Be Made Configurable?

Below is a list of fields in a gate that can be configured and an example of how the configuration may apply:

Gate Element	Example Configuration
Thresholds	Test coverage ≥ 80%, p95 latency ≤ 300ms
Severity levels	"fail", "warn", or "notify only"
Gating scope	Which services, branches, or environments it applies to
Conditional logic	Only apply gate for production deployments
Gate activation	Enable/disable gate via feature flag
Gate failure action	Block pipeline, trigger approval, or open ticket

Common Configuration Approaches

When implementing quality gates in CI/CD pipelines, organizations have several options for managing and applying configuration. Each approach offers different trade-offs in terms of flexibility, maintainability, and auditability. Common strategies include storing configuration alongside code in YAML or JSON files, using centralized services to manage policies across multiple teams, leveraging environment variables and secrets to adjust behaviour per environment, and adopting policy-as-code frameworks like Open Policy Agent to enforce complex gating logic programmatically. Understanding these approaches helps teams choose the right method for their workflow and governance needs.

- **YAML/JSON Files in Repo**
  - Example: .qualitygates.yml
  - Versioned with code, service-specific, easy to audit
- **Centralized Configuration Service**
  - Stores policies for many teams
  - Enables dynamic updates without code changes
- **Environment Variables & Secrets**
  - Useful for toggling gates across environments (e.g., staging vs. prod)
- **Policy-as-Code**
  - Tools like Open Policy Agent (OPA) use Rego to evaluate gating logic based on configs

Tooling That Supports Configurable Gates

Many of the same tools mentioned through this book cater for configurability within their quality gates:

Platform	Config Support Example
GitHub Actions	workflow_dispatch, env, YAML-based input parameters
GitLab CI	Dynamic variables, rules, include external config files
Jenkins	Shared libraries + parameters or config files

Azure DevOps	Variable groups, runtime parameters, gated approvals
Spinnaker	Pipeline templates with configuration overrides

Best Practices

Below is a list of best practices worth considering when introducing configurable quality gates into your delivery processes:

- **Define defaults and override logic**: Use safe defaults with override capability for advanced teams
- **Document gate configuration clearly**: Help teams understand what each gate does and how to modify it safely
- **Apply validation and linting**: Prevent misconfigurations that silently disable critical gates
- **Separate logic from thresholds**: Keep gating logic in code/policy, but make thresholds adjustable via config
- **Audit config changes**: Log and review updates to gating rules as part of change management

What to Monitor

When monitoring quality gates across a large organisation, it's useful to track not just the raw metrics but also what they reveal about your processes and why they matter for maintaining an effective, reliable pipeline.

Metric	What It Measures	Why It Matters
Number of gate configurations	Tracks the total number of active gate settings across services	Helps identify complexity and potential configuration drift

		that could affect consistency and maintainability
Most/least customized gates	Measures which gates are heavily customized versus standardized	Highlights areas where standardization could reduce risk and simplify management
Gate config change frequency	Tracks how often gate configurations are updated	Indicates responsiveness to evolving requirements and helps assess stability of gate policies
Gate failure rates by config value	Measures the failure rate for different configuration settings	Provides insights for tuning thresholds and improving gate effectiveness over time

Making quality gates configurable turns your CI/CD pipeline into a living system, one that adapts to the context of each team, application, and deployment. It balances central governance with team autonomy, allowing organizations to enforce quality standards without compromising speed or flexibility.

Strategies for Early vs. Late Gating in CI/CD

In Continuous Integration and Continuous Delivery (CI/CD), quality gates can be placed at multiple points in the delivery pipeline, from initial code commits to final production deployment. Choosing the right placement strategy for each gate is critical to balancing fast feedback, efficient pipelines, and high confidence in releases.

This is where early vs. late gating strategies come in. The goal is to apply the right checks at the right time, minimizing feedback delay while ensuring that critical quality standards are met before production.

What Is Early vs. Late Gating?

Gate Timing	Description	Purpose
Early Gating	Gates applied as soon as possible (pre-commit, commit, build, unit test)	Fast feedback, catch issues cheaply
Late Gating	Gates applied closer to deployment (staging, pre-prod, release)	High-confidence checks, real-world fidelity

Why the Distinction Matters

In a CI/CD pipeline, the timing of quality gates plays a crucial role in balancing speed, feedback, and confidence in code quality. Early gating refers to applying gates as soon as possible in the development workflow, such as during pre-commit hooks, commit-time checks, build validations, or unit tests. By catching issues at this stage, developers receive fast feedback, allowing them to correct problems at the lowest possible cost. Early gating prevents defective code from propagating downstream, reduces rework, and accelerates the overall development cycle.

In contrast, late gating occurs closer to deployment, during stages such as staging, pre-production, or final release checks. These gates provide high-confidence validation by evaluating code in environments that closely mirror production. Late gating is particularly valuable for catching integration issues, performance bottlenecks, security vulnerabilities, or compliance violations that may not be visible during earlier stages. By testing under real-world conditions, late gates help reduce the risk of failures in live systems and ensure that releases meet expected quality standards.

Effectively combining early and late gating allows teams to benefit from both fast feedback and high-confidence verification. Early gates maximize efficiency and reduce the cost of fixing issues, while late gates provide assurance that the system behaves correctly under production-like conditions. Together, they form a balanced approach to maintaining quality throughout the CI/CD pipeline.

Early Gating Strategies

Early gates are most effective when applied to checks that are fast, deterministic, and developer-friendly. These are validations that can be executed quickly without relying on runtime conditions or external dependencies, allowing developers to receive immediate feedback on their changes. Because early gates run before code reaches shared environments, they help maintain a clean and stable codebase while supporting agile development practices such as trunk-based development.

Common examples of early gates include linting and code formatting checks, which enforce coding standards consistently across the team, and static code analysis, which can identify potential security vulnerabilities or maintainability issues before code is merged. Unit test execution and code coverage checks ensure that functionality behaves as expected and that new changes are adequately tested. Additional early gates may include pre-commit hooks, license compliance verification, business rule validation in isolation, and basic secret scanning to prevent sensitive information from entering the repository.

The benefits of applying early gates are significant. They allow issues to be detected before they reach shared or downstream environments, reducing the cost and complexity of fixing defects. By failing fast, early gates prevent wasted build and test cycles, promoting more efficient use of CI/CD resources. They also encourage local accountability among developers, who can address issues immediately, and enable trunk-based development by ensuring that only validated, high-quality changes are merged into the main branch. Together, these practices create a robust foundation for faster, safer, and more reliable software delivery.

Apply early gates for checks that are:

- Fast and deterministic
- Static (i.e., don't rely on runtime conditions)
- Developer-friendly

Common early gates include:

- Linting and code formatting
- Static code analysis (security, maintainability)
- Unit test execution
- Code coverage checks
- Pre-commit hooks
- License compliance
- Business rule validation (in isolation)
- Basic secret scanning

Benefits:

- Catch issues before they hit shared environments
- Reduce build waste by failing fast
- Promote local accountability
- Enable trunk-based development

Late Gating Strategies

Late gating strategies are best applied to checks that require integrated systems, realistic environments, or context that cannot be replicated earlier in the pipeline. These gates are particularly useful for performance and scalability testing, evaluations that may require manual intervention or stakeholder review, and validations that depend on environment-specific conditions. By running these checks closer to deployment, teams can gain high-confidence assurance that the software will behave as expected in production.

Common examples of late gates include load and stress testing in staging environments to evaluate system performance under realistic traffic conditions, and security vulnerability scans on deployable artifacts to identify risks before release. End-to-end (E2E) and smoke tests in pre-production ensure that critical workflows function correctly, while feature flag toggles and canary analysis help validate new functionality in controlled subsets of users.

Late gates may also include manual approval processes for regulated environments, chaos or fault-injection testing to assess system resilience, SLA/SLO conformance checks, and observability or anomaly monitoring to detect unexpected behaviours.

The benefits of applying late gates are significant. They allow teams to catch production-specific or runtime regressions that early gates might miss, and they verify non-functional aspects of quality, such as performance, reliability, and user experience. Late gating ensures that software releases are truly ready for real-world conditions, providing confidence that the deployed system will meet both technical and business expectations.

Apply late gates for checks that require:

- Integrated systems or realistic environments
- Performance and scalability testing
- Manual intervention or stakeholder review
- Environment-specific context

Common late gates include:

- Load and stress tests in staging
- Security vulnerability scans on deployable artifacts
- End-to-end (E2E) and smoke tests in pre-prod
- Feature flag toggles or canary analysis
- Manual approval for regulated environments
- Chaos / fault-injection tests
- SLA / SLO conformance checks
- Observability and anomaly monitoring

Benefits:

- Catch production-specific or runtime regressions
- Verify non-functional and user-facing quality
- Ensure release readiness under real-world conditions

Hybrid Gating Strategy: Shift-Left, Layer Right

A hybrid gating strategy combines the best of both early and late gating approaches, enabling teams to "shift left" where possible for fast feedback, while still applying thorough validation closer to production. This layered approach ensures that simple, deterministic checks are performed early in the development cycle, preventing defects from propagating, while more complex, environment-dependent, or high-risk validations occur later, where they can catch issues that only manifest under realistic conditions. By structuring gates across multiple stages, teams can balance speed, risk, and confidence, ensuring each change is rigorously validated before reaching users.

Example Layered Approach:

1. **Pre-Commit**: Linting, secrets, unit tests (run locally or in Git hook)
2. **Build-Time**: Code coverage, SAST, license checks, commit message validation
3. **Post-Build (CI)**: Integration tests, artifact signing, dependency scanning
4. **Pre-Staging**: Performance benchmarks, environment-specific tests
5. **Pre-Prod**: Regression suite, SLA checks, business rule enforcement
6. **Release**: Canary deployment gates, manual approval, anomaly detection, rollback triggers

Each gate builds on previous checks and aligns with stage-specific risk tolerance.

Best Practices

Below are best practices to consider when apply early or late stage Gating:

- **Fail fast and early**: Reserve late stages for validation, not triage
- **Don't duplicate slow gates** across environments unless required
- **Allow conditional gating**: e.g., bypass late performance gates for internal-only microservices
- **Use progressive thresholds** (green/yellow/red) to reduce false blocks
- **Time-box late gates** to keep pipeline duration in check

What to Monitor

By measuring not just outcomes but also timing and effort, teams can identify bottlenecks, optimize gate placement, and improve overall pipeline performance.

Metric	What It Reveals	Why It Matters
Time to feedback at each gate stage	Identifies bottlenecks and delays in receiving results	Helps teams accelerate feedback loops and reduce developer wait times, improving productivity and early issue detection
% of failures by gate timing	Shows whether issues are being caught early or late in the pipeline	Indicates the effectiveness of early gates and highlights areas where additional checks may be needed
Rework rate after late gate failures	Measures the amount of corrective work required when issues are caught late	Provides insight into the efficiency of early gates and the cost of defects that escape early detection
Cost of running late gates	Tracks the resources required for late-stage validations	Helps optimize gate placement and frequency based on return on investment, balancing thoroughness with pipeline efficiency

Early vs. late gating isn't a binary decision, it's a strategic layering of quality control across the pipeline. Early gates keep development lean and confident. Late gates protect production and user trust. Done right, this layered model supports velocity without compromising reliability.

Conclusion: Configurability breeds flexibility and control

Designing effective gate policies and thresholds is a critical step in ensuring a CI/CD pipeline enforces quality without slowing delivery. Policies define what checks should be applied at each stage, while thresholds determine acceptable levels of risk or deviation before a gate blocks progress. When setting these thresholds, teams must balance sensitivity, catching defects early - with practicality - avoiding excessive false positives that disrupt development flow. Thoughtful policy design considers stage-specific risk tolerance, feedback speed, and the cumulative effect of layered gates, enabling a pipeline that is both efficient and robust.

This understanding naturally leads into the next chapter, which explores pipeline orchestration and gate integration. There, we will examine how gates are implemented, coordinated, and automated within CI/CD pipelines, ensuring that each policy and threshold functions seamlessly as part of a holistic delivery process.

Pipeline Orchestration and Gate Integration

Purpose of chapter: This chapter explores how to orchestrate CI/CD pipelines and integrate quality gates effectively, ensuring that checks are automated, coordinated, and aligned with overall delivery goals.

We are now going to dive deeper into how to orchestrate and integrate quality gates into your CI/CD pipeline. Up to this point, the discussion has been largely conceptual, focusing on why gates matter, when to apply them, and how to design effective policies and thresholds. In this chapter, the emphasis shifts to the practical side: we will explore how these gates can be implemented, automated, and coordinated across different stages of your pipeline.

We've already shown many aspects of this chapter in previous chapters – but look to try and tie in many of the individual gate elements in a more flow and evaluate how to orchestrate the different elements and gates to flow better together.

You will see concrete examples of how to define, trigger, and enforce gates in code, how they interact with one another, and how they contribute to a smooth, reliable delivery process. By bridging the gap between theory and practice, this chapter provides a clear roadmap for embedding quality controls directly into your CI/CD workflow, helping teams move faster while maintaining confidence in their releases.

Integrating Gates into different CI/CD Platforms

For quality gates to be effective, they must be deeply integrated into your CI/CD pipelines, not just as isolated scripts or checks, but as first-class citizens of your delivery flow. Whether you're using Jenkins, GitHub Actions, GitLab CI, Azure DevOps, or another platform, integrating gates at the right stages ensures that only code that meets defined quality standards moves forward.

This section explores how to embed quality gates into popular CI/CD tools, offering strategies and best practices for each platform.

What Does "Gate Integration" Mean?

Gate integration means connecting automated quality checks, such as tests, security scans, policy evaluations, or performance benchmarks, directly into your pipeline workflow in a way that:

- Enforces pass/fail logic
- Provides clear feedback
- Allows thresholds or rules to be configured
- Supports conditional promotion or rollback

It's the glue between your gate logic and the build/deploy machinery.

Gate Integration by Platform

We have been providing a lot of different scripts through the book – but we will now look at how these ill work in more detail across different tools and different approaches to integrating gates into them. The intention is not to go into detail on how each platform works, but rather provide a high level view of how it operates and best practices to consider when using these different platforms.

Jenkins

Approach: Jenkins pipelines use either declarative (Jenkinsfile) or scripted Groovy syntax. Gates are integrated as individual steps or shared library functions.

Examples:

```
stage('Static Analysis') {
  steps {
    sh 'run-sonarqube-analysis.sh'
    junit 'reports/*.xml'
  }
}
stage('Gate: Code Coverage') {
  steps {
    script {
      def coverage = readCoverage('coverage.json')
      if (coverage < 80) {
        error("Coverage threshold not met!")
      }
    }
  }
}
```

Plugins:

- Quality Gates Plugin
- SonarQube Scanner for Jenkins
- OWASP Dependency-Check Plugin

- Build Failure Analyzer

Best Practices:

- Use shared libraries to centralize gate logic
- Use the post block for conditional cleanup or notifications
- Integrate gates with tools like JIRA or GitHub for visibility

GitHub Actions

Approach: Gates are defined as jobs or steps in a workflow YAML file. Failures at any point prevent merging (if branch protection rules are configured).

Example:

```
jobs:
  lint:
    runs-on: ubuntu-latest
    steps:
      - run: npm run lint

  test:
    runs-on: ubuntu-latest
    steps:
      - run: npm test

  gate-checks:
    needs: [lint, test]
    steps:
      - run: ./check-quality-gates.sh
```

Features:

- Native support for secrets, matrix builds, and status checks
- Reusable workflows for cross-repo standardization

- GitHub Advanced Security for built-in code scanning

Best Practices:

- Configure branch protection rules to enforce gates before merges
- Use Actions Marketplace for prebuilt scan/test actions
- Leverage workflow_dispatch and environment for gated deployments

GitLab CI

Approach: Gates are implemented using stages and rules in .gitlab-ci.yml. Jobs can block merges or deploys depending on outcome.

Example:

```
stages:
  - lint
  - test
  - quality-gates

lint:
  script: npm run lint

quality-gate:
  stage: quality-gates
  script: ./run-quality-checks.sh
  allow_failure: false
```

Features:

- rules: and only: directives for conditional gating
- Merge request approvals and security scans integrated into GitLab Premium
- Support for manual and scheduled gates

Best Practices:

- Use artifacts: to pass gate data between jobs
- Use environments: and deployment: for stage-specific gates
- Integrate with GitLab's Code Quality or SAST/DAST tools

Azure DevOps

Approach: Azure Pipelines integrates gates using pipeline steps or release gates (via environments and approvals).

Gate Types:

- Pre-deployment conditions (approvals, triggers)
- REST API callouts to external quality systems (e.g., SonarQube, Checkmarx)

Best Practices:

- Use environment checks to run gates before deployment
- Integrate with Azure Policy or Defender for advanced compliance checks

Spinnaker, ArgoCD, FluxCD

These GitOps/CD-first tools support gates in the form of:

- Manual judgments
- Webhook or REST-based policy engines
- Analysis phases (e.g., in Argo Rollouts)

They often integrate with Prometheus, Kayenta, OPA, or custom gate evaluators for progressive delivery and rollback logic.

Gate Reusability and Templates

Across all platforms, gate integration becomes easier and more scalable when you:

- **Use shared pipeline templates** (e.g., reusable workflows in GitHub or includes in GitLab)
- **Externalize gate logic** to scripts, APIs, or policies-as-code
- **Use metadata or config files** to parameterize thresholds

Best Practices for Gate Integration

1. **Fail early, fail fast**: Place inexpensive gates near the start of the pipeline.
2. **Use named statuses**: Make it clear which gate failed (e.g., security-scan-fail).
3. **Log clearly**: Include summary results and links to reports.
4. **Visualize outcomes**: Use dashboards, badges, or status checks to improve visibility.
5. **Fail gates conditionally**: Allow yellow-level gates to pass with warnings (using exit codes or API responses).
6. **Test locally**: Ensure gates can be dry-run outside the full CI/CD context when needed.

No matter your CI/CD platform, the key to successful quality gate integration lies in consistency, transparency, and flexibility. By embedding gates directly into pipeline workflows, while keeping them configurable and observable, you create a robust, scalable foundation for secure, reliable, and high-quality software delivery.

Managing Secrets, Identities, and Access in CI/CD Pipelines

As CI/CD pipelines automate more of the software delivery lifecycle, they often need access to sensitive information, API keys, tokens, credentials, certificates, and more. Without proper management, these secrets can become a major security risk. Similarly, ensuring proper access control and identity management across the pipeline is essential to uphold integrity, traceability, and compliance.

Mismanaged secrets and identities are among the top attack vectors in software supply chains. So, managing them securely must be a core component of any quality gate strategy.

Why Secrets and Access Matter in CI/CD

CI/CD pipelines interact with:

- Cloud services (AWS, Azure, GCP)
- Databases and internal APIs
- Artifact repositories and registries
- Deployment tools and infrastructure

Every one of these interactions requires authentication and authorization. If secrets are hardcoded, exposed in logs, or improperly shared between jobs, they can be compromised, leading to unauthorized access, data leaks, or even production outages.

Proper secret and access management:

- Prevents credential leaks and abuse
- Ensures least-privilege access
- Provides auditability and traceability
- Reduces blast radius from a compromised pipeline

Common Types of Secrets in CI/CD

Secret Type	Examples
API Keys	GitHub tokens, Stripe keys, Slack webhooks
Cloud Credentials	AWS IAM keys, Azure service principals
SSH Keys	Deployment and git access keys
Certificates and TLS Keys	For service-to-service encryption
Database Credentials	Access to staging or test databases
Signing Keys	For container or artifact integrity verification

Managing Secrets Securely

Effective secret management is a foundational requirement for secure CI/CD pipelines. Credentials such as API keys, tokens, certificates, and passwords must be handled in a way that minimizes exposure, limits blast radius, and supports auditability. Treating secrets as first-class security assets, rather than configuration details, helps prevent some of the most common and damaging security incidents in modern software delivery.

Use a Dedicated Secrets Manager

Secrets should never live in source control or be hardcoded into pipeline definitions. Instead, store and retrieve them from a centralized secrets management solution designed for secure storage, access control, and auditing. Commonly used tools include HashiCorp Vault, AWS Secrets Manager, Azure Key Vault, Google Secret Manager, Doppler, 1Password, Bitwarden.

Best practices when using a secrets manager include:

- Fetch secrets dynamically at runtime rather than injecting them permanently into the pipeline.
- Prefer short-lived credentials or tokens over long-lived static secrets.
- Rotate secrets automatically and regularly to reduce the impact of potential compromise.
- Audit access to secrets and alert on unusual usage patterns.

Avoid Hardcoding or Logging Secrets

Hardcoded secrets remain one of the most frequent causes of security breaches. Secrets should never be stored in:

- Environment variables committed to a repository.
- Configuration files under version control.
- Build output, console logs, or error messages.

Most modern CI/CD platforms support secret masking in logs, this should always be enabled to prevent accidental disclosure during troubleshooting. In addition, scanning repositories and pipelines for leaked secrets should be part of your standard security gates.

Scope Secrets to Jobs and Environments

Remember that not every pipeline stage needs access to every secret. Applying the principle of least privilege significantly reduces risk:

- Expose secrets only to the specific job or step that requires them.

- Use environment scoping so that production secrets are never available in non-production pipelines.
- Leverage ephemeral or just-in-time secrets that expire automatically after job completion.

By combining centralized secret management, strict access controls, and short-lived credentials, teams can significantly reduce the likelihood of credential leakage while still enabling fast, automated delivery pipelines.

Identity and Access Management (IAM)

Managing access in CI/CD pipelines goes far beyond handling secrets. Identity and Access Management (IAM) defines who is allowed to trigger pipelines, approve changes, configure quality gates, and deploy software to sensitive environments. Weak IAM controls can undermine even the most sophisticated quality and security gates, making access governance a critical pillar of a secure and trustworthy delivery process.

Apply the Principle of Least Privilege

Every identity, human or machine, should have only the permissions required to perform its specific function, and nothing more. Over-privileged access increases the blast radius of mistakes or compromises.

- Grant narrowly scoped permissions aligned to the task being performed.
- Avoid using shared or highly privileged accounts for automation.
- For example, CI service accounts should not have full administrative access to cloud subscriptions or

production environments unless absolutely required.

Regularly review and prune permissions to ensure access remains appropriate as teams, tools, and pipelines evolve.

Use Service Identities for Pipelines

Modern pipelines should rely on dedicated machine identities rather than static credentials. Service identities provide stronger security, better traceability, and simpler rotation.

- Use identity federation mechanisms such as OIDC or workload identity federation instead of long-lived API keys.
- Platforms like GitHub Actions, GitLab CI, and Azure Pipelines natively support federated authentication with major cloud providers.
- This approach allows pipelines to request short-lived credentials on demand, significantly reducing the risk of credential leakage.

Enforce Approval Gates and Role-Based Access Control

Not all pipeline actions should be fully automated. High-risk operations, such as production deployments or security gate overrides, often require an additional layer of control.

- Introduce manual approval gates for sensitive stages, especially in regulated or high-impact environments.
- Apply Role-Based Access Control (RBAC) to clearly define who can approve deployments, modify gate policies, or override failures.

- Ensure approval roles are limited to appropriate seniority or responsibility levels and are auditable.

These controls help balance automation with accountability without slowing down routine development work.

Ensure Auditability and Traceability

Visibility into who did what, when, and why is essential for both security and compliance.

- Log all access to pipelines, secrets, environments, and configuration changes.
- Track manual approvals, gate overrides, and emergency deployments.
- Integrate pipeline logs with centralized audit systems, such as SIEM tools or cloud-native audit trails.

Strong audit and traceability practices not only support incident response and compliance audits, but also reinforce trust in the CI/CD process by making access and decisions transparent and accountable.

CI/CD Platform Support for Secret Management

Platform	Secret Management Capabilities
GitHub Actions	Encrypted secrets, OIDC for cloud access, masked logs
GitLab CI	CI/CD variables (masked/protected), Vault integration
Jenkins	Credentials plugin, environment variable masking
Azure Pipelines	Azure Key Vault integration, pipeline secrets
CircleCI	Contexts and encrypted environment variables
Spinnaker	Encrypted secrets and secret manager integrations

Example: Injecting Secrets Securely

GitHub Actions (yaml script):

```
env:
  STRIPE_SECRET_KEY: ${{ secrets.STRIPE_KEY }}
```

GitLab CI (yaml script):

```
variables:
  DATABASE_PASSWORD: $DATABASE_PASSWORD
```

Jenkinsfile (groovy script):

```
withCredentials([string(credentialsId:          'db-
password', variable: 'PASSWORD')]) {
  sh './run-tests.sh --password=$PASSWORD'
}
```

Best Practices Summary

Below is a summary of best practices to follow when dealing with secrets.

- Never hardcode secrets
- Rotate secrets frequently
- Use ephemeral or short-lived tokens
- Enforce least privilege access
- Log and audit all access to secrets
- Prefer identity-based auth (OIDC, IAM roles)

What to Monitor

Tracking and monitoring secrets-related metrics helps ensure that sensitive credentials are handled securely throughout the pipeline, while also providing early warning signs of misuse, overexposure, or policy violations.

Metric	What It Measures	Why It Matters
Secret usage frequency	How often individual secrets are accessed or injected into pipeline jobs	Helps identify unused secrets that should be removed and overused secrets that may indicate poor scoping or risk concentration
Secret exposure in logs	Occurrences where secret values or fragments appear in build or runtime logs	Prevents accidental credential leaks that could lead to security incidents or unauthorized access
Access attempt logs	Records of successful and failed attempts to access secrets	Enables detection of suspicious or unauthorized access patterns early
Rotation frequency	How regularly secrets are rotated or renewed	Supports compliance requirements and reduces the blast radius of compromised credentials
Scope of secrets	How widely secrets are shared across pipelines, jobs, or environments	Ensures secrets follow least-privilege principles and are not unnecessarily exposed across workflows

Secrets and access are the linchpins of CI/CD security. Without proper controls, even the most robust quality gates can be undermined by a single leaked token. By treating secrets and identity management as a first-class concern in your gating strategy, you ensure not just the correctness of your software, but also its safety, integrity, and trustworthiness.

Scalable, Maintainable Pipeline Patterns

As engineering teams and services grow, so does the complexity of CI/CD pipelines. Without thoughtful design, these pipelines quickly become bloated, duplicated, and fragile, making them hard to maintain, audit, or evolve.

To build scalable, maintainable pipelines, teams must apply proven patterns such as templating, reusability, and the DRY (Don't Repeat Yourself) principle. These patterns reduce redundancy, enforce consistency, and streamline the process of adding new services or modifying existing workflows.

Why Pipeline Scalability Matters

- **Too many custom pipelines** → hard to manage and troubleshoot
- **Inconsistent gates and checks** → risk of quality drift
- **Repetitive logic** → higher chance of errors and more maintenance work
- **Changing policies** → painful when each pipeline needs manual updates

Scalable patterns make it possible to enforce quality gates and other standards reliably and automatically, across hundreds of services and repositories.

Key Goals of Scalable Pipelines

Below are some of the key objectives that can be gained from having pipelines that are scalable:

- **Reusability** – Common logic should be shareable and not rewritten per project.
- **Configurability** – Each service should adjust only what's unique to them.
- **Standardization** – Consistent structure and behaviour across teams.
- **Observability** – Clear logs and structure for fast troubleshooting.
- **Evolution-friendly** – Easy to roll out improvements or changes org-wide.

Core Patterns and Strategies

We are now going to look at some core patterns and strategies that should be considered for establishing healthy code governance.

Pipeline Templating

Pipeline templating is a foundational technique for building scalable, maintainable CI/CD systems. Rather than defining full pipelines independently for every repository, templating allows teams to define reusable workflow components - such as build steps, test gates, or security scans - that can be shared, versioned, and consistently applied across projects. These templates act as standardized building blocks, ensuring that quality gates are implemented uniformly while still allowing teams to configure details to suit their specific needs.

Most modern CI/CD platforms provide native support for templating and reuse, making it easier to balance central governance with team autonomy:

GitHub Actions supports reusable workflows that can be invoked from other repositories or workflows. This allows organisations to define standard linting, testing, or security gate workflows centrally and pass parameters such as language versions or thresholds when used:

```
jobs:
  call-lint:
    uses:
org/.github/.github/workflows/lint.yml@main
    with:
      node-version: '18'
```

GitLab CI offers includes and YAML anchors, enabling teams to pull in shared pipeline definitions or reference reusable job templates:

```
include:
  - template: 'Workflows/Security.gitlab-ci.yml'

.lint-template:
  script:
    - npm run lint
```

Jenkins achieves reuse through shared libraries, where common pipeline logic is implemented as versioned functions or classes and consumed by individual Jenkinsfiles.

Azure DevOps provides pipeline templates with parameterized YAML, allowing teams to compose pipelines from centrally managed templates while controlling environment- or project-specific behaviour.

The benefits of pipeline templating are significant, especially when quality gates are involved. Templates make it possible to update a gate, such as changing a security threshold or adding a new compliance check, once and have that change propagate across dozens or hundreds of pipelines. This dramatically reduces duplication, minimizes configuration drift, and simplifies audits, as there is a single source of truth for how quality is enforced. Over time, templating becomes a key enabler of both consistency and velocity, allowing organisations to scale quality gates without scaling complexity.

DRY Pipelines (Don't Repeat Yourself)

As CI/CD adoption grows across teams and repositories, one of the fastest ways pipelines become brittle and unmanageable is through copy-and-paste reuse. DRY (Don't Repeat Yourself) pipeline design focuses on eliminating duplicated logic by centralizing common quality gate behaviour and making it reusable, configurable, and easy to evolve over time. This approach is especially important for quality gates, where inconsistent implementations can lead to uneven enforcement and confusion across teams.

Rather than embedding gate logic directly into every pipeline definition, organizations should extract shared behaviour into reusable components:

- **Centralize gate logic** in scripts, shared workflows, or libraries that can be invoked from multiple pipelines.
- **Use parameters or configuration files** to customize behaviour per project, such as different thresholds, languages, or environments.
- **Modularize pipeline steps** into callable functions or jobs that perform a single, well-defined responsibility.

For example, a reusable quality gate that enforces a minimum code coverage threshold can be implemented once and reused everywhere:

```
steps:
  - name: Check coverage
    run: ./gates/check_coverage.sh --threshold 80
```

By externalizing the gate logic, teams can adjust the threshold, reporting format, or failure behaviour without rewriting pipeline YAML in every repository. This also makes it easier to test and version gate logic independently of application code.

DRY pipelines reduce maintenance overhead, improve consistency, and make it significantly easier to audit how quality is enforced across an organization. When combined with templating, they form a powerful pattern for scaling CI/CD pipelines, allowing teams to move quickly while ensuring that quality gates remain reliable, predictable, and aligned with organizational standards.

Pipeline as Code + Config as Code

A key principle for building scalable and adaptable quality gates is to clearly separate *how* a gate works from *what* rules it enforces. Gate logic, such as running tests, parsing reports, or evaluating results, should be implemented once in reusable scripts or workflows. Configuration, such as thresholds, enabled checks, or severity levels, should live outside the pipeline logic in declarative files or policy definitions. This separation dramatically improves flexibility, clarity, and long-term maintainability.

In practice, this often means introducing dedicated configuration files alongside application code, such as `.qualitygates.yml` or `ci-settings.json`. These files define which gates are active, the thresholds they enforce, and any environment- or team-specific variations. For example, one team might enforce 90% code coverage on new services, while another gradually ramps up from 70% on legacy systems, all without changing the underlying gate implementation.

For more advanced scenarios, organizations can adopt policy-as-code using tools like Open Policy Agent (OPA) and Rego. Policies define pass/fail conditions in a declarative, testable format that can be versioned and reviewed like application code. This approach enables consistent enforcement across pipelines, infrastructure, and environments while still allowing fine-grained control and exceptions, where justified.

Separating logic from configuration enables declarative gating, supports team-specific thresholds, and makes overrides and inheritance explicit and auditable. As pipelines scale, this pattern becomes essential for balancing centralized governance with local autonomy, allowing quality gates to evolve with both technical maturity and business needs without becoming rigid or hard-coded.

Centralized Shared Libraries

As pipelines mature, reusable scripts and templates alone are often not enough. Centralized shared libraries take reuse a step further by packaging quality gate logic into well-defined, versioned components that can be consumed consistently across all pipelines. These libraries become the backbone of standardized quality enforcement, enabling organizations to roll out improvements or fixes to gate logic without manually updating every repository.

Common approaches include:

- **Jenkins Shared Libraries**, written in Groovy, which expose reusable pipeline steps and utilities.
- **GitHub Actions reusable composite actions**, which bundle multiple steps into a single, versioned action.
- **Shared Bash or Python libraries** that implement gate logic and can be invoked from any CI system.

By versioning and documenting these libraries, teams gain predictable upgrade paths and can adopt new gate behaviour incrementally. This reduces the risk of breaking changes, simplifies onboarding, and makes it easier to audit exactly which gate logic is in use across the organization.

Dynamic Gate Evaluation

Not every change requires the same level of scrutiny, and applying all gates to every pipeline run can slow delivery without improving outcomes. Dynamic gate evaluation allows pipelines to adaptively decide which quality gates to apply based on contextual information available at runtime.

Pipelines can evaluate metadata such as:

- **Service type**, for example applying UI accessibility gates to frontend services but not backend APIs.
- **Change type**, enforcing stricter checks for infrastructure or security-related changes than for simple documentation updates.
- **Target environment**, with lightweight gates in development and progressively stricter gates in staging and production.
- **Historical risk**, increasing gate strictness for services or teams with frequent failures or past incidents.

When combined with configuration-driven logic and conditional pipeline jobs, dynamic evaluation enables pipelines to be both intelligent and efficient. Quality enforcement becomes risk-aware rather than one-size-fits-all, preserving fast feedback for low-risk changes while ensuring that high-impact deployments receive the scrutiny they deserve.

Visual Pipeline Design and Documentation

As CI/CD pipelines grow in complexity, their effectiveness increasingly depends on how well they are understood by the teams that use and maintain them. Visual pipeline design and clear documentation help demystify quality gates by making gate flow, dependencies, and decision points explicit rather than implicit in YAML or scripts.

Using pipeline graphs and diagrams allows teams to quickly see where quality gates sit, which stages depend on them, and how failures propagate through the pipeline. Most CI platforms provide built-in visualizations, and these can be complemented with architecture diagrams or flowcharts for more complex pipelines. Alongside visuals, each job or stage should clearly document its purpose, inputs, outputs, and failure conditions, setting clear expectations for developers interacting with the pipeline.

Providing onboarding templates for new repositories further reinforces consistency. These templates give teams a ready-made, well-documented starting point that includes standard quality gates, recommended configurations, and links to further guidance. Together, visualization and documentation improve maintainability, reduce onboarding time, and promote cross-team alignment around how quality is enforced.

Observability and Feedback Loops

Maintaining healthy pipelines requires continuous visibility into how quality gates perform in practice. Observability ensures that gates do not silently degrade, become overly strict, or introduce unnecessary friction over time.

Effective pipelines expose gate outcomes directly in developer workflows, such as through GitHub Checks, GitLab pipeline badges, or status indicators in pull requests. Beyond individual runs, teams should collect and analyse metrics that reveal broader trends, including overall pipeline duration, the most common gate failures, and how often gates are skipped or overridden.

Regularly running pipeline linting or drift detection tools helps identify inconsistencies, outdated configurations, or deviations from approved templates. Combined with dashboards and review rituals, these feedback loops turn pipeline data into actionable insight, allowing teams to continuously refine their quality gates while keeping pipelines reliable, transparent, and aligned with delivery goals.

Best Practices

Below is a summary of best practices to consider when looking into making your pipelines more scalable:

- Create a library of pre-approved gates that teams can consume easily
- Use versioned templates **to** avoid breaking changes in pipelines
- Keep gate logic small and testable
- Encourage teams to own their config, but inherit shared logic
- Make pipelines testable locally to reduce CI trial-and-error

Scaling CI/CD pipelines isn't about building bigger pipelines, it's about building smarter ones. With templating, modularity, and DRY principles, you can construct pipelines that are easier to manage, quicker to evolve, and more effective at enforcing quality gates consistently across a growing organization.

Event-Driven vs. Scheduled Checks in CI/CD Quality Gates

As pipelines grow more complex and automation expands, engineering teams often need to make decisions about when certain quality checks should run. Two primary approaches dominate: event-driven checks **and** scheduled checks. Each serves a distinct purpose in ensuring software quality while balancing cost, speed, and system load.

Understanding when to trigger checks is just as important as what those checks are.

What Are Event-Driven and Scheduled Checks?

CI/CD pipelines can be triggered in different ways depending on the workflow requirements, as outlined below:

Type	Description
Event-Driven	Triggered immediately by specific actions or changes (e.g., code push, pull request, merge)
Scheduled	Run on a regular interval regardless of recent activity (e.g., nightly, weekly)

Event-Driven Checks

Event-driven gates are reactive checkpoints in a CI/CD pipeline, they execute in response to specific events in the software lifecycle rather than running on a fixed schedule. These gates ensure that quality checks are closely tied to changes in the codebase, providing timely feedback to developers and maintaining high confidence in code integrity.

Common Triggers

Event-driven gates typically respond to key development actions, such as:

- **Push to a branch:** Validates changes as soon as code is pushed, catching errors early.
- **Opening or updating a pull request:** Ensures that proposed changes meet coding standards and pass automated tests before review.

- **Merging to main or protected branches:** Confirms that only verified changes enter critical branches.
- **Tagging a release:** Runs release-specific validations like versioning checks or final security scans.
- **Deployment to an environment:** Triggers environment-specific gates to verify deployment readiness or configuration compliance.

Ideal Use Cases

Event-driven gates are particularly suited for scenarios where immediate validation is valuable:

- **Pre-merge validation:** Run unit tests, linting, and code coverage checks to catch issues before code is merged.
- **Release gates:** Perform security scans or compliance checks before deploying to production.
- **Infrastructure drift detection:** Identify configuration changes or environment inconsistencies in real-time.
- **Real-time policy enforcement:** Enforce team or organizational policies, such as required reviewers, commit message formats, or branch protection rules.

Tools and Configurations

Popular CI/CD platforms support event-driven triggers in various ways:

- **GitHub Actions:** on: push, on: pull_request
- **GitLab CI:** only: [merge_requests], rules: changes

- **Jenkins:** Webhooks combined with multibranch pipeline triggers
- **ArgoCD:** GitOps reconciliation triggered on repository commits

Benefits

Below is a list of benefits that event-driven checks provide in the delivery process:

- Provides fast feedback to developers, allowing issues to be resolved quickly.
- Ensures that quality checks are aligned with code changes, reducing the chance of regressions.
- Avoids unnecessary pipeline runs, saving compute resources and reducing wait times.

Watchouts

- High-frequency commits can generate noise and excessive pipeline runs if triggers are not filtered carefully.
- Event-driven gates may miss issues that develop between events, such as gradual dependency rot or environment drift that occurs outside of monitored events.

Scheduled Checks

Scheduled gates operate on a fixed, time-based cadence, running whether or not code changes have occurred. These gates are proactive, designed to continuously monitor the health, security, and compliance of a codebase or environment. Unlike event-driven gates, scheduled checks do not rely on developer actions to trigger them, making them ideal for ongoing maintenance and periodic validation tasks.

Common Frequencies

Scheduled gates can be configured to run at intervals that match the risk or importance of the components being monitored:

- **Nightly:** Standard daily checks for general pipeline health.
- **Every 15 minutes:** High-frequency checks for critical or high-risk components.
- **Weekly:** Broader system health checks or audits.

Ideal Use Cases

Scheduled gates are best suited for tasks that benefit from regular monitoring or long-running analysis:

- **Dependency freshness and security scanning:** Detect outdated libraries or vulnerabilities on a consistent basis.
- **Flaky test detection:** Identify tests that intermittently fail over time rather than just on code changes.
- **Long-running regression or load tests:** Ensure performance and stability across the system.
- **Dead code or unused resource audits:** Spot inefficiencies or unused assets that may accumulate unnoticed.
- **Post-deployment SLO/SLA verification:** Measure service-level objectives after deployments to ensure compliance.
-

Tools and Configurations

Most CI/CD platforms support time-based scheduling using either built-in features or external schedulers:

- **GitHub Actions:** `on: schedule` with cron expressions
- **GitLab CI:** Cron schedules configured in the pipeline UI
- **Jenkins:** CRON syntax in build triggers for precise timing
- **ArgoCD / Flux:** Periodic reconciliation combined with alert rules
- **Third-party schedulers:** Tools like Airflow or CircleCI schedules for complex workflows

Benefits

Below is a list of benefits that scheduled checks provide in the delivery process:

- Detects time-sensitive or environmental issues that might not be triggered by specific code events.
- Reduces the need for developers to manually trigger checks, freeing up time and reducing human error.
- Ideal for non-blocking "watchdog" gates, such as drift detection, anomaly spotting, or system audits.

Watchouts

- Scheduled gates can become stale if results are not clearly surfaced or acted upon.
- There is a risk of neglect if they are disconnected from the main delivery pipeline.

- Requires monitoring to ensure jobs don't silently fail, as missed runs could lead to undetected issues.

Combine Both for a Resilient Strategy

Event-driven gates catch errors fast, while scheduled checks uncover hidden degradation over time.

Hybrid Approach Example:

Gate Type	Trigger	Description
Lint & Unit Tests	On PR	Block merge if coding or test standards fail
Security Scans	On PR + Nightly	Block release if high-severity CVE detected
Load Testing	Nightly	Alerts if regression in response time detected
License Compliance	On Tag	Validate before shipping a release
Dependency Updates	Weekly	Warn teams of outdated or vulnerable packages

Best Practices

Below is a list of best practices to follow when trying to apply a hybrid approach between both event-driven and scheduled pipeline checks:

- **Use filters**: Run only when relevant files change (e.g., skip frontend gates if only backend files are touched)
- **Visualize scheduled check results** in dashboards or PR comments
- **Make scheduled jobs fail noisily**, don't hide broken watchdogs
- **Tag gates with severity** (fail-fast, warn-only, advisory)
- **Use GitOps or state-monitoring tools** to automate drift detection on a schedule

Both event-driven and scheduled gates have their place in a mature CI/CD strategy. Event-driven checks power fast feedback and real-time safety nets, while scheduled checks provide background confidence and protect against the slow decay of quality over time. Together, they form a defence-in-depth model for maintaining high standards in automated delivery.

Conclusion: Orchestrating Pipelines That Tell a Story

In this chapter, we explored how to orchestrate complex CI/CD pipelines and integrate various quality gates effectively. We discussed strategies for sequencing jobs and stages, handling dependencies, and ensuring that gates, such as testing, security scans, and compliance checks, are executed at the right points in the workflow.

The focus was on creating pipelines that are not only automated but also intelligent, allowing teams to catch issues early, reduce feedback loops, and prevent unnecessary work from propagating downstream. By combining practical examples with clear patterns for gate integration, this chapter aimed to provide actionable guidance on designing maintainable, scalable, and reliable pipelines.

Building on the foundation of well-orchestrated pipelines, the next chapter shifts attention to observability and feedback loops. Even the most efficiently designed pipeline is only as effective as the insights it provides. Observability allows teams to monitor gate outcomes, detect bottlenecks, and respond proactively to failures.

Feedback loops - through dashboards, alerts, and metrics, ensure that developers, testers, and DevOps engineers have the data they need to continuously improve both the pipeline and the software it delivers. In this chapter, we will explore practical approaches for tracking performance, exposing meaningful metrics, and creating a culture of continuous feedback that drives smarter decisions across the organization.

Observability and Feedback Loops

Purpose of chapter: This chapter explores how observability and feedback loops turn pipeline data into actionable insights, enabling teams to detect issues early, optimize performance, and continuously improve their delivery process.

Observability and feedback loops are critical for making the delivery process transparent, measurable, and continuously improvable. By exposing detailed information on pipeline performance, gate outcomes, and deployment metrics, teams can quickly detect failures, bottlenecks, or inefficiencies before they impact production. This visibility ensures that issues are addressed at the right time, reducing downtime and preventing small problems from escalating into larger ones.

Beyond detection, feedback loops provide actionable insights to developers, testers, and DevOps engineers. Dashboards, alerts, and automated reports allow teams to understand trends, measure improvements, and validate whether changes to the pipeline or application are delivering the desired outcomes. Over time, these insights help optimize test coverage, reduce cycle times, and improve the overall reliability and predictability of software delivery. In essence, observability and feedback loops turn raw pipeline data into a tool for learning, adaptation, and continuous improvement, making the delivery process faster, safer, and smarter.

Logging, Tracing, and Metric Collection in CI/CD Quality Gate Pipelines

As pipelines grow in complexity and automation deepens, observability becomes a cornerstone of both reliability and quality enforcement. To ensure that gates are functioning as expected, and that their failures are actionable, teams must adopt robust logging, tracing, and metric collection practices. Without observability, even well-designed gates can fail silently, slow down delivery, or create debugging nightmares.

Why Observability Matters in CI/CD

In the context of quality gates, observability enables teams to:

- **Understand** why a gate passed or failed
- **Debug** broken or flaky pipeline steps
- **Track** quality trends over time (e.g., test flakiness, security issues)
- **Alert** proactively on regressions or performance degradation
- **Audit** pipeline decisions for compliance or review

Whether you're building, testing, scanning, or deploying, if you can't see it, you can't improve it.

Observability Components

We will now look at the different aspects of observability that need to be configured in order to have a more complete picture of what is going on in both your software and the delivery process itself.

Logging

Logging forms the backbone of observability in CI/CD pipelines by providing a clear, time-ordered record of what happened during each pipeline execution. When a quality gate fails, or behaves unexpectedly, logs are often the first and most reliable source of truth for understanding why. Well-designed logging enables faster debugging, more effective post-mortems, and greater trust in automated gate decisions.

At a minimum, logs should clearly capture gate decision logic, making it obvious why a pipeline passed or failed. For example, a message such as *"Security scan failed: 2 high-severity CVEs detected in dependencies"* immediately tells a developer what action is required. Test outputs should be logged in a summarized and structured format, highlighting key results rather than overwhelming teams with raw output. Where pipelines interact with external quality systems, such as code coverage services, performance benchmarks, or SLA validation APIs, those interactions and their responses should also be recorded.

Context is equally important. Logs should include relevant metadata such as the commit hash, branch, pipeline stage, job name, tool versions, and environment. This context makes it possible to correlate failures across runs, environments, or services and is essential for tracing issues back to specific changes.

To maximize usefulness, adopt structured logging (for example, JSON) so logs can be parsed, searched, and aggregated automatically. Always avoid logging secrets or credentials, and rely on CI tooling to mask sensitive values if they appear in output. Tagging logs by stage, job, or gate name further improves traceability, especially in complex pipelines with many parallel steps.

Finally, logs should be centralized in a common logging platform such as ELK, Loki, or cloud-native services like CloudWatch. Centralization allows teams to analyse trends across pipelines, correlate failures with deployments, and retain historical data for audits or incident investigations. When logging is treated as a first-class concern, quality gates become more transparent, explainable, and easier to evolve over time.

What to Log:

- Gate decision logic (e.g., "Security scan failed: 2 high severity CVEs")
- Test outputs (summarized in structured format)
- API calls to external quality systems (e.g., coverage thresholds, SLA validations)
- Environment context (e.g., version, commit hash, job name)

Best Practices:

- Use structured logging (e.g., JSON) for machine parsing
- Avoid logging secrets or credentials
- Tag logs by stage, job, or gate name
- Centralize logs (e.g., ELK, Loki, CloudWatch)

Tracing

While logs tell you *what* happened, tracing helps you understand *how* it happened across a sequence of steps, services, and systems. In modern CI/CD pipelines, especially those orchestrating microservices, external quality tools, or chained workflows, tracing provides end-to-end visibility into execution flow and timing. This makes it an invaluable capability for diagnosing slow pipelines, flaky gates, and complex failure scenarios.

In a CI/CD context, tracing can be used to follow a pipeline execution across stages such as build, test, security scanning, and deployment. It allows teams to pinpoint where time is being spent, for example, whether delays are caused by long-running tests, slow responses from security scanners, or queuing between stages. Traces also help visualize how a deployment or quality scan progressed, showing dependencies and execution order rather than isolated steps.

Tracing becomes particularly powerful when correlating gate outcomes with system behaviour. For instance, a performance gate failure can be directly linked to a trace showing a latency spike in a downstream service during a canary deployment. This end-to-end perspective helps teams move beyond "the gate failed" to understanding the underlying cause and impact.

To implement tracing consistently, many organizations adopt OpenTelemetry as a standard for collecting and propagating trace data across pipelines and services. Traces can then be visualized using tools such as Jaeger, Zipkin, Honeycomb, or Grafana Tempo. Some CI platforms, including GitHub Actions, support trace correlation through mechanisms like traceparent headers, enabling pipeline steps to be linked with application runtime traces.

By adding tracing to CI/CD observability, teams gain a powerful diagnostic tool that complements logs and metrics. Together, these signals make quality gates more transparent, reduce mean time to resolution, and provide the insight needed to continuously optimize both pipeline performance and gate effectiveness.

Use Cases in CI/CD:

- Understand delays in pipeline stages (e.g., long test execution or slow scan response)
- Visualize how a deployment or scan progressed
- Correlate a gate failure with a service's behaviour (e.g., performance gate tied to a latency spike)

Tooling:

- OpenTelemetry for tracing standardization
- Jaeger, Zipkin, Honeycomb, or Grafana Tempo for trace visualization
- GitHub Actions trace correlation with traceparent headers

Metric Collection

Metrics are quantitative measurements collected over time that provide a high-level view of how well your CI/CD pipelines and quality gates are performing. Unlike logs or traces, which focus on individual executions, metrics reveal patterns and trends, making them essential for understanding long-term health, identifying regressions, and guiding continuous improvement.

In the context of quality gates, metrics can track both pipeline efficiency and quality outcomes. Common examples include pipeline duration, stage execution times, pass/fail rates for specific gates, frequency of retries or overrides, and defect or vulnerability trends over successive releases. These measurements allow teams to spot emerging issues early, such as a security scan that is gradually slowing down builds or a test suite that is becoming increasingly flaky.

Metrics also underpin effective alerting and visualization. By defining thresholds on key indicators, such as an increase in failed builds or a drop in test coverage, teams can trigger alerts when quality or performance deviates from acceptable ranges. Dashboards built with tools like Grafana, Datadog, or native CI analytics provide a shared, real-time view of pipeline health, helping teams align on priorities and outcomes.

Most importantly, metrics turn quality gates from binary pass/fail mechanisms into learning tools. By analysing trends over time, organizations can refine thresholds, rebalance gate placement, and make data-informed decisions about where to invest in automation or optimization. When used thoughtfully, metrics create a feedback loop that continuously improves both software quality and delivery speed.

Examples of CI/CD Metrics:

Monitoring pipeline and quality metrics provides visibility into both delivery efficiency and gate effectiveness, enabling teams to identify bottlenecks, recurring risks, and opportunities for continuous improvement across the CI/CD lifecycle.

Metric	What It Measures	Why It Matters
Pipeline duration (per stage)	Time taken to complete each pipeline stage	Helps identify slow or inefficient stages that delay feedback and delivery
Gate failure rate (per type)	Frequency with which specific quality gates fail	Highlights recurring quality issues and misconfigured or overly strict gates

Code coverage percentage	Proportion of code exercised by automated tests	Indicates test effectiveness and areas of untested risk
Test pass/failure counts	Number of successful versus failed tests per run	Reveals instability, flaky tests, or regressions introduced by changes
Vulnerabilities over time	Trend of security findings across builds or releases	Tracks security hygiene and whether vulnerabilities are being reduced or accumulating
Deployment frequency	How often code is successfully deployed	Provides insight into delivery maturity and helps correlate speed with quality outcomes
MTTR (Mean Time to Recovery)	Average time to recover from a failed pipeline or production incident	Reflects overall pipeline reliability and the effectiveness of recovery practices

Best Practices:

- Emit metrics as part of pipeline steps (e.g., `echo "quality_gate_passed=1"` → Prometheus scrape)
- Use tags/labels for dimensional analysis (e.g., repo, service, environment)
- Set SLIs/SLOs (e.g., <2% gate failure rate, <15 min pipeline duration)

Tooling Landscape

The tooling ecosystem that supports observability and quality gates in CI/CD pipelines is broad and continuously evolving. New tools emerge, existing platforms converge, and capabilities that once required specialist products are increasingly built directly into CI/CD and cloud platforms. For this reason, it is often more important to understand the *purpose* a tool serves than to become overly attached to a specific product. The categories below represent common capabilities rather than a fixed or exhaustive list.

- **Logging tools** focus on collecting, indexing, and searching pipeline and application logs. Stacks such as the ELK Stack (Elasticsearch, Logstash, Kibana), Loki, and Fluent Bit are commonly used to centralize logs from CI jobs, security scans, and deployments, making it easier to investigate failures and perform post-incident analysis.
- **Tracing tools** provide end-to-end visibility into execution flows across pipelines and services. OpenTelemetry has become the de facto standard for collecting and propagating trace data, while tools like Jaeger, Zipkin, and Grafana Tempo visualize how work moves through pipeline stages and external systems, helping teams diagnose latency and dependency issues.
- **Metrics platforms** aggregate numerical data over time, enabling trend analysis, alerting, and performance tracking. Prometheus, Datadog, CloudWatch, and New Relic are commonly used to capture pipeline durations, gate pass/fail rates, test stability, and operational signals tied to deployments.
- **Dashboarding tools** such as Grafana, Kibana, and Datadog bring logs, traces, and metrics together into a unified view. These dashboards provide at-a-glance insight into pipeline health, quality trends, and bottlenecks, supporting both day-to-day development and strategic decision-making.
- **CI integration tooling** connects observability data directly into developer workflows. Platforms like GitHub Actions, GitLab Pipelines, and Jenkins (via monitoring plugins) increasingly expose native insights, status checks, and hooks that make

quality gate outcomes visible where developers already work.

As this landscape continues to change, organizations should prioritize tools that integrate well with their pipelines, support open standards, and evolve with their delivery practices. Flexibility and interoperability are key to ensuring observability remains effective as CI/CD systems and quality gates mature.

Observability and Gate Reliability

Gate observability isn't just nice to have, it's critical. Without it:

- Test failures may be hard to reproduce
- Security scan results may be ignored or misinterpreted
- Performance regressions may go undetected
- The root cause of gate flakiness may remain elusive

A well-instrumented pipeline allows engineering and DevOps teams to trust their automation, and act on its results.

Best Practices Summary

- Log every gate's decision and its input data
- Track metrics like gate pass rate, scan duration, or alert frequency
- Trace across service boundaries when pipelines interact with external systems
- Correlate observability data with code commits, authors, and change types
- Automate alerts for anomalies or gate instability

CI/CD observability is the nervous system of your pipeline. By logging meaningfully, tracing execution flows, and collecting actionable metrics, you enable faster debugging, better decision-making, and more reliable quality enforcement. In a world of automated gating, visibility isn't optional, it's essential.

Dashboards for Quality Status in CI/CD Pipelines

As engineering teams adopt automated quality gates across their CI/CD pipelines, visibility becomes crucial. Dashboards for quality status provide a centralized, real-time, and historical view of how software quality evolves throughout the delivery process. They turn raw data, test results, scan outcomes, code coverage, gate pass/fail rates, into actionable insights for developers, QA, security, and leadership.

These dashboards aren't just vanity metrics, they serve as the health monitors of your delivery process.

Why Quality Dashboards Matter

- **Transparency** – Developers and stakeholders can see the impact of their changes on quality gates.
- **Early Warning System** – Highlights regressions, test failures, or policy violations before they reach production.
- **Continuous Improvement** – Enables teams to track trends and iterate on quality practices.
- **Communication Tool** – Aligns cross-functional teams around shared quality and release readiness goals.
- **Audit and Compliance** – Records historic gate decisions for regulatory or internal review.

What to Include on a Quality Status Dashboard

An effective quality status dashboard does more than report whether the latest build passed or failed, it provides a clear, shared view of software quality across the delivery lifecycle. The best dashboards balance real-time status with historical trends, helping teams understand not only where they are today, but whether quality is improving or degrading over time. When designed well, these dashboards become a daily decision-making tool for engineers, testers, security teams, and leadership alike.

Current Gate Status

At a glance, teams should be able to see the outcome of all critical quality gates for the latest pipeline runs. This includes build and test results, security scan outcomes, linting and code quality checks, compliance flags such as license violations, and performance thresholds. Clear visual indicators, such as green, amber, and red states, make it easy to identify blocking issues and understand which gate is responsible for a failure without digging into logs.

Trends Over Time

Trend data transforms quality gates from binary checkpoints into learning tools. Tracking gate pass and failure rates over time, by day, week, or service, helps identify systemic issues, such as a brittle test suite or an overly strict gate. Metrics like test flakiness, vulnerability counts by severity, code coverage progression, and deployment success rates reveal whether quality initiatives are having the desired long-term impact or need adjustment.

Test Quality Insights

Test-related views help teams focus on stability and efficiency rather than just volume. Highlighting the most frequently failing tests, identifying flaky tests by occurrence, and showing the longest-running or slowest test suites enables teams to target improvements where they will have the greatest effect. Average test execution time per job is particularly useful for balancing fast feedback with adequate coverage.

Security and Compliance Metrics

Security and compliance sections should emphasize risk and remediation progress rather than raw scan output. Key indicators include the number of open CVEs, time to fix vulnerabilities, license usage by type, and the number of policy exceptions currently in place. These metrics help teams prioritize remediation work and give stakeholders confidence that risk is being actively managed.

Access and Secrets Checks

Dashboards should also surface signals related to access control and secrets hygiene. Metrics such as secrets exposure incidents, expired or unused secrets, and the number of pipelines failing secret scans provide early warning signs of governance or security gaps that might otherwise go unnoticed.

Pipeline Performance

Finally, pipeline performance metrics ensure that quality gates themselves are not becoming a bottleneck. Average pipeline duration, slowest stages, queuing or blocking issues, and the frequency of manual approvals or interventions all help teams optimize flow. When quality gates are visible alongside performance data, teams can continuously refine their pipelines to maintain both speed and confidence.

Below is a summary of this information that can be tracked through your quality dashboard:

Current Gate Status

- Build and test gate results (pass/fail)
- Security scan status (pass/warnings/fail)
- Linting/code quality checks
- Compliance flags (e.g., license violations)
- Performance thresholds

Trends Over Time

- Gate pass/failure rate (daily, weekly, per service)
- Test flakiness or instability metrics
- Security vulnerability counts by severity
- Code coverage progression
- Deployment success rate

Test Quality Insights

- Top failing tests
- Flaky tests by frequency
- Longest-running tests
- Average test execution time per job

Security and Compliance Metrics

- Number of open CVEs
- Time to fix for vulnerabilities
- License usage by type

- Number of policy exceptions

Access and Secrets Checks

- Secrets exposure incidents
- Expired or unused secrets
- Number of failing secret scans per pipeline

Pipeline Performance

- Average pipeline duration
- Slowest pipeline stages
- Queuing or blocking issues
- Frequency of manual interventions or approvals

Tooling Options

The tooling ecosystem for CI/CD observability and quality reporting is broad and continuously evolving, with platforms increasingly converging around integrated views of metrics, logs, traces, and pipeline data. Rather than selecting a single "best" tool, most mature organizations combine multiple tools based on their existing stack, scale, and governance requirements. The following options are commonly used to build effective quality status dashboards, each with distinct strengths.

Grafana: Grafana excels at highly customizable, real-time dashboards and is often the centrepiece of an observability stack. It integrates seamlessly with Prometheus for metrics, Loki for logs, and Tempo or Jaeger for traces, making it ideal for correlating pipeline performance, gate outcomes, and system health. Grafana is particularly well suited for trend analysis, cross-service comparisons, and executive-level quality overviews.

Kibana: Kibana is a strong choice when log data is the primary source of truth, especially in environments built around the ELK stack. It enables powerful log-based dashboards that can surface gate decisions, failure reasons, security scan outputs, and audit trails. Kibana is often used for forensic analysis and compliance reporting, where detailed, searchable historical records are required.

Datadog: Datadog provides a unified platform for metrics, logs, traces, and application performance monitoring, with native CI/CD and cloud integrations. Its strength lies in fast setup, rich out-of-the-box dashboards, and strong correlation across pipeline activity, deployments, and runtime behaviour. Datadog is well suited for organizations looking for an opinionated, low-maintenance observability solution with strong alerting capabilities.

GitHub Insights: GitHub Insights offers native visibility into GitHub Actions, checks, pull requests, and workflow outcomes. While less flexible than dedicated observability tools, it provides immediate, contextual feedback close to the developer workflow. It is most effective for surfacing build status, test results, and basic trends without introducing additional tooling.

GitLab Value Streams: GitLab Value Stream Analytics integrates quality metrics, DORA metrics, and pipeline data directly into the GitLab platform. This tight integration enables teams to track flow efficiency, deployment frequency, failure rates, and quality trends end to end. It is particularly useful for organizations standardizing on GitLab as a single DevSecOps platform.

Jenkins Plugins: Jenkins offers a wide ecosystem of plugins for visualizing build pipelines, test results, code coverage, and historical trends. While dashboards often require more customization and maintenance, Jenkins remains a flexible option for teams with complex or highly customized pipelines that need fine-grained control over reporting.

Sentry / Honeycomb: Tools like Sentry and Honeycomb focus on advanced debugging, performance analysis, and high-cardinality observability. When integrated with CI/CD pipelines, they help correlate failed gates or deployments with runtime errors and performance regressions. These tools are especially valuable for tying pipeline quality signals to real production impact.

In practice, quality dashboards often combine native CI visibility (e.g., GitHub or GitLab) with observability platforms (such as Grafana or Datadog) to provide both immediate feedback and long-term insight. As the tooling landscape continues to evolve, the key is to favour integrations, open standards, and adaptability over rigid, single-purpose solutions.

Tool	Strengths
Grafana	Highly customizable dashboards, works with Prometheus, Loki, Tempo
Kibana	Great for log-based dashboards from ELK stack
Datadog	Unified metrics, logs, APM, and CI/CD integrations
GitHub Insights	Native visibility into Actions and checks
GitLab Value Streams	Quality trends and DORA metrics integrated
Jenkins Plugins	Build pipeline, test results, and trend visualizations
Sentry / Honeycomb	Advanced debugging and performance observability

Best Practices for Dashboard Design

When designing your respective dashboards, below are some best practices to consider:

- Segment by service / team to allow focused analysis
- Use red / yellow / green indicators to signal health at a glance
- Enable filtering by branch / environment (e.g., prod vs. staging)
- Make it self-serve and always visible (link from PRs or engineering homepages)
- Integrate with alerting tools (e.g., Slack, email, PagerDuty) for live triggers

Example: Dashboard Use Case

Below is an example use case of how a dashboard can be used to identify issues in the delivery process:

A product team wants to ship a new feature. They check their "Release Readiness" dashboard and see:

- 100% of tests passed in staging
- One security warning (low severity)
- Code coverage held steady at 85%
- Performance gate flagged a 20% increase in response time

Instead of blindly deploying, they investigate the performance regression and delay release until it's resolved, avoiding a production slowdown.

From Dashboards to Decisions

As shown in the above example, dashboards should not only display information, they should enable informed action. Connect your dashboard insights to:

- Auto-blockers (e.g., halt promotion if gates fail)
- Exceptions tracking (e.g., security waivers)

- Ownership (e.g., direct failing gate alerts to service owners)

Dashboards are the front line of quality visibility in a modern DevOps environment. When thoughtfully implemented, they become powerful tools for:

- Enforcing gates consistently
- Responding quickly to failures
- Driving conversations around quality
- Elevating engineering accountability and trust

Well-designed dashboards ensure that quality gates don't operate in the dark, but instead act as transparent, data-driven enablers of safe, fast delivery.

Alerting and Notification Practices in CI/CD Quality Gates

In fast-moving development environments, quality gates only matter if teams are made aware when they fail, and why. That's where alerting and notification practices become critical. When done well, alerts help teams respond quickly, maintain quality standards, and reduce downtime. When done poorly, they lead to alert fatigue, missed signals, and degraded trust in the gating system.

The key is to build a targeted, actionable, and non-intrusive alerting strategy that empowers, not overwhelms, your developers and stakeholders.

Why Alerting Matters for Quality Gates

- **Real-time visibility** when critical gates (e.g., security, tests, performance) fail
- **Contextual insight** into the root cause of failure

- **Prompt remediation** and reduced Mean Time to Resolution (MTTR)
- **Feedback loops** between delivery, quality, and operations
- **Confidence in automation**, knowing it will speak up when needed

Common Notification Channels

Below are some common communication channels that can be used to notify teams of quality gate failures or metrics:

Channel	Use Case
Email	Formal gate reports, stakeholder summaries
Slack/MS Teams	Real-time pipeline and gate updates, team discussions
GitHub/GitLab PR UI	Inline gate feedback in pull/merge requests
PagerDuty/On-call	Critical gate failures that block release or affect production
Dashboards	Persistent visualizations of alerts and gate history
SMS/Push	Rarely used, reserved for high-severity events

Best Practices for Alerting in CI/CD

Below we look at some important best practices when it comes to alerting in more detail. Alerting is an important aspect of responding to failures and remediating them and so it's important teams work on getting these aspects correctly.

Define Alert Severity and Actionability

Not all quality gate failures carry the same level of risk or urgency. Treating every failure as equally critical leads to alert fatigue, slower response times, and reduced trust in the alerting system. Instead, alerts should be classified by severity and expected response, ensuring teams know exactly how to act when an alert is triggered.

Severity	Example	Expected Action
Critical	Critical security CVE, failed production deploy gate	Immediately block merge or deployment, page on-call or security team
High	Major test suite failure, broken contract tests	Notify owning team immediately, require fix before proceeding
Medium	Code coverage drop, flaky test detected	Post notification (e.g., Slack), triage during standup or backlog refinement
Informational	Lint warnings, deprecated API usage	Log to dashboard or include in daily/weekly summary

Clearly defining severity levels establishes consistent expectations, aligns alerts with business risk, and prevents unnecessary escalation for low-impact issues.

Make Alerts Contextual and Actionable

An alert is only useful if it enables fast diagnosis and resolution. Every alert should provide enough context so the recipient can take action without hunting for additional information.

A well-formed alert should answer:

- **What failed?** (gate name, rule, or threshold)
- **Why did it fail?** (specific violation or metric)
- **Who owns it?** (team or individual responsible)
- **Where do I fix it?** (links to reports, code, or remediation guidance)

Example Slack Alert:

> **Security Gate Failed**
>
> **Repository:** payments-service
>
> **Blocked by:** CVE-2024-1098 (HIGH) in log4j
>
> **Owner:** @secops
>
> **Fix Guidance:** [View Scan Report] | [Update Dependency]

This format reduces cognitive load and shortens mean time to remediation by making the next step explicit.

Throttle to Prevent Alert Fatigue

Excessive or noisy alerts erode trust and are often ignored. Alerting systems should be tuned to emphasize signal over noise.

Effective throttling techniques include:

- **Debouncing flapping gates**, such as intermittently failing or flaky tests
- **Batching low-severity notifications** into daily or weekly summaries
- **Suppression windows** for known or accepted issues
- **Escalation rules**, where alerts trigger only if a gate fails X *times within Y minutes*

By filtering out transient or low-risk events, teams remain responsive to genuinely important failures.

Route Alerts to the Right People

Alerts should reach the people who can actually resolve the issue, nothing more, nothing less. Misrouted alerts slow resolution and increase frustration.

Common routing strategies include:

- Using CODEOWNERS or service.yaml files to map repositories to owners
- Applying labels or tags such as @backend, @infra, or @mobile for team-based routing
- Automatically creating tickets in JIRA, ServiceNow, or incident platforms for trackable follow-up

Accurate ownership mapping ensures accountability while avoiding unnecessary broadcast alerts.

Integrate Notifications into Dev Workflow

Alerts are most effective when they appear where developers already work. Pulling engineers into separate tools or dashboards for basic feedback slows response times.

Best practices include:

- Commenting directly on pull requests with gate results
- Using GitHub Checks **or** GitLab Job Summaries to show detailed failure context
- Auto-tagging PRs with labels like *"requires attention"* when gates fail
- Including remediation hints or links directly in CI logs

This tight feedback loop keeps quality gates from feeling like external blockers and instead positions them as part of the development process.

Audit and Improve Your Alerts

Alerting systems should evolve alongside the pipeline and the organization. Regular review ensures alerts remain relevant, trusted, and effective.

Improvement activities include:

- Tracking alert resolution time and the percentage of ignored or dismissed alerts
- Gathering direct team feedback on alert usefulness and clarity
- Maintaining an alert catalogue that documents alert types, severity, owners, and intent
- Periodically revisiting thresholds, wording, and delivery channels as systems and risk profiles change

Over time, this continuous tuning turns alerting from a reactive safety net into a proactive driver of quality and reliability.

Real-World Examples

Seeing alerts and quality signals in context helps teams understand not just *what* failed, but *how* quality gates fit naturally into day-to-day engineering workflows. The following examples illustrate how different delivery touchpoints - chat, pull requests, and reporting - can be used to surface actionable feedback without overwhelming teams.

Example 1: Test Gate Slack Alert

Scenario:
An integration test fails during a pull request build for a backend service. The failure is significant enough to block the merge, but it is not a production-impacting incident.

Slack Alert:

Integration Tests Failed – user-service
Failing Test: TestUserSignupFlow
Category: Flaky test detected
Estimated Time to Fix: ~4 hours
Owner: @user-platform-team
Details: View test logs | Rerun test | Mark as flaky

Why this works:

- The alert is targeted to the owning team rather than broadcast globally.
- It distinguishes between a hard failure and flakiness, avoiding unnecessary escalation.
- It provides immediate next actions (view logs, rerun, classify), keeping resolution inside the developer workflow.

Example 2: GitHub Check

Scenario:
A pull request introduces or exposes a dependency with a known critical vulnerability. The security gate blocks the merge and reports the issue directly in the PR.

GitHub Check Output:

```
**Security Gate Failed**
```

```
- Critical vulnerability detected: `CVE-2024-1582`
- Affected file: `requirements.txt`
- Impact: Remote code execution risk
- Recommended fix: Upgrade `flask` to `>= 2.3.0`

View full vulnerability report
Apply suggested dependency upgrade
```

Why this works:

- Feedback is in line with the pull request, where the change was introduced.
- The alert explains the impact, not just the rule violation.
- Clear remediation guidance reduces friction and avoids back-and-forth with security teams.

Example 3: Weekly Quality Digest (Email or Dashboard)

Scenario:
Engineering leadership and teams need a high-level view of quality trends without reacting to every individual alert. A weekly digest aggregates signals into a single, consumable report.

Weekly Quality Summary:

- **95% of pipelines** passed all quality gates
- **3 flaky tests flagged**
    - 2 acknowledged
    - 1 unresolved
- **1 new CVE detected** in analytics-service
- **Average pipeline duration:** 14m 12s
  (↑ 2 minutes compared to last week)

Why this works:

- Emphasizes **trends over time**, not just point-in-time failures.
- Helps teams spot systemic issues (e.g., increasing pipeline duration).
- Supports leadership conversations around stability, investment, and technical debt without micromanaging individual failures.

These examples demonstrate that effective quality gate feedback is multi-channel and purpose-driven:

- **Real-time alerts** (Slack, PR checks) drive fast remediation.
- **Aggregated summaries** (dashboards, weekly digests) support learning, prioritization, and continuous improvement.

By tailoring feedback to the audience and context, quality gates become a trusted guide for better engineering decisions rather than a source of friction or noise.

Summary Guidelines

Below are some summary guidelines to consider when building alerting into your pipelines:

- Alert only when action is needed
- Route to the right people, in the right context
- Make messages short, clear, and linked to evidence
- Balance real-time and batch notifications
- Continuously tune alert volume and usefulness

A quality gate that fails silently is worse than no gate at all. But over-alerting without clarity is just as damaging. Effective alerting transforms quality gates into living feedback systems that protect codebases, support fast iteration, and keep teams informed without overwhelming them.

Leveraging Quality Data for Decisions in CI/CD Pipelines

Modern CI/CD pipelines generate a wealth of quality data, from test results and code coverage to security scans and performance metrics. But collecting data isn't enough. The true value lies in turning quality signals into smart decisions. Whether you're releasing to production, prioritizing technical debt, or adjusting team practices, data-informed decision-making is essential for sustainable, high-quality software delivery.

Why Quality Data Matters

- **Informs Go/No-Go decisions**: Should this build ship to production?
- **Shapes prioritization**: Which bugs, refactors, or tests should come first?
- **Identifies risk**: Where are your weak spots in code, test, or security?
- **Enables continuous improvement**: Which parts of your SDLC need investment?
- **Builds stakeholder trust**: Back decisions with transparent, evidence-based metrics.

Sources of Quality Data

Below is a list of various sources from which data should be collected in order to gain a comprehensive understanding of all activities, interactions, and outcomes within your software development and delivery processes. Gathering information from these sources helps identify bottlenecks, monitor quality, uncover risks, and ensure that every stage of the pipeline is performing optimally.

Data Type	Examples
Test Results	Pass/fail rates, flakiness, execution time
Code Quality Metrics	Code smells, cyclomatic complexity, linting issues
Coverage Reports	Line, branch, or path coverage
Security Scans	CVEs, dependency risks, policy violations
Performance Tests	Latency, throughput, memory footprint
Build & Deployment Logs	Failure rates, durations, rollback frequency
Static Analysis Tools	Maintainability scores, duplication, style issues
Operational Telemetry	SLA/SLO adherence, incident frequency, drift

Decision Use Cases

In modern software delivery, teams generate an enormous amount of data from tests, builds, deployments, and security scans. The real value comes not from collecting this data, but from using it to make informed, actionable decisions. This section outlines key decision use cases where quality gates, metrics, and analytics directly guide engineering and operational choices. By leveraging these insights, teams can ensure release readiness, prioritize technical debt and refactoring, optimize test suites, maintain security and compliance, and continuously monitor team performance and delivery health. Each use case illustrates how data-driven decisions reduce risk, improve efficiency, and support high-quality, reliable software delivery.

Release Readiness Decisions

Quality gates and metrics provide objective evidence to determine whether a release is ready to proceed. By evaluating each gate, teams can reduce risk and avoid deploying unstable or insecure software. Key considerations include:

- **All blocking gates passed** – Ensure all critical tests (unit, integration, regression), security scans, and performance benchmarks are successful before approving release.
- **Code coverage above agreed baseline** – Maintain a minimum standard (e.g., 85%) to reduce the risk of untested functionality slipping into production.
- **No unacknowledged critical bugs or CVEs** – Prevent high-risk defects or vulnerabilities from reaching users.
- **Performance within acceptable thresholds** – Confirm that new code does not degrade response times, throughput, or other key performance indicators.

Tooling Examples: GitHub/GitLab Checks, Release Dashboards, Jira integrated with CI/CD gates. These tools centralize visibility, making it easier for release managers to make informed, timely decisions.

Technical Debt and Refactoring

Monitoring trends in quality data helps teams prioritize engineering work that improves long-term maintainability and reliability. Decisions are data-driven rather than reactive:

- **Modules with high test flakiness or poor coverage** – These become candidates for stabilization or targeted testing improvements.
- **Functions with high complexity but low change frequency** – May indicate areas suitable for refactoring to reduce technical debt without impacting current delivery.

- **Frequent gate failures in a particular service** – Signals the need for test reliability improvements or automation enhancements.

Tooling Examples: SonarQube, CodeClimate, internal dashboards. These provide metrics on code complexity, duplication, coverage, and maintainability trends to guide refactoring and technical debt reduction.

Test Optimization and Cleanup

Data-driven test management ensures that the test suite remains efficient, reliable, and aligned with business risk. Teams can make actionable decisions, such as:

- **Remove or quarantine consistently flaky tests** – Avoid wasting pipeline resources and reduce false negatives that slow delivery.
- **Parallelize longest-running suites** – Shorten pipeline execution times without sacrificing coverage.
- **Add tests in high-risk but uncovered code areas** – Focus efforts where failures would have the largest impact.
- **Use historical trends to prioritize regression testing** – Run tests more strategically based on past failures, changes, and risk.

Tooling Examples: Test analytics platforms like Launchable or ReportPortal, plus code coverage reports. These tools provide insights into test efficiency, reliability, and historical patterns.

Security & Compliance Readiness

Security decisions must balance risk and velocity. Gate data helps teams enforce policies while allowing safe releases:

- **Delay deployments for critical CVEs or policy violations** – Reduce exposure to vulnerabilities that could compromise production.
- **Auto-approve low-severity, acknowledged findings for staging only** – Streamline workflow while maintaining awareness of minor risks.
- **Monitor time-to-remediate vulnerabilities** – Track security team performance and detect systemic issues in vulnerability management.

Tooling Examples: Snyk, Dependabot, OSS Review Toolkit, custom dashboards. These tools automate vulnerability detection, reporting, and remediation tracking, making risk-based decisions faster and more consistent.

Team Performance and Delivery Health

Quality gate data is valuable not just for technical decisions but also for understanding team performance and enabling continuous improvement:

- **Frequency and causes of gate failures** – Identify recurring issues, whether technical or process-related, that block delivery.
- **Progress in coverage, flakiness, and cycle time** – Assess whether the team is improving quality and efficiency over time.
- **Impact of test debt on release speed** – Determine whether poor-quality tests or coverage gaps are slowing safe delivery.

Tooling Examples: DORA metrics, team scorecards, pipeline telemetry. These provide a holistic view of engineering performance, helping teams plan improvements, allocate resources, and measure progress.

Turning Data into Action

To go from passive dashboards to active improvement:

1. **Automate alerts** for threshold violations (e.g., coverage < 80%)
2. **Visualize trends**, not just one-off failures
3. **Correlate metrics** (e.g., "flaky tests" + "slow deploys")
4. **Tie data to ownership** (e.g., map metrics to teams, not just services)
5. **Review quality metrics regularly** in standups, retros, or leadership reviews

Common Metrics That Drive Decisions

Metric	Decision Use Case
Code Coverage %	Enforce minimum standards before merge
Test Flake Rate	Identify tests to fix, refactor, or isolate
Vulnerabilities by Severity	Block release or trigger triage process
Gate Pass/Fail Ratio	Assess pipeline health, release confidence
Deployment Success Rate	Track operational reliability over time
SLA/SLO Breach Rate	Trigger incident management or rollback policy

Quality gates are not just pipeline blockers, they're feedback instruments. The data they generate is a goldmine for proactive, high-impact decisions across engineering, security, product, and leadership. By turning that data into insight and action, teams can move fast without sacrificing confidence, stability, or customer trust.

Conclusion: Feedback is essential to improvement

Effective pipeline orchestration and the strategic integration of quality gates are the backbone of a reliable CI/CD process. By sequencing jobs intelligently and applying gates at the right points, teams can catch issues early, prevent wasted effort, and maintain a consistent level of quality throughout the delivery process. Early feedback not only accelerates problem resolution but also builds confidence across development, testing, and operations teams, enabling them to focus on meaningful work rather than firefighting downstream failures.

To fully realize the value of observability, it is not enough to simply surface metrics and alerts, teams must also know how to effectively detect, interpret, and remediate quality gate failures. In the next chapter, Handling Gate Failures and Exceptions, we explore practical strategies for responding to failures, managing exceptions, and ensuring that gates provide fast, actionable feedback without disrupting delivery flow.

Handling Gate Failures and Exceptions

Purpose of the Chapter: This chapter focuses on handling gate failures and exceptions in CI/CD pipelines, providing strategies to detect, respond to, and resolve issues when quality gates do not pass. Its goal is to help teams maintain pipeline reliability, minimize disruption to delivery, and turn failures into actionable insights for continuous improvement.

Quality gates serve as critical checkpoints that ensure only code meeting agreed standards progresses through the delivery process. However, gates are not infallible, tests fail, security scans flag vulnerabilities, and performance metrics can fall outside acceptable thresholds. Handling these failures effectively is essential, not only to prevent broken or risky code from reaching production but also to maintain developer confidence and pipeline efficiency. Without a structured approach, gate failures can cause delays, frustrate teams, and obscure the underlying causes of issues.

This chapter explores strategies for managing gate failures and exceptions in a systematic way. It covers techniques for detecting failures early, categorizing and prioritizing them, and deciding on the right course of action, whether that's immediate remediation, temporary bypass with acknowledgment, or rerunning pipelines after fixes. By implementing robust handling processes, teams can turn gate failures into actionable insights, continuously improve test reliability, and maintain a smooth, predictable CI/CD workflow.

Retry Logic and Handling Transient Issues in CI/CD Quality Gates

In complex CI/CD pipelines, not all failures are equal. Some are caused by genuine quality violations, while others are transient issues, temporary, flaky, or environment-related hiccups that don't reflect the true quality of the software. Recognizing and gracefully handling these transient failures is essential for maintaining developer trust in the pipeline, improving velocity, and ensuring only meaningful gate results block delivery.

That's where smart retry logic comes in.

Why Retry Logic Matters

Retry logic is a critical mechanism in CI/CD pipelines that helps ensure tests and scans produce reliable results, minimizing the impact of transient failures while maintaining developer productivity and pipeline stability. By implementing it, you can gain the following benefits:

- **Reduces flakiness**: Automatically revalidates test or scan outcomes that may have failed due to timing or infrastructure blips.
- **Improves pipeline stability**: Prevents false negatives from breaking builds unnecessarily.
- **Saves developer time**: Eliminates manual reruns for known intermittent issues.

- **Enables smarter automation**: Incorporates logic that can distinguish between persistent and transient issues.

What Are Transient Failures?

Non-deterministic failures, often referred to as "flaky" or transient failures, are those that may fail in one pipeline run but pass on a subsequent attempt without any code changes. Understanding these types of failures is essential for designing robust retry strategies and maintaining stable CI/CD pipelines. Examples include:

Type	Common Symptoms
Flaky tests	Pass/fail intermittently across runs
Network timeouts	External API or DB unresponsive briefly
Tooling hiccups	Scan tools or runners crash or hang unexpectedly
Resource contention	Jobs fail due to memory/CPU limits in CI runners
Race conditions	Non-deterministic behaviour in concurrent code/tests

Strategies for Retry Logic

Retry logic in CI/CD pipelines is essential for managing transient or non-deterministic failures without slowing down delivery or causing unnecessary manual intervention. By implementing smart retries, teams can reduce flakiness, maintain pipeline stability, and focus on genuine issues rather than intermittent noise.

Automatic Retries on Specific Gates

Certain stages in the pipeline are more prone to intermittent failures, such as integration tests, end-to-end suites, or tools that occasionally time out.

Configuring automatic retries for these stages ensures that transient issues do not block releases unnecessarily.

Examples include:

- Integration or end-to-end test suites that occasionally fail due to timing issues.
- Static analysis tools or scanners that may timeout sporadically.
- Health checks for external APIs or services that may be briefly unresponsive.

Sample YAML configuration:

```
retry:
  max: 2
  when:
    - runner_system_failure
    - test_flaky
```

This configuration automatically retries the job up to two times for known system failures or flaky tests.

Context-Aware Retries

Not all failures are equal, some can be identified as transient or predictable based on patterns. Context-aware retry logic uses failure messages, historical trends, or even machine learning to make smarter decisions about when to retry.

Strategies include:

- **Regex-based detection:** Automatically identify failures that match common transient patterns, such as "timeout" or "port in use."

- **Historical flake rate analysis:** Use tools like Launchable or FlakyBot to track which tests fail frequently without code changes.
- **Machine learning-based anomaly detection:** Advanced pipelines can predict which failures are likely transient based on historical and environmental data.

Advanced example: Only retry a failed test if it:

- Has passed in more than 50% of the last 10 runs.
- Failed due to a recognized transient issue, such as a network error.

Backoff and Cooldown Policies

Retrying too aggressively can overload services or waste CI/CD resources. Backoff and cooldown policies control retry frequency to protect both infrastructure and pipeline efficiency.

Key techniques include:

- **Exponential backoff:** Increase the wait time between retries progressively.
- **Randomized delays:** Avoid "retry storms" when multiple jobs fail simultaneously.
- **Max retry budgets:** Limit the total number of retries per pipeline to prevent excessive resource consumption.

Selective Rerun of Failed Jobs or Tests

Instead of rerunning the entire pipeline, targeted reruns can save time and reduce compute costs while still ensuring reliability.

Strategies include:

- Rerun only failed test suites or individual pipeline steps.
- Use built-in retry mechanisms or plugins, such as pytest-rerunfailures, mocha-retry, or GitHub Actions' continue-on-error combined with conditional reruns.
- Focus on flaky or critical stages without affecting successful jobs.

Human-in-the-Loop (Optional Retry)

For certain flaky or high-risk stages, it may be safer to allow developers or release managers to manually approve retries. This approach balances automation with oversight.

Approaches include:

- One-click rerun buttons in CI/CD dashboards for developers.
- Pull request comment triggers (e.g., /retry tests) to initiate retries.
- Slack bots or chatops integrations that allow authorized users to approve or deny reruns (e.g., "approve override").

This combination of automated, context-aware, and optionally human-approved retries ensures pipelines remain stable, efficient, and resilient, turning transient failures into manageable events rather than blockers.

Tool Support

The following table highlights common CI/CD tools and platforms, along with the built-in or configurable retry mechanisms they provide to handle transient failures and improve pipeline reliability.

Tool/Platform	Retry Support
GitHub Actions	continue-on-error, workflow reruns, strategy.fail-fast
GitLab CI	Native retry keyword with conditions
Jenkins	Plugins for retrying failed stages, test rerun tools
CircleCI	when: on_fail, reusable job retries
Buildkite	Retry step configuration and flaky test detection

When Not to Retry

Not every failure should be retried automatically. Avoid retries in situations where doing so could mask real problems or introduce unnecessary risk:

- **Deterministic failures:** If a test fails due to a true defect or failed assertion, retrying will not resolve the issue.
- **Compliance or policy violations:** Failures related to security, licensing, or regulatory checks (e.g., CVEs, license issues) require immediate attention rather than automated retries.
- **Intermittent real issues:** Some bugs only surface under certain conditions, blind retries could hide these problems instead of exposing them.
- **Performance bottlenecks:** Excessive retries can obscure underlying issues, such as slow startup times or resource contention, making pipelines appear more stable than they actually are.

Whenever retries are used, ensure they remain visible and measurable. Track how often retries succeed to detect hidden instability, identify flaky tests, and continuously improve pipeline reliability.

Metrics to Track

Tracking retry-related metrics provides insight into pipeline reliability, highlights flaky or unstable areas, and helps teams understand the impact of retries on delivery velocity. The table below outlines key metrics to monitor, what they measure, and why they matter.

Metric	What It Measures	Why It Matters
Retry success rate	The percentage of retries that successfully resolved a failed job or test	Indicates how effective retry logic is in addressing transient failures and whether failures are truly intermittent or persistent
Top causes of retry	Categorizes the primary reasons for retries (e.g., test flake, network issue, infrastructure failure)	Helps identify root causes of instability and guides targeted improvements in tests, infrastructure, or tooling
Pipelines with most retries	Counts retries per pipeline, highlighting services or components with frequent failures	Reveals which services are unstable or prone to flakiness, allowing teams to prioritize reliability efforts
Time added due to retries	Measures the additional pipeline duration caused by retries	Quantifies impact on delivery velocity, enabling teams to balance reliability and speed

Best Practices

Implementing retry logic effectively requires more than just enabling automatic retries. Following best practices ensures retries improve pipeline reliability without introducing risk or inefficiency. Key practices and their benefits include:

- **Retry only on known transient failures**: Focus retries on tests or stages that are prone to intermittent issues, such as network blips or flaky tests, to avoid masking real defects that need immediate attention.
- **Use backoff and maximum retry limits**: Implement exponential backoff and caps on retries to prevent overloading CI/CD infrastructure and consuming excessive resources unnecessarily.
- **Log retry reason and result**: Maintain visibility into why a retry occurred and whether it succeeded. This traceability helps diagnose patterns and informs future improvements in test or pipeline stability.
- **Combine with flake tracking**: Integrate retry logic with tools that track test flakiness and historical failure patterns. This enables long-term stabilization by identifying and addressing consistently unreliable tests.
- **Prefer targeted retries**: Instead of rerunning entire pipelines, retry only the failed job, test suite, or stage. This approach saves time, reduces compute costs, and keeps pipelines efficient without compromising reliability.

Retries are not a crutch, they're a resilience strategy. When implemented thoughtfully, they help pipelines adapt to real-world instability, improve developer confidence, and maintain flow without compromising on gate integrity. The goal isn't to hide failures, but to distinguish noise from signal, and act accordingly.

Graceful Degradation vs. Hard Stops in CI/CD Quality Gates

When a quality gate fails during CI/CD, how the pipeline responds can significantly impact developer productivity, delivery speed, and overall trust in the automation. Two common approaches to handling gate failures are graceful degradation and hard stops.

Both have their place, knowing when to apply which approach is the key to designing resilient, developer-friendly pipelines that uphold quality standards without becoming bottlenecks.

What Is a Hard Stop?

A hard stop is a gate configuration in a CI/CD pipeline that enforces an immediate, non-negotiable halt whenever a check fails. Unlike soft or advisory gates, a hard stop ensures that no further steps in the pipeline are executed until the issue is addressed and the gate passes. This mechanism is critical for maintaining strict quality, security, and compliance standards.

When to Use: Hard stop gates are best applied in scenarios where failing to address an issue immediately could result in significant risk or downstream problems. Common use cases include:

- **Security vulnerabilities:** Critical CVEs or other high-risk findings detected during automated security scans.
- **Failed mandatory tests:** Unit, integration, or end-to-end tests that are essential for verifying functionality.
- **Code quality violations:** Instances where code metrics (e.g., cyclomatic complexity, linting errors) exceed defined thresholds.
- **Non-compliance issues:** Legal, licensing, or regulatory policy violations that must be resolved before proceeding.
- **Production deployment gates:** Ensuring that any release to production meets all quality and safety criteria.

Example:

```
jobs:
  - name: "Security Scan"
    if: scan_status != "pass"
    fail_pipeline: true
```

In this example, if the security scan does not pass, the pipeline immediately stops, preventing any further deployment or processing.

Benefits:

- **Strong quality enforcement:** Ensures only code that meets predefined standards progresses through the pipeline.
- **Prevents defects from propagating:** Stops problematic changes early, reducing the risk of failures in later stages or production.
- **Encourages immediate feedback and correction:** Teams address issues as they arise, fostering a culture of accountability and rapid improvement.

Risks:

- **Potential bottlenecks from false positives or flaky tests:** A failing gate due to an unreliable check can halt progress unnecessarily.
- **Team frustration under delivery pressure:** Hard stops can slow down work if failures are frequent or not well-understood.
- **Pipeline reruns or bypass requests:** Frequent halts may lead to repeated executions or attempts to bypass the gate, potentially undermining its purpose.

Best Practices:

- Combine hard stops with monitoring and alerting to quickly identify true failures versus flakiness.
- Limit hard stops to critical gates where immediate action is non-negotiable.
- Pair with softer advisory gates for areas where stopping the pipeline is not strictly necessary, balancing speed with quality.

What Is Graceful Degradation?

Graceful degradation is a gate configuration in CI/CD pipelines that allows the pipeline to continue even if a particular check fails. Instead of halting the build, it typically generates warnings, logs the failure, sends notifications, or requires conditional approvals. This approach provides flexibility, enabling teams to maintain development velocity while still capturing and reporting issues. Graceful degradation is particularly useful in lower environments, experimental branches, or for gates that are informative rather than mandatory.

When to Use: Graceful degradation gates are appropriate when failures are **non-critical**, or when halting the pipeline would unnecessarily slow progress. Common use cases include:

- **Non-critical quality signals:** Minor linting errors, style violations, or code formatting issues.
- **Flaky or unstable tests:** Tests that occasionally fail due to timing, external dependencies, or known instability.
- **Low-severity security warnings:** Findings that do not pose immediate risk but should still be tracked.
- **Experimental or early-stage branches:** Environments where strict enforcement may hinder innovation or testing.

- **Gates with exception policies:** Checks where known deviations are allowed under documented conditions.

Example:

```
jobs:
  - name: "Lint Check"
    continue-on-error: true
    notify: "frontend-team"
```

In this example, the pipeline continues even if the lint check fails, while sending a notification to the frontend team to address the issue at a convenient time.

Benefits:

- **Maintains development flow:** Avoids unnecessary halts, keeping pipelines moving and developers productive.
- **Encourages continuous feedback:** Issues are reported without blocking progress, allowing teams to act when convenient.
- **Supports progressive adoption of new gates:** Teams can gradually enforce new quality or security checks without disrupting current workflows.

Risks:

- **Delayed issue resolution:** Teams may deprioritize fixing non-blocking failures, letting problems accumulate.
- **Gate credibility erosion:** Frequent use of downgraded or ignored gates can weaken trust in the CI/CD process.
- **Normalization of risk:** Exceptions must be tracked carefully to prevent repeated bypassing of genuine issues.

Best Practices:

- Clearly document which gates can degrade and under what conditions.
- Combine graceful degradation with notifications, dashboards, or metrics to ensure visibility.
- Periodically review degraded gates to determine whether they should be upgraded to hard stops as quality standards evolve.

Choosing the Right Approach: Decision Matrix

Knowing when to allow a quality gate to be a hard stop or rather stop more graceful will likely differ from team to team based on the importance of certain rules. Some teams dealing with security or financial systems may choose to take more gates stricter than others. However, the below is a good is a good guideline to follow in understanding which approach should be following certain scenarios.

Quality Gate Type	Recommended Action
Critical security scan	Hard Stop
Flaky E2E test	Graceful (with alert)
Unit test failure	Hard Stop
Performance regression (minor)	Graceful (with dashboard note)
License violation (non-blocking env)	Graceful (with audit trail)
Infrastructure timeout	Retry + alert
CVE with known mitigation	Graceful (with approval gate)

Patterns to Balance Both Approaches

Below is some best practices and patterns to follow to help you balance your approach on which type of gating approach to use.

- **Soft Fail with Approval Gates**
    1. Continue the pipeline but require manual approval to deploy.

    2. Useful for low/medium severity issues where trade-offs are needed.
- **Policy-as-Code Controls**
    1. Define severity levels and response actions in version-controlled files.
    2. Tools: OPA (Open Policy Agent), Conftest, custom YAML policies.
- **Fail Staging, Not Dev**
    1. Enforce hard stops only from staging onward.
    2. Let dev and PR environments use graceful degradation for feedback.
- **Progressive Enforcement**
    1. Start with graceful mode, then switch to hard stops as maturity improves.
    2. E.g., start with lint warnings, hard fail after 30 days of adoption.

Visibility Is Non-Negotiable

Regardless of the strategy:

- Log every gate decision (pass, soft fail, hard stop)
- Notify teams with details of failures
- Track metrics (soft failure frequency, ignored warnings, delayed fixes)
- Audit overrides to ensure they remain exceptions, not norms

Graceful degradation and hard stops aren't rivals, they're tools. Use hard stops to enforce non-negotiable standards, and graceful degradation to support flow and flexibility where possible. The art of modern CI/CD lies in designing pipelines that are not only technically sound, but also strategically adaptive, balancing speed, stability, and risk.

Manual Override and Approval Workflows in CI/CD Quality Gates

While automation is the backbone of modern CI/CD pipelines, there are times when human judgment is necessary, particularly when a quality gate fails under circumstances that require nuance. Manual override and approval workflows provide a structured way for responsible individuals or teams to evaluate exceptions, approve critical deployments, and maintain governance without becoming a bottleneck.

When implemented thoughtfully, these workflows preserve speed and flexibility without sacrificing accountability or quality.

Why Manual Overrides Matter

Human approval gates complement automated checks by enabling informed, accountable decisions in situations where exceptions or contextual judgment are required.

- Supports contextual decision-making when automated gates can't account for all scenarios.
- Provides governance for exceptional cases such as security waivers, urgent hotfixes, or experimental rollouts.
- Reduces unnecessary blockages from non-critical failures (e.g., false positives, known flaky tests).
- Creates an auditable trail for why a build proceeded despite failed checks.

Common Use Cases

The following table illustrates common scenarios where a pipeline may continue despite gate failures, highlighting examples of controlled exceptions or overrides.

Scenario	Example
Known flaky test	Allow deploy while test is under stabilization
Low-severity CVE	Approve deploy with temporary exception
Performance threshold exceeded slightly	Proceed with caution due to business urgency
Urgent production fix	Bypass non-blocking gates to restore service
Experimental feature or rollout	Override for testing in non-prod or limited environments

Implementation Patterns for Handling Gate Exceptions

When automated gates fail, there are situations where teams need controlled flexibility to proceed without compromising governance. Several implementation patterns have emerged to balance strict enforcement with practical decision-making.

Pull Request-Based Approvals

Pull request (PR) workflows can allow exceptions while maintaining visibility and accountability. In this pattern, a gate failure does not automatically block merging if a designated reviewer approves the change.

This approach is ideal for handling known false positives, minor non-critical issues, or when human judgment is required.

Key Points:

- Gates fail, but merging can proceed with reviewer approval.

- Reviewer roles can include tech leads, security engineers, or QA specialists.
- Ensures accountability through PR comments and documented approval.

Tools: GitHub/GitLab protected branches, CODEOWNERS, PR status checks

Example:

Security scan failed (1 MEDIUM CVE)
Approved by @security-lead with justification
Comment: "False positive on transitive dependency. Logged ticket for vendor update."

Pipeline Pause and Manual Approval Steps

Some pipelines implement a pause-and-approve approach, where execution halts automatically on gate failure and requires a manual step to resume. This pattern is particularly useful for production deployments, high-risk changes, or critical environments where human oversight is necessary.

Tooling Support:

Tool	Feature
GitHub Actions	environment: production with designated reviewers
GitLab CI	manual job triggers (when: manual)
Jenkins	input step with approval conditions
Azure DevOps	Environment approvals with designated approvers

This ensures that no pipeline progress occurs without explicit authorization while maintaining an auditable trail of who approved the continuation.

Override Tokens or Slack/ChatOps Commands

For agile or high-velocity workflows, teams may use secure tokens or ChatOps commands to approve continuation of a blocked build. This pattern integrates CI/CD approvals into communication platforms like Slack or Teams, providing rapid intervention while maintaining logs.

Key Points:

- Requires a secure token or bot authorization.
- Enables workflow triggers or API-based automation.
- Ensures that overrides are logged with approver and reason.

Example:

```
/override build-1024 --reason "known flaky UI test"
```

The system records the override, logs the approver and reason, and resumes the pipeline.

Waiver Policies and Exception Logs

To maintain governance, organizations define waiver policies that outline acceptable categories of overrides. All exceptions are logged to an audit dashboard or compliance registry to enable review and traceability.

Examples of Waiver Categories:

- "Approved CVE list" for known low-severity vulnerabilities
- "Test exception list" for flaky or non-critical automated tests

Governance and Audit Best Practices

Maintaining strict oversight is essential to prevent misuse of overrides. Key practices include:

1. **Track every override** – record who approved, why, and when.
2. **Tie overrides to issue tickets** – link to JIRA, ServiceNow, or similar systems for traceability.
3. **Set expiration limits** – e.g., overrides valid for 7 days only.
4. **Regular reviews** – periodically audit exceptions to ensure policies are enforced.
5. **Limit approvers** – enforce role-based access control (RBAC) so only authorized personnel can approve overrides.

By combining these patterns, organizations can maintain a balance between automation, speed, and governance, ensuring that pipelines remain resilient without sacrificing compliance or traceability.

When to Allow Manual Overrides

The table below outlines common quality signals in a CI/CD pipeline and the circumstances under which manual overrides may be permitted, along with relevant notes for governance and risk management.

Quality Signal	Manual Override Allowed?
Critical CVE	Rarely (only if mitigated and approved by security)
Medium/Low CVE	With security sign-off and tracking ticket
Test flakiness	With dev/QA approval and quarantine strategy
Coverage drop	If justified and not systemic
SLA/SLO performance drift	Only in pre-prod or with rollback plan
Broken linting/style	With low risk; enforce later

Metrics to Monitor

The table below presents key metrics for monitoring manual overrides in CI/CD pipelines, detailing what each metric measures and why it is important for maintaining governance and improving process effectiveness.

Metric	What It Measures	Why It Matters
Number of overrides per release or team	Frequency of manual approvals across releases or teams	Helps identify high-dependency areas and potential pipeline risks
Repeat offenders	Instances of the same test, gate, or check being bypassed multiple times	Highlights recurring issues that may need permanent fixes or process improvement
Time between override and issue resolution	Duration from manual override to actual issue resolution	Ensures issues are addressed promptly and prevents accumulation of technical debt
Approvers and average decision time	Who is approving overrides and how quickly decisions are made	Helps evaluate responsiveness, identify bottlenecks, and ensure accountability
Compliance ratio (overrides vs. actual failures fixed)	Proportion of overrides that led to actual resolution versus ignored issues	Measures effectiveness of overrides and ensures exceptions do not undermine quality standards

Balancing Flexibility with Control

Balancing flexibility with control requires clear practices that allow necessary exceptions while ensuring risk, accountability, and long-term quality are not compromised.

Practice	Purpose
Require justification + ticket ID	Prevent careless or unexplained overrides
Limit override scope (e.g., non-prod only)	Contain risk
Notify teams on override usage	Increase visibility and accountability
Build dashboards of override usage	Spot patterns, improve automation or training

Manual override workflows are not loopholes, they are safety valves. When clearly defined, well-governed, and transparently executed, they help teams move fast while still upholding quality, security, and operational trust. They remind us that human judgment still matters, especially in a world increasingly driven by automation.

Post-Failure Analysis and Learning Loops in CI/CD Quality Gates

A quality gate failure is not just a signal to stop a release, it's an opportunity to learn, improve, and harden the delivery pipeline. Post-failure analysis and structured learning loops transform reactive debugging into proactive quality engineering. The most mature teams don't just fix the failure, they fix the *reason it happened undetected*, and evolve their processes accordingly.

When consistently applied, this feedback cycle leads to better automation, faster resolution times, and more resilient systems.

Why Post-Failure Analysis Matters

- **Identifies root causes** instead of masking symptoms

- **Improves the pipeline** by addressing system-level weaknesses
- **Tracks recurring issues** (e.g., flaky tests, slow builds, misconfigured tools)
- **Builds team knowledge** and strengthens quality culture
- **Feeds continuous improvement** into both code and process

What Triggers Post-Failure Analysis?

Post-mortems aren't just for outages. They're valuable for significant failures at any CI/CD stage, such as:

Trigger Event	Example
Repeated gate failures	Test suite fails in 3+ consecutive builds
Manual override usage	Security gate bypassed due to false positive
Production rollback or hotfix	A critical issue slipped past quality gates
New gate implementation failure	New coverage check blocks all PRs unexpectedly
High-priority defect post-release	Indicates quality gate missed an issue

Steps of Post-Failure Analysis

Post-failure analysis ensures that gate failures lead to learning and improvement, not just pipeline reruns. By consistently capturing context, identifying root causes, and acting on insights, teams can reduce repeat failures and continuously strengthen their CI/CD processes.

Capture the Event Context

Begin by clearly documenting what happened and under what conditions. Capturing accurate context early prevents assumptions and ensures that analysis is based on facts rather than speculation.

Record the following details:

- Pipeline or job that failed (including stage and environment)
- The failing gate and relevant logs or error messages
- Associated commit, pull request, or feature flag
- Who was involved, including approvers, reviewers, and any manual overrides or actions taken

Supporting tools and sources:

- CI/CD logs, artifacts, and pipeline metadata
- GitHub or GitLab pull request history and comments
- Quality and security dashboards (e.g., SonarQube, SAST/DAST tools, dependency scanners)

This step establishes a shared understanding of the failure before deeper analysis begins.

Perform Root Cause Analysis (RCA)

Once the context is captured, shift focus from *what failed* to *why it failed*. Structured RCA techniques help teams avoid superficial conclusions and uncover systemic issues.

Recommended techniques:

- **5 Whys:** Iteratively ask "why" until the underlying cause is identified
    - Why did the test fail?
    - Why was the issue not detected earlier?
    - Why did existing gates not prevent it?

- **Fishbone (Ishikawa) diagrams:** Visualize contributing factors across technical, process, and human dimensions

Key categories to explore:

Dimension	Example Root Causes
Code	Bug in logic, poor test design, unhandled edge case
Test	Flaky, outdated, or missing test coverage
Tooling	Misconfigured scanner, outdated dependency
Process	Lack of peer review, override without context
Environment	Resource limits, infra instability

The goal is to identify root causes, not symptoms, and to determine whether the issue is isolated or systemic.

Document and Share Findings

Insights lose value if they are not captured and shared. Use a lightweight, consistent format so documentation remains practical rather than burdensome.

Post-Failure Review Template:

Below are some key questions that should be answered when reviewing failures:

- What failed and when?
- What was the root cause?
- What did we learn?
- What actions will we take?
- How will we prevent this from happening again?

Sharing mechanisms:

- Confluence or Notion pages for longer-term reference

- Slack or Teams channels (e.g., #quality-reviews) for visibility
- Sprint retrospectives or weekly team syncs for discussion and alignment

This transparency helps teams learn collectively and avoids repeating the same mistakes across projects.

Drive Improvements

Post-failure analysis should always result in concrete actions. Each identified issue should translate into a measurable improvement.

Common improvement actions include:

- Fixing or rewriting flaky or brittle tests
- Adjusting gate thresholds, retries, or tolerances
- Adding new checks to cover previously missed scenarios
- Updating documentation, standards, or onboarding material
- Investing in improved tooling (e.g., flake tracking, observability dashboards)

All actions should be tracked with clear ownership and deadlines to ensure accountability.

Close the Loop

Closing the loop ensures that post-failure analysis leads to lasting improvement, not one-off fixes.

Build habits such as:

- Revisiting past failures during retrospectives
- Verifying whether corrective actions were effective

- Logging and analysing recurring themes (e.g., repeated security scan timeouts or flaky environments)

Over time, these patterns can guide strategic investments and process changes that significantly reduce pipeline instability.

Metrics to Support Learning Loops

The table below highlights key metrics for evaluating the effectiveness of post-failure analysis, showing what each metric measures and why it matters for continuous improvement of quality gates.

Metric	What It Measures	Why It Matters
Repeat failure frequency	How often the same gates fail for the same underlying reasons	Indicates systemic issues that are not being addressed permanently
Time to detect and fix	Duration from failure occurrence to issue resolution	Reflects how timely, visible, and actionable feedback is for teams
Override recurrence	Frequency of repeated manual overrides for the same issues	Reveals whether teams are improving gates or relying on manual workarounds
RCA completion rate	Percentage of failures that undergo root cause analysis	Ensures failures are analysed rather than ignored
% of failures leading to improvements	Proportion of failures that result in concrete corrective actions	Measures whether learning is translating into meaningful and lasting change

Automating Parts of the Loop

Automation can significantly strengthen post-failure analysis by ensuring that issues are tracked, followed up, and learned from without relying on manual effort.

- Auto-link failure logs to JIRA tickets for RCA tracking
- Tag PRs or builds with "needs post-mortem" if failure criteria met
- Use bot reminders to follow up on assigned corrective actions
- Integrate dashboards with trends (e.g., test failures per service per sprint)

Best Practices

The following best practices are useful to following when looking into implement learning loops and applying those learnings to your delivery processes:

- **Analyse both technical and human factors** to uncover deeper process and systemic issues, not just surface-level failures.
- **Keep reviews blameless and constructive** to build trust and psychological safety rather than fear or defensiveness.
- **Share findings widely, not just within the immediate team**, to prevent the same mistakes from being repeated across the organization.
- **Track corrective actions through to closure** to ensure lessons learned result in real, lasting change rather than forgotten insights.

Every gate failure is a story. By analysing it with curiosity instead of blame, and turning insights into improvements, teams can break the cycle of firefighting and move toward sustainable delivery.

Post-failure analysis and learning loops are how good CI/CD practices evolve into great ones.

Conclusion: Feedback is essential to improvement

Effective pipeline orchestration and the strategic integration of quality gates are the backbone of a reliable CI/CD process. By sequencing jobs intelligently and applying gates at the right points, teams can catch issues early, prevent wasted effort, and maintain a consistent level of quality throughout the delivery process. Early feedback not only accelerates problem resolution but also builds confidence across development, testing, and operations teams, enabling them to focus on meaningful work rather than firefighting downstream failures.

As pipelines mature, the next challenge is ensuring that quality gates themselves continue to evolve and provide maximum value. The following chapter delves into the continuous improvement of gates, exploring how teams can monitor gate effectiveness, refine thresholds, and adjust policies based on real-world results. By treating gates as living components rather than static checks, organizations can maintain high standards of quality, reduce false positives, and ensure that pipelines keep pace with changing business needs and technical landscapes. This sets the stage for a culture of ongoing learning and optimization, where pipelines not only deliver code but also continuously learn from it.

Continuous Improvement of Quality Gates

Purpose of chapter: This chapter explores how to continuously refine and improve quality gates, ensuring they remain effective, relevant, and aligned with evolving pipeline and business needs. By monitoring performance, adjusting thresholds, and learning from past results, teams can maximize gate value and maintain high delivery quality over time.

Quality gates are not "set it and forget it" mechanisms, they are living, evolving components of your CI/CD pipeline. As codebases grow, team practices shift, and business priorities evolve, the rules that define your gates must be continuously reviewed and refined to remain effective, relevant, and non-disruptive.

This ongoing calibration ensures your gates deliver high signal and low friction, catching what matters while staying aligned with delivery goals.

Why Gate Rules Need Continuous Review

The following are important high level reasons as to why gate rules need to be constantly reviewed within either a team or a large organisation:

- Outdated rules can block unnecessarily (e.g., enforcing deprecated linting checks)

- Overly strict gates slow velocity or create developer workarounds
- Overly lenient gates miss real issues, reducing trust in pipeline safeguards
- Changing risks require new types of checks (e.g., adding AI code requires model scanning)

How Often Should Gate Rules Be Reviewed?

There's no one-size-fits-all, but the following cadence is common:

Review Cadence	Scope
Sprintly	High-friction gates, recent failures, overrides
Monthly	Threshold tuning, new failure patterns
Quarterly	Full gate inventory, effectiveness analysis, cleanup
On-demand	After major incidents, regressions, or process changes

What to Review in Gate Rules

To ensure quality gates remain effective and valuable over time, they should be reviewed regularly against a consistent set of criteria. The following dimensions help teams assess whether a gate is still relevant, trustworthy, developer-friendly, and aligned with evolving technology and risk landscapes

1. **Relevance**
    - Is this gate still needed?
    - Is the risk it covers still a concern?
    - Are there better tools or practices available now?
2. **Signal Quality**
    - How often does the gate catch real issues vs. false positives?
    - Does it correlate with bugs, incidents, or regressions?

3. **Developer Experience**
    - Are developers constantly working around or overriding it?
    - Does it introduce unnecessary delays?
4. **Performance**
    - Does it add significant time to the pipeline?
    - Is it parallelizable or cacheable?
5. **Coverage & Blind Spots**
    - Are there quality areas not covered (e.g., accessibility, infra drift)?
    - Are new languages, frameworks, or services excluded?

Techniques for Refinement

As systems, teams, and risks evolve, quality gates must evolve with them. Continuous improvement of gates focuses on maximizing signal value while minimizing unnecessary friction, ensuring that enforcement remains fair, effective, and trusted.

Threshold Tuning

Threshold tuning involves adjusting acceptable limits based on risk tolerance, maturity, and observed impact rather than static or arbitrary targets.

Key practices include:

- **Gradual increases in test coverage thresholds:** Raise minimum coverage only when teams demonstrate readiness and stability, avoiding sudden enforcement that disrupts delivery.
- **SLO-based threshold calibration:** Adjust service-level objective gates using real production baselines rather than theoretical targets, ensuring gates reflect actual system behaviour.
- **Environment-specific thresholds:** Apply looser performance limits in development environments

to support rapid iteration, while tightening thresholds in staging or pre-production where production parity matters.

This approach helps gates evolve in step with team capability and system complexity.

Gate Downgrades or Phasing

Not all gates need to be enforced at full strength immediately. Downgrading or phasing gates allows teams to adopt new controls without creating sudden bottlenecks.

Common patterns include:

- **Hard stop to warning transitions:** Temporarily converting a blocking gate into a non-blocking warning during rollout or remediation periods.
- **Progressive enforcement:** Introducing a new gate as informational, then escalating to a hard failure over a defined period (e.g., a 30-day ramp-up).

These techniques build trust and adoption while maintaining a clear path toward stronger enforcement.

Rule Consolidation

As pipelines grow, overlapping or redundant gates can dilute signal quality and increase noise. Rule consolidation focuses on simplifying enforcement while preserving coverage.

Examples include:

- **Merging similar static analysis checks** into a single, unified report to reduce duplication and confusion.

- **Using meta-gates** that aggregate multiple signals - such as test results, security findings, and performance metrics - into a holistic pass/fail decision.

Consolidation improves clarity for developers and makes gate outcomes easier to interpret.

Feedback Collection

Developer feedback is critical to maintaining high-quality gates. Without it, gates risk becoming obstacles rather than safeguards.

Effective feedback mechanisms include:

- **Inline feedback prompts** after gate failures (e.g., "Was this a false positive?").
- **Regular developer surveys** (e.g., quarterly) to identify pain points, blind spots, or opportunities for improvement.

This feedback helps teams distinguish genuine quality signals from friction or tooling issues.

Historical Analysis

Historical data provides valuable insight into whether gates are delivering real value over time.

Key analysis activities include:

- **Reviewing trends** in gate failures, manual overrides, and downstream incidents.
- **Identifying low-value gates**, such as those with consistently high failure rates but little correlation to bugs, outages, or regressions.

Using historical evidence ensures that gate decisions are data-driven, enabling teams to retire, refine, or strengthen gates based on proven impact.

Together, these practices ensure that quality gates remain relevant, trusted, and effective, continuously adapting to changing risks, technologies, and delivery pressures.

Example Gate Refinement Table

Below is a table providing an example of how different lessons can be applied to different stages of the pipeline quality gates and some of the reasons why:

Gate	Original Rule	Refined Rule	Reason
Unit Test Coverage	90% minimum	80% minimum for new code only	Legacy code skewing metrics
Linting Error Gate	Block on any warning	Block only on error-level violations	Too noisy, slowed delivery
Dependency CVE Gate	Block on any severity	Block only on High/Critical	Reduced noise, matched risk appetite
Load Test Gate (staging)	Pass only if latency < 300ms	Pass if latency <300ms 95% of time	Accounted for natural variability

Tooling Tips

Most modern CI/CD platforms support dynamic gate rules and parameterization:

Platform	Refinement Capability
GitHub Actions	Conditional checks, matrix testing, dynamic inputs
GitLab CI	Variable-based thresholds, manual approvals
Jenkins	Pipeline-as-code logic with scripted gates

Azure DevOps	Gate policies tied to variable conditions

Also consider integrating:

- Policy-as-code tools (e.g., Open Policy Agent, TFSec)
- Dashboards to track gate metrics over time (Grafana, Datadog)

Best Practices

Sustaining effective quality gates requires treating them as living assets that evolve alongside teams, tools, and delivery practices. The following practices help ensure gates remain reliable, relevant, and trusted over time.

- **Version-control gate configurations** to enable traceability, safe rollback, and collaborative updates, ensuring changes are reviewed and auditable like any other code change.
- **Involve both developers and QA in gate reviews** so rules reflect real-world workflows and do not introduce unnecessary friction or unrealistic expectations.
- **Pilot rule changes before full rollout** to catch regressions, false positives, or performance impacts early without disrupting all teams at once.
- **Automate feedback collection from gate failures** to prioritize improvements using real usage data rather than assumptions or anecdotal evidence.
- **Treat quality gates as part of the product itself**, maintaining them with the same rigor as production code to preserve trust, reliability, and long-term value.

Strong pipelines aren't just about having gates, they're about having the *right* gates, continuously refined based on evolving systems, teams, and risks. By making gate review part of your engineering rhythm, you don't just preserve quality, you scale it.

Collecting Feedback from Teams on Quality Gates

To continuously improve quality gates in CI/CD pipelines, one of the most powerful, and often underutilized, tools is direct feedback from engineering teams. Developers, testers, DevOps engineers, and security analysts interact with these gates daily. Their experience is a vital signal in understanding whether the gates are valuable, disruptive, overly strict, or missing key risks.

Without regular feedback, quality gates risk becoming obstacles rather than enablers of velocity and quality.

Why Team Feedback Matters

Team feedback is essential to ensuring quality gates remain practical, trusted, and effective, bridging the gap between automated enforcement and real-world development workflows.

- **Reality check**: Reveals where gates are misaligned with actual developer workflows
- **Surface pain points**: Highlights friction caused by false positives or confusing messages
- **Prioritizes improvements**: Guides which gates to relax, remove, or reinforce
- **Drives adoption**: Developers are more likely to support and maintain gates they helped shape

- **Encourages a quality culture**: Turns quality from top-down enforcement into team-owned excellence

What to Ask: Key Feedback Areas

When gathering team feedback on quality gates, it's important to structure discussions around a few key areas that reveal both strengths and weaknesses in the current setup.

Start by assessing **usefulness**. Do the gates consistently catch issues that matter, such as real defects, security risks, or performance regressions, or do they mainly surface noise? Understanding this helps determine whether a gate is delivering meaningful value.

Next, consider **clarity**. Gate failures should be easy to understand and clearly actionable. If developers struggle to interpret error messages or are unsure how to fix a failure, the gate may be creating confusion rather than improving quality.

Evaluate **friction** by identifying which gates introduce unnecessary delays, extra steps, or cognitive overhead. Excessive friction often leads to frustration, workarounds, or pressure to bypass gates entirely.

Reliability is another critical factor. Feedback should highlight whether failures are consistent and reproducible or whether they are flaky and intermittent, which can quickly erode trust in the pipeline.

Look at **coverage** to uncover blind spots. Teams can often identify important quality concerns, such as accessibility, infrastructure drift, or configuration issues, that are not currently enforced by any gate.

Examine **override behaviour** to understand when and why gates are typically bypassed. Frequent overrides may indicate misaligned thresholds, low signal quality, or unclear policies.

Finally, invite **improvement ideas** directly from the team. Developers and testers often have practical suggestions for making gates faster, clearer, or more relevant based on their day-to-day experience.

Together, these areas provide a well-rounded view of how quality gates are performing and where targeted improvements will have the greatest impact.

Area	Example Questions
Usefulness	Does this gate catch valuable issues?
Clarity	Are gate failures understandable and actionable?
Friction	Which gates are causing unnecessary delays or confusion?
Reliability	Are failures consistent or flaky?
Coverage	Are there quality concerns not being gated?
Override Behaviour	When and why are gates typically bypassed?
Improvement Ideas	What changes would make the gates more helpful?

Methods for Gathering Feedback

Collecting effective feedback on quality gates requires using multiple, complementary channels. Different methods capture different types of insight, ranging from quick sentiment checks to deep, contextual understanding, helping teams improve gates without adding unnecessary process overhead.

Lightweight Surveys

Lightweight surveys are an efficient way to gather broad feedback with minimal disruption. These can be run on a regular cadence, such as quarterly pulse surveys or as part of sprint retrospectives.

Best practices include:

- Keeping surveys short and focused, typically three to five questions, to maximize response rates.
- Asking targeted questions about usefulness, clarity, and friction rather than open-ended prompts only.
- Allowing anonymous responses to encourage honest and candid feedback.

Sample tooling: Google Forms, Typeform, Slack-based surveys, or GitHub/GitLab issues for structured input.

Retrospective Discussions

Team retrospectives provide a natural forum for deeper conversations about pipeline experiences. Including CI/CD and gate feedback as a recurring agenda item ensures that issues are surfaced consistently rather than only when failures occur.

Effective approaches include:

- Actively inviting teams to share both frustrations and success stories related to automation.
- Adding a standing "CI/CD feedback" section to retrospectives.
- Converting insights into actionable improvement items tied directly to pipeline or gate changes.

Example prompt: *"Was there any test, gate, or automation that slowed you down this sprint? If so, was the delay justified?"*

Embedded Feedback in Pipelines

Embedding feedback directly into the pipeline experience captures insights at the moment of friction, when context is freshest.

Common patterns include:

- Adding optional prompts to build or gate failure notifications, such as:
  - "Was this gate failure helpful?" [Yes] [No]
  - "Leave a comment on this gate outcome"
- Storing feedback alongside build metadata to provide rich, contextual insights during analysis.

Tooling integration options:

- GitHub Checks API
- Custom Slack or Microsoft Teams bots
- ChatOps commands (e.g., /gate-feedback)

Gate Owner Check-ins

Assigning clear ownership ensures feedback leads to action. Gate owners or component leads act as stewards of gate quality.

Their responsibilities typically include:

- Monitoring feedback trends, failure patterns, and override behaviour.

- Acting as advocates and translators between development teams and platform or security stakeholders.
- Hosting short, focused check-ins with teams when friction or dissatisfaction spikes.

This ownership model prevents gates from becoming "nobody's problem."

Metrics-Backed Feedback

Qualitative feedback is most effective when combined with objective data. Metrics help validate perceptions and reveal patterns that might otherwise be missed.

Common supporting metrics include:

- Gate failure frequency
- Manual override rates
- Pipeline duration by stage
- Volume of PR comments or discussions related to specific gates

By triangulating what teams feel with what the data shows, organizations can prioritize improvements based on both experience and measurable impact.

Anti-Patterns to Avoid

When collecting feedback on quality gates, certain anti-patterns can undermine trust and reduce the value of the feedback loop if not actively avoided.

- Ignoring feedback loops leads to rigid, resented gates that fail to evolve with real team needs.

- Assuming 'no complaints' means no issues is risky, as silence often indicates teams have stopped trusting or engaging with the gates.
- Punishing or discouraging override feedback suppresses honest input and drives issues underground instead of resolving them.
- Creating survey fatigue through overly long or frequent surveys results in low engagement and poor-quality feedback.

Pitfall	Why It's Harmful
Ignoring feedback loops	Leads to rigid, resented gates
Assuming "no complaints = no issues"	Silence may mean teams have stopped trusting gates
Punishing override feedback	Discourages honest input
Survey fatigue	Low engagement if too long or too frequent

Best Practices

Applying feedback effectively requires intentional practices that turn input into action while reinforcing trust and shared ownership of quality gates.

- **Close the loop on feedback** by showing teams how their input directly influenced gate changes, reinforcing that feedback is valued and acted upon.
- **Track recurring themes over time** to distinguish systemic issues from one-off noise and prioritize the most impactful improvements.
- **Involve teams directly in gate reviews** to build shared ownership and collective responsibility for pipeline health.
- **Celebrate gates that provide real value**, highlighting when automation prevented defects or incidents rather than focusing only on failures.

- **Make feedback easy and optional** to encourage honest participation without adding friction or forcing compliance.

A great quality gate doesn't just catch defects, it serves the team using it. Collecting feedback is how we ensure our gates stay relevant, trusted, and tuned to real-world needs. It's the heartbeat of continuous improvement in delivery pipelines.

Evolving Gates with Changing Tech and Business Needs

Quality gates are only as effective as their ability to adapt. In fast-moving technology environments, the systems we build, the tools we use, and the risks we face are constantly shifting. Gates that worked well yesterday may be obsolete, or even counterproductive, tomorrow.

That's why one of the defining characteristics of a mature CI/CD strategy is the ability to evolve gate policies and practices alongside both technical advancements and business priorities.

Why Gate Evolution Is Essential

Quality gates cannot remain static, because the technical, security, and business contexts they protect are constantly changing.

- **New architectures introduce new risks** (e.g., microservices require inter-service contract testing, not just unit tests)
- **New testing paradigms demand new checks** (e.g., shift from manual QA to model-based testing or contract testing)
- **Security landscapes evolve constantly** (e.g., need to add container scanning or SBOM checks)

- **Business goals shift** (e.g., focusing on speed to market may justify trade-offs on performance testing early in dev)
- **Tooling ecosystems improve** (e.g., better static analysis tools, AI-based test generators, smarter policy engines)

If your gates stay static, they become either blockers or bypassable noise, both of which erode trust in your pipeline.

Signals That It's Time to Evolve a Gate

Over time, there are clear signals that indicate when quality gates need to be revisited or reworked. These signals often emerge from a combination of developer behaviour, incident patterns, and changes in business or technology direction. When gates begin to fail frequently without leading to action, are routinely overridden due to false positives, or miss real production issues, their effectiveness is called into question.

Similarly, shifts in business priorities or underlying technology, such as a new focus on mobile experience or a move to serverless architectures, can expose gaps in existing gate coverage. Recognizing and responding to these signals early helps ensure that gates continue to provide meaningful protection rather than becoming ignored noise or false assurance.

Signal Type	Example Prompt
Reduced signal value	"This gate fails often, but no one takes action."
High override rate	"We keep bypassing this due to known false positives."
Missed incidents	"A production bug wasn't caught because the gate was too shallow."
New business requirements	"We need to prioritize mobile experience now."

Tech stack shifts	"We're using serverless now, how do we test cold starts?"

What It Means to "Evolve" a Gate

Evolving a quality gate means deliberately adapting it to remain effective as systems, risks, and priorities change. Rather than treating gates as static rules, mature teams view them as living controls that must be refined to continue providing meaningful protection without becoming blockers or noise.

Add new quality dimensions

As software responsibilities expand beyond basic functionality, gates must cover a broader definition of quality.

This can include:

- Introducing checks for accessibility, data privacy, or AI fairness, ensuring systems meet regulatory, ethical, and user-experience expectations.
- Expanding from purely functional validation to include observability, resilience, and compliance checks, such as ensuring proper logging, tracing, or audit coverage.

These additions reflect a shift toward holistic quality rather than narrowly focused test coverage.

Refactor for new architecture

Architectural changes often invalidate existing gates if they are not updated accordingly.

Examples include:

- Moving from monolithic integration tests to contract testing when adopting microservices, ensuring services can evolve independently without breaking consumers.
- Adding chaos or resilience tests in distributed systems to validate behaviour under failure scenarios such as latency spikes, partial outages, or dependency failures.

Refactoring gates alongside architecture changes prevents blind spots and outdated assumptions.

Update thresholds and tolerance

Thresholds that made sense at one stage of a product's lifecycle may become either too lax or too restrictive over time.

Common adjustments include:

- Tightening performance SLOs as traffic grows and user expectations increase.
- Temporarily loosening test coverage requirements to unblock early MVPs, with a clear plan to raise standards as stability improves.

This ensures gates remain aligned with both maturity and risk tolerance.

Modernize tooling

Outdated or inefficient tools can undermine even well-designed gates by slowing pipelines or producing low-quality signals.

Modernization efforts may involve:

- Replacing slow, monolithic static scanners with faster, incremental tools that integrate more smoothly into CI pipelines.
- Migrating from ad-hoc scripts to centralized policy and gate platforms such as Open Policy Agent (OPA), enabling consistency, reuse, and better governance.

Better tooling improves signal quality while reducing friction.

Reprioritize based on business risk

Not all quality risks are equal, and gate evolution must reflect business context.

For example:

- In fintech, gates may focus more heavily on audit logging, data integrity, and transactional consistency.
- In gaming or real-time systems, performance, latency, and responsiveness may take precedence over other checks.

Reprioritization ensures that gates protect what matters most to the business at any given time.

Ultimately, evolving a gate is about maintaining relevance and trust, ensuring that quality enforcement continues to support delivery, reliability, and business outcomes rather than standing in their way.

Framework for Evaluating and Evolving Gates

Before keeping, changing, or removing a quality gate, teams should periodically evaluate it against a set of guiding questions to ensure it remains relevant, effective, and aligned with both technology and business goals.

Question	Considerations
Is the gate still relevant?	Is the quality concern it targets still valid and critical?
Is it aligned with current tech?	Does it apply to the current architecture / tooling?
Is it actionable and efficient?	Does it fail for clear reasons, and does it fail fast?
Does it support business goals?	Does it help us move faster *and* more safely?
Can it be improved with new tech?	Are there better or more scalable tools or frameworks available?

Practices to Support Gate Evolution

To ensure quality gates continue to provide value over time, teams should adopt practices that support their ongoing evolution, maintenance, and safe adaptation to changing technology and business needs.

- **Regular reviews** (quarterly or at major release points)
- **Feedback loops** (see previous section on collecting team feedback)
- **Safe experimentation** (pilot new gates in dev / staging before enforcing)
- **Version control for gate logic** (treat gates as code)
- **Modular pipelines** (makes it easier to swap or enhance gates)

Real-World Examples of Evolution

The following examples illustrate how quality gates can evolve in practice, showing the before-and-after changes and the reasons driving each improvement.

Before	After	Why?
Static HTML linting	Accessibility and UX gates	New business focus on inclusive design
Blocking flaky UI tests	Quarantined with retry logic + alerting	Reduced noise, improved velocity
Legacy security scan with long runtime	Container-level scanning + SBOM integration	Improved speed and supply chain visibility
Code coverage > 90%	Risk-weighted test strategy (critical paths prioritized)	Business needed speed, not broad testing

A quality gate isn't a rule carved in stone, it's a contract between your engineering practices and your evolving product and platform realities. The best teams actively evolve their gates to stay ahead of risks, reduce delivery friction, and ensure their CI/CD pipelines serve both technical excellence and business outcomes.

Gate A/B Testing and Experimentation in CI/CD Pipelines

Introducing or modifying quality gates can sometimes have unintended consequences, from slowing pipelines and generating false positives to unintentionally blocking critical releases. To mitigate this risk, A/B testing and experimentation offer a safe, data-driven way to evaluate new gates or gate changes before full rollout.

Just as we use feature flags and controlled rollouts in product development, we can apply similar practices to our pipeline logic, ensuring changes are effective, efficient, and developer-friendly.

Why Experiment with Quality Gates?

Experimenting with quality gates allows teams to validate their effectiveness, measure impact, and build confidence before full enforcement, reducing risk and increasing adoption.

- Validate that new gates catch meaningful issues without overwhelming teams
- Compare performance impact, failure rates, and developer sentiment
- Ensure pipeline throughput isn't harmed by stricter checks
- Prevent gate misconfigurations or false positives from becoming widespread
- Increase trust and adoption through transparent rollout strategies

What Can Be A/B Tested?

A/B testing of quality gates allows teams to evaluate different configurations, tools, and enforcement strategies in a controlled way. By comparing alternative approaches side by side, teams can understand which gates catch meaningful issues most effectively, which minimize false positives, and which maintain developer productivity. Examples include testing different static analysis tools or rulesets, comparing security scanners, experimenting with test coverage thresholds, and measuring the impact of stricter versus more lenient performance or latency gates. Teams can also trial approaches to handling flaky tests, such as retry logic versus quarantining, or different CI/CD policies, such as hard stops versus soft fails with notifications.

Deployment gates can similarly be evaluated by comparing manual approvals to automated rollouts based on service-level objectives. This type of experimentation provides data-driven insights that guide gate evolution, helping teams balance quality enforcement with pipeline efficiency and developer experience.

Gate Type	A/B Test Example
Static code analysis	Compare two linters or rulesets
Security scanning	Evaluate different scanners (e.g., Snyk vs. Trivy)
Test thresholds	80% vs. 90% code coverage pass/fail levels
Performance gates	Latency threshold: <300ms vs. <500ms
Flaky test detection	Retry-based logic vs. test quarantine
CI policies	Hard stop vs. soft fail with notification
Deployment gates	Manual approval vs. automated rollout based on SLOs

How to Run Gate A/B Tests

Running A/B tests on quality gates is a strategic approach to evaluate effectiveness, minimize disruption, and guide data-driven improvements before full enforcement. Rather than applying new gates blindly, this approach allows teams to observe behaviour, measure impact, and gradually adapt pipelines, reducing risk and improving trust in the automation.

Shadow Mode / Observation Mode

Shadow mode, also known as observation mode, lets a new gate run alongside the existing pipeline without enforcing a pass/fail outcome. The gate logs all findings silently, giving teams insight into its impact without interrupting developers or blocking deployments.

Key practices:

- Record detailed outcomes of the gate, including which commits or builds would have failed, and any false positives.

- Collect data over a defined period (e.g., two to four weeks) to capture variations across teams, workloads, and environments.
- Use the collected data to evaluate accuracy, reliability, and signal quality before deciding whether full enforcement is appropriate.

Example:
Run a new security scan in shadow mode for two weeks and log all detected vulnerabilities. Review which findings are actionable, which are false positives, and how often it would have blocked deployments before enabling it as a hard stop.

Split by Branch, Environment, or Team

Targeted rollout limits exposure and allows focused observation. Instead of applying the new gate across all pipelines, teams can choose specific branches, environments, or teams for testing.

Strategies include:

- **Branch-based rollout:** Apply gates to main or release branches first while leaving feature branches unaffected.
- **Environment-based rollout:** Run gates only in staging or pre-production to validate without impacting production velocity.
- **Team-based rollout:** Pilot the gate with a single service team to gather feedback and iterate on configuration before wider adoption.

Example:
Apply stricter performance checks only in pre-production for the payments service. Track failures, false positives, and developer feedback before extending enforcement to production or other teams.

Progressive Enforcement

Gradual enforcement helps teams adapt to new gates without causing unexpected disruptions. This approach phases the gate from passive observation to active enforcement, giving teams time to respond to failures and refine thresholds.

Typical stages:

1. **Shadow mode:** Gate runs and logs results, but does not block the pipeline.
2. **Soft fail with warning:** Gate signals a failure but allows the pipeline to proceed, giving teams a chance to address issues while maintaining delivery flow.
3. **Hard fail:** Gate fully blocks the pipeline when it fails, enforcing compliance.

By moving through these stages, teams can validate signal quality, educate developers, and identify exceptions before full enforcement, increasing trust and adoption.

Flag-Based Toggle Control

Feature flags or configuration toggles provide dynamic control over gate behaviour, enabling experimentation and selective activation. They make it easy to turn gates on or off per branch, environment, or service, and to safely rollback if issues arise.

Best practices for toggle-based control:

- Store gate logic in version-controlled configuration files (e.g., YAML, JSON) to ensure changes are auditable and repeatable.

- Allow overrides in specific branches, services, or environments without affecting the global pipeline.
- Log toggle usage for traceability and governance, ensuring every activation, deactivation, or override is recorded.

This approach provides flexibility for experimentation, incremental adoption, and rapid response to misconfigurations or unexpected impact.

By combining shadow mode, selective rollouts, progressive enforcement, and toggle-based controls, teams can safely test and refine new quality gates. These methods reduce the risk of false positives, minimize disruption to developers, and provide the data needed to make confident, evidence-based decisions about gate enforcement.

Metrics to Track During Experiments

The following metrics help teams evaluate the effectiveness and impact of new or updated quality gates, ensuring they provide meaningful protection without unnecessary friction.

Metric	What It Measures	Why It Matters
Gate failure rate	Frequency of gate rejections	Reveals whether the gate is too strict, too lenient, or appropriately calibrated
False positive/negative rate	Accuracy of gate outcomes	Ensures failures are meaningful and reduces noise that can erode trust
Pipeline duration impact	Time added to builds or deployments	Measures whether the gate slows delivery, affecting

		developer productivity
Override frequency	How often teams bypass the gate	Highlights potential misalignment with workflows or thresholds that are too strict
Defects caught post-merge	Issues detected after merge that the gate would have blocked	Indicates whether the gate is improving overall code quality and preventing regressions
Developer sentiment	Perceived value or frustration from engineers	Helps gauge adoption, trust, and potential resistance to the gate

Best Practices for Gate Experimentation

Running experiments on quality gates is most effective when guided by disciplined practices that ensure measurable outcomes, minimize risk, and maintain team trust.

- **Document experiment goals** to keep testing focused, measurable, and aligned with desired outcomes.
- **Timebox experiments** to avoid indefinite uncertainty and ensure decisions are made promptly.
- **Communicate with affected teams** to build buy-in, prevent surprises, and reduce friction during the trial.
- **Start with high-risk, low-blast areas** to minimize potential disruption from misconfigurations or false positives.
- **Log and analyse everything** so that decisions are driven by data rather than assumptions or anecdotal evidence.

- **Treat pipeline experiments like product experiments**, applying the same rigor, iteration cycles, and feedback loops to drive continuous improvement.

Example: Experimenting with a New Security Scanner

Implementing a new security scanner in a CI/CD pipeline illustrates how careful experimentation can reduce risk while improving both speed and quality.

Step 1 – Shadow Mode: Run the new scanner (e.g., Trivy) in parallel with the existing security scanner without enforcing failures. This allows teams to observe its detection capabilities and logging behaviour without impacting deployment flow.

Step 2 – Data Collection: Track key metrics such as CVE detection overlap, false positives, and scan runtime. Collecting this data over a defined period helps determine whether the new tool offers measurable improvements over the legacy solution.

Step 3 – Split Testing: Limit the experiment to a subset of services, such as containerized applications, so that any misconfigurations or unexpected behaviour only affects a small, controlled environment. This approach reduces potential disruption while providing meaningful insight.

Step 4 – Progressive Rollout: Introduce enforcement gradually: first in soft-fail mode, where failures are logged but do not block the pipeline, then escalate to hard-fail mode after a validation period (e.g., 30 days) once confidence in accuracy and usability is established.

Step 5 – Team Feedback Loop: Collect qualitative feedback from developers on usability, clarity of findings, and workflow impact. Combining this with quantitative metrics ensures the decision to adopt the new scanner is evidence-based.

Outcome:
Trivy replaces the legacy scanner, offering faster scans, more relevant findings, and fewer false positives, while maintaining developer trust and pipeline throughput.

Step	Implementation
Shadow Mode	Run Trivy in parallel with existing scanner
Data Collection	Track CVE detection overlap and false positives
Split Testing	Apply Trivy only to containerized services
Progressive Rollout	Soft fail first, then hard fail after 30 days
Team Feedback Loop	Survey developers on usability and findings clarity

Gates shape the quality and speed of delivery, but only if they're the right gates, used the right way. By experimenting before enforcing, you minimize risk, increase trust, and evolve your CI/CD pipeline with confidence and control.

Conclusion: Continuous Improvement equals Continuous Quality

In this chapter, we explored how quality gates are not static checkpoints but living components of a CI/CD pipeline that must evolve with changing codebases, team practices, and business priorities. We discussed strategies for monitoring gate effectiveness, collecting metrics on pass/fail rates, execution times, and false positives, and adjusting thresholds or policies based on real-world results. By continuously refining gates, teams can reduce unnecessary failures, improve developer confidence, and ensure that every gate contributes meaningfully to overall software quality. This approach fosters a culture of learning, where feedback from the pipeline drives smarter decisions and more reliable software delivery.

With a solid understanding of gate design and continuous improvement, the next chapter focuses on real-world implementations. Here, we will move from theory to practice, examining how organizations integrate these concepts into actual pipelines, overcome common challenges, and tailor solutions to their unique environments. By studying practical examples, readers will gain insight into the tools, patterns, and best practices that make high-performing pipelines a reality in diverse engineering contexts.

Case Studies and Real-World Implementations

Purpose of chapter: This chapter demonstrates how quality gates are applied in real-world CI/CD pipelines, highlighting practical lessons, challenges, and strategies for effective implementation. Case studies show how teams balance enforcement, speed, and developer experience to achieve measurable improvements in software quality.

We've covered a lot of ground around the topic of quality gates, but now let's look at some actual use-case and implementations where companies have done some of these steps successfully. It's important to understand that the topics discussed in this book are not just great theory, but have been implemented by many tech companies with success. Yes, for many organisations grappling with older technology, the challenges may look different and not everything may be as applicable – but it's still useful to learn from these different approaches, along with other implementation lessons that have been experienced in practice and then see how they may apply in different circumstance's

Some of the world's most innovative and high-performing tech companies, like Netflix, Google, and Spotify, have set the benchmark for how quality gates can enable, rather than hinder, speed and innovation. Rather than treating quality gates as red tape, these companies have integrated them as intelligent, adaptive controls that ensure every release meets a high bar for performance, security, and user experience.

Let's explore how these organizations have successfully used quality gates as strategic levers within their software delivery pipelines.

Netflix: Automating Confidence with Guardrails, Not Roadblocks

Netflix deploys code thousands of times per day across its globally distributed architecture. To support this velocity, they've embraced quality gates that act as automated safety nets, not bottlenecks.

Highlights:

- Automated canary analysis (ACA) evaluates new deployments against baseline metrics like error rates, CPU/memory, and user impact. Deployments only proceed if results fall within safe thresholds.
- Netflix's Kayenta tool automates ACA as a gating mechanism, plugging into Spinnaker pipelines and supporting progressive delivery strategies.
- Instead of hard-stopping builds, gates recommend rollbacks or alert humans when anomalies are detected, providing a balance between autonomy and oversight.
- Their culture emphasizes "Freedom and Responsibility", so gates are seen as enabling safe freedom rather than enforcing rigid control.

Key Lesson: Use intelligent, data-driven quality gates to automate trust, not limit speed.

Google: Engineering Quality as a First-Class Signal

With large-scale deployments and a global user base, Google prioritizes reliability, security, and scalability at every stage of the development lifecycle. Their pipelines emphasize proactive quality gating via tooling and culture.

Highlights:

- Google uses presubmit checks extensively, automated tests, static analysis, style enforcement, and even performance benchmarks before code is allowed to merge.
- Build Cop roles monitor CI gate health, ensuring test flakiness or pipeline degradation is addressed immediately, preserving signal quality.
- Security scanning (e.g., for CVEs) and code review policies are automated and enforced across all projects, ensuring policy compliance without developer overhead.
- At scale, Google emphasizes gate modularity and composability: different products can extend or tune gates based on domain-specific risks.

Key Lesson: Treat every gate failure as a data point for system improvement, not just an individual fault.

Spotify: Fast Flow Meets Structured Quality

Spotify practices Continuous Delivery at Scale, with squads deploying independently using Backstage (their open-source developer portal) and pipelines integrated with quality guardrails.

Highlights:

- Teams define service-specific quality requirements via templates in Backstage (e.g., minimum test coverage, SLOs, or secure dependencies).
- Gates are driven by platform-defined golden paths, so while teams move fast, they stay aligned with org-wide best practices.
- Spotify uses progressive delivery techniques with gates checking real-time KPIs like user engagement or feature adoption in canary releases.
- Emphasis on developer experience: if a gate is too noisy or misaligned, it gets flagged and improved rapidly through feedback loops.

Key Lesson: Empower teams to define and manage gates with platform support and sensible defaults, not rigid mandates.

Shared Practices Across Industry Leaders

All the above approaches shared similar shared practices that many in the industry have since adopted to improve their quality gating practices:

Practice	Benefit
Progressive gates (canary, shadow, soft fail)	Reduces risk while supporting fast delivery
Real-time data in gating	Ensures decisions reflect true production behaviour
Automated rollback & alerts	Maintains availability even when something slips
Scalable templates or golden paths	Accelerates consistency across many teams
Feedback-driven refinement	Keeps gates relevant, trusted, and high signal

These industry leaders show that quality gates aren't barriers, they're enablers of high-performance software delivery. The secret isn't just the tools, but how they're integrated into culture, feedback loops, and continuous improvement practices. Gates at Netflix, Google, and Spotify help answer the core CI/CD question: *"Can we release this safely, right now?,* "and give teams the confidence to say yes.

Anti-Patterns and Lessons Learned from Quality Gate Implementation

While quality gates are critical to building trust in CI/CD pipelines, they can easily become counterproductive if implemented poorly. From real-world failures to recurring frustrations in engineering teams, there are several anti-patterns that organizations fall into when adopting or scaling quality gates.

Understanding these missteps, and learning from them, is key to making quality gates effective, sustainable, and widely adopted.

Common Anti-Patterns

Even well-intentioned quality gates can backfire if implemented poorly; recognizing common anti-patterns helps teams avoid pitfalls that reduce trust, slow delivery, or create unnecessary friction.

The "Too Many Gates, Too Early" Trap

What happens: Teams introduce every possible check at once - test coverage, linting, vulnerability scanning, performance thresholds, manual approvals - without phasing or evaluating impact.

Impact:

- Slows down development drastically

- Creates noise and alert fatigue
- Leads to gate fatigue and widespread bypassing

Lesson Learned: Start with high-value, low-friction gates first. Roll out progressively, using shadow mode and data to justify expansion.

Overly Rigid Thresholds

What happens: A gate blocks deployment if test coverage is <90% or performance exceeds 300ms, even if the service is experimental, legacy, or in early development.

Impact:

- Creates bottlenecks with no clear benefit
- Incentivizes gaming metrics (e.g., writing meaningless tests)
- Frustrates developers and slows feedback loops

Lesson Learned: Use risk-based and context-aware thresholds. Coverage on critical paths matters more than blanket enforcement.

Ignoring Feedback from the Ground

What happens: Gate failures are viewed as developer incompetence rather than signals to improve the gate. Teams have no input into what's enforced.

Impact:

- Gates become resented and routinely overridden
- False positives go unaddressed
- Leads to brittle, fragile pipelines

Lesson Learned: Listen to the people closest to the gates. Collect feedback regularly, act on trends, and communicate changes transparently.

Manual Intervention as the Default

What happens: Gates rely heavily on human approvals or manual QA before deployments can continue.

Impact:

- Slows down delivery
- Adds inconsistency and risk of human error
- Breaks the promise of continuous delivery

Lesson Learned: Reserve manual approval for exception handling only, and aim for automated, policy-driven gates by default.

No Observability on Gate Outcomes

What happens: Teams have no visibility into which gates are failing, how often, or why.

Impact:

- Can't detect flaky tests, slow scans, or recurring pipeline issues
- Difficult to prioritize improvement
- Undermines confidence in the CI/CD system

Lesson Learned: Treat gates like any other system: add dashboards, metrics, and alerting. Observe them continuously.

One-Size-Fits-All Gating

What happens: Every team and every service is subject to the exact same rules, regardless of context, risk, or maturity.

Impact:

- Doesn't scale across diverse products
- Leads to gate erosion (e.g., turning everything into warnings)
- Prevents teams from optimizing for their domain

Lesson Learned: Support configurable, modular, and service-specific gates, with central guidance and sensible defaults.

Gates Without Ownership

What happens: No one is assigned to maintain or evolve gates. They're added once and forgotten.

Impact:

- Gates drift out of date with tools and architecture
- Broken gates remain broken
- Developers lose trust in the system

Lesson Learned: Assign clear ownership for each gate or gate type. Include them in sprint and platform planning cycles.

Hard-Failing on Flaky or Non-Deterministic Gates

What happens: Pipelines fail due to tests or scans that produce different results based on environment, timing, or dependencies.

Impact:

- Teams waste time on re-runs and retries
- False sense of risk and broken feedback loops
- Encourages bypassing the pipeline

Lesson Learned: Use flake detection and soft-fail quarantine mechanisms. Don't let flakiness compromise trust in gates.

Summary Table

The following table highlights common anti-patterns in quality gate implementation, the negative consequences they can cause, and recommended approaches to avoid or mitigate them.

Anti-Pattern	Consequence	Better Approach
Too many gates at once	Fatigue, slow pipelines	Phase rollout, prioritize by risk
Hard thresholds without context	Blocks progress, gaming behaviour	Use risk-weighted and progressive thresholds
Ignoring team feedback	Gate erosion and mistrust	Regular feedback loops and reviews
Manual gating by default	Slows automation and delivery	Automate, use manual approval only as fallback
Lack of visibility	Poor decision-making and debugging	Dashboards, logs, alerts
Uniform rules across services	Poor fit for diverse needs	Support customization via templates/configs
No ownership or maintenance	Gate rot and pipeline instability	Assign gate owners with evolution responsibility
Flaky tests block builds	Reduced confidence in CI/CD	Detect flakiness, rerun or quarantine logic

The biggest lesson? Quality gates should serve the team, not the other way around. When gates are misapplied, they become bureaucratic noise. But when designed thoughtfully, measured constantly, and refined continuously, they become powerful tools that accelerate innovation while preserving trust.

Gate Maturity Models

As organizations grow in engineering scale, complexity, and delivery velocity, their use of quality gates must evolve. What starts as simple test automation can eventually mature into a dynamic, context-aware system of safeguards that empower delivery rather than constrain it.

A Gate Maturity Model helps teams:

- Assess the current state of quality gates
- Identify gaps and inefficiencies
- Plan an evolution roadmap aligned with engineering and business goals

The 5 Levels of Gate Maturity

We start by looking at a practical 5-level maturity model that aligns with many industry best practices and can be easily incorporated into most organizations. These 5-level maturity models start from level 0 to 4 and provide a clear progression from ad-hoc or minimal gate usage to fully optimized, data-driven, and automated quality gate practices, helping organizations benchmark current capabilities and plan targeted improvements.

Level 0: No Gates (Ad Hoc Quality)

Description: Quality assurance is informal or manual. Pipelines may exist but lack enforcement checks.

Characteristics:

- No automated tests or static analysis
- Manual reviews and approvals only
- Frequent production issues
- Reactive rather than preventive

Risks:

- High defect leakage
- Inconsistent delivery quality
- High reliance on individual developer diligence

Level 1: Basic Gates (Minimum Viable Control)

Description: Teams introduce basic checks to enforce minimum standards.

Characteristics:

- Basic unit test gate (pass/fail)
- Linting or style checks
- Code reviews required before merge
- Static thresholds (e.g., >80% test coverage)

Benefits:

- Prevents obvious issues from reaching production
- Establishes a culture of pipeline ownership

Limitations:

- Hardcoded rules
- Lack of flexibility or context-awareness
- Poor signal-to-noise ratio if not maintained

Level 2: Structured Gates (Risk-Aligned Controls)

Description: Gates are tied to testing strategy and aligned with component criticality.

Characteristics:

- Test pyramid enforced (unit, integration, E2E)
- CVE scanning, licensing checks, secret detection
- Performance testing in staging
- Environment-specific gates
- Soft fail logic for low-risk gates

Benefits:

- Reduced false positives
- More consistent quality across teams

Limitations:

- Some gates still feel arbitrary
- Limited feedback mechanisms

Level 3: Adaptive Gates (Context-Aware & Configurable)

Description: Gates adjust behaviour based on context, history, and service criticality.

Characteristics:

- Gates configurable per service/domain via templates or policy-as-code
- Risk scoring influences threshold strictness
- Data-informed test gating (e.g., flakiness detection, confidence scoring)
- Progressive gates (shadow mode, canaries, SLA/SLO-based release guards)

Benefits:

- Better alignment with team autonomy and product risk
- Developers trust and engage with gates

Limitations:

- Requires better observability and feedback systems
- Gate configuration complexity increases

Level 4: Predictive & Autonomous Gates (High-Trust Systems)

Description: Gates are predictive, data-driven, and continuously evolving with minimal human intervention.

Characteristics:

- ML-based anomaly detection and gate tuning
- Historical data used to suppress noise and optimize thresholds
- Auto-remediation and rollback based on gate outcomes
- Real-time dashboards with quality telemetry

- Continuous experimentation and A/B testing of gates

Benefits:

- High delivery velocity with strong quality assurance
- Near-zero friction gating
- Continuous improvement loop driven by data

Summary Table

Below is a high-level summary of the different maturity levels of this model:

Level	Name	Focus	Key Features
0	No Gates	Manual quality	No automation, reactive debugging
1	Basic Gates	Standardization	Unit tests, linters, coverage checks
2	Structured Gates	Risk alignment	Integration/E2E tests, security/perf checks, gating by env
3	Adaptive Gates	Contextual control	Configurable, risk-based thresholds, test flake mitigation
4	Predictive & Autonomous	Intelligent automation	ML-based scoring, auto-remediation, A/B testing of gates

How to Use the Maturity Model

Advancing the maturity of your quality gates requires a structured approach, from understanding your current state to planning and tracking targeted improvements over time.

1. **Assess your current state**
   - Map each stage of your pipeline to a maturity level
   - Evaluate gates across dimensions (testing, security, performance, observability)
2. **Identify next-level goals**
   - Choose practices from the next maturity level to adopt gradually
   - Focus on high ROI improvements (e.g., flaky test handling, progressive gating)
3. **Build an evolution roadmap**
   - Align gate improvements with sprint cycles or platform upgrades
   - Use feedback loops and observability to guide decisions
4. **Track maturity as a KPI**
   - Use this model in quarterly reviews or platform team metrics
   - Demonstrate progress toward better developer experience and release confidence

A mature gating system isn't about having *more* gates, it's about having the *right* gates, evolving with your technology, your teams, and your business. This maturity model gives you a shared language and structure to track that evolution and guide your quality culture toward continuous improvement.

Auditing Quality Over Time

Quality gates are not a "set-it-and-forget-it" mechanism. To remain effective, they must be part of a continuous feedback loop that includes regular auditing, a structured process to evaluate whether your gates are actually driving better software quality, reducing risk, and enabling safe delivery at scale.

Auditing quality over time enables teams to:

- Measure long-term effectiveness of gates
- Uncover trends in delivery health
- Justify investments in tooling and process
- Continuously align pipeline enforcement with evolving business and engineering needs

Why Audit Quality Gates?

Regularly reviewing and assessing your quality gates helps ensure they continue to provide real value. By examining relevance, detecting quality drift, and validating the return on enforcement, teams can identify areas for refinement and improvement. These assessments not only support continuous evolution of gates but also help demonstrate adherence to compliance requirements and best practices, ensuring that gates remain effective, trusted, and aligned with both technical and business objectives.

Reason	Value Delivered
Ensure gates are still relevant	Prevent outdated, redundant, or noisy gates
Detect quality drift	Identify rising defect rates, flakiness, or gate bypasses
Validate ROI of enforcement	Measure whether strict gates improve outcomes
Support continuous improvement	Data-informed refinements and evolution plans
Prepare for compliance	Demonstrate quality practices for audits or regulators

What to Audit

Tracking key metrics and signals provides teams with a data-driven view of how quality gates are performing. By monitoring gate effectiveness, failure trends, false positives, and pipeline health, organizations can identify weaknesses, reduce friction, and ensure gates are catching meaningful issues. Additional measures such as flaky test frequency, security and compliance gaps, release quality, and developer sentiment help guide continuous improvement and maintain a balance between enforcement and productivity.

Category	Sample Metrics / Signals
Gate effectiveness	Number of defects caught by each gate vs. number missed
Failure trends	Frequency and cause of gate failures (e.g., test, security, SLO)
False positives	Instances where gates failed but were overridden or ignored
Pipeline health	Avg. pipeline duration, stage duration, stability rate
Flaky tests	Retry rates, quarantined test frequency
Security & compliance	CVE aging, license violations, policy enforcement gaps
Release quality	Post-release incidents, rollbacks, user-reported bugs
Developer friction	Survey feedback, gate skip/bypass rates

How to Conduct a Quality Audit

Conducting a quality audit for CI/CD pipelines allows teams to systematically assess the effectiveness, reliability, and alignment of their quality gates with business and technical objectives. By reviewing gate configurations, analysing failure trends, evaluating signal quality, and gathering developer feedback, organizations can identify gaps, reduce pipeline friction, and prioritize improvements. A structured audit not only strengthens software quality and release confidence but also provides a clear basis for evolving gates, aligning teams, and demonstrating compliance with internal policies or regulatory requirements.

The following steps are useful to follow when conducting these audits:

Establish a Baseline

Start by gathering historical data:

- Gate pass/fail rates
- Pipeline durations
- Incident and bug trends
- Manual approvals or override frequency

This creates a foundation to track change over time.

Map Gates to Quality Outcomes

Link gates to actual outcomes:

- Did the security scan gate prevent a vulnerable release?
- Did a flaky test cause a false fail and delay?
- Did gating performance in staging reduce post-release latency issues?

Use this to assess **value vs. cost** of each gate.

Review at Regular Intervals

Include quality audits as part of:

- Quarterly engineering reviews
- Sprint or release retrospectives
- Incident postmortems

Flag which gates need:

- Tuning
- Removal
- Replacement
- Expansion to new pipelines / services

Report with Visual Dashboards

Use dashboards to visualize quality over time:

- Gate failure heatmaps
- Build health over time
- Deployment frequency vs. gate strictness
- Post-release incident correlation

Tools like Grafana, DataDog, Backstage, or custom dashboards via CI tools (e.g., GitHub Actions Insights, GitLab Analytics, Azure DevOps) work well here.

Include Human Feedback

Combine metrics with qualitative insights:

- What are developers skipping or overriding?
- Are any gates seen as noise or friction?
- Are there requests for new gates (e.g., chaos, accessibility)?

Surveys, retros, or embedded feedback mechanisms (like Slack prompts or GitHub comment bots) can help.

Auditing a Security Gate

Auditing security gates helps identify gaps in accuracy, usability, and effectiveness, providing actionable insights to improve both protection and developer experience. The following examples show typical findings and the steps taken to address them.

Audit Finding	Action Taken
CVE scan gate had 90% false positive rate	Switched scanner to one with better filtering
40% of CVE gate failures were overridden	Added alert-only phase and custom exception logic
Teams asked for better visibility	Added per-repo dashboards + Slack summaries

Best Practices

Following best practices when auditing quality gates ensures the process is efficient, insightful, and aligned with both technical and business priorities.

- **Audit both data and sentiment** – Combine quantitative metrics with developer experience to get a complete view of gate effectiveness.
- **Timebox audits** – Keep audits lightweight and regular (e.g., quarterly) to maintain consistency without overburdening teams.
- **Make gate outcomes traceable** – Log why gates passed or failed, creating an auditable record for review and follow-up.
- **Track trends, not snapshots** – Focus on movement and patterns over time rather than isolated incidents to identify systemic issues.
- **Align audits with business risk** – Prioritize auditing gates that impact critical systems or high-value features to maximize ROI and safety.

Without auditing, quality gates risk becoming stale, noisy, or misaligned with actual delivery needs. With it, they become living systems, measured, tuned, and continuously improved. Auditing is the key to ensuring that your quality strategy isn't just enforced, but also effective, evolving, and empowering.

Conclusion: Learning from the industry is a good way to improve

Examining real-world implementations of quality gates shows that success is not just about the tools or rules, but about thoughtful design, measurement, and iterative improvement. Case studies, audits, and A/B experiments highlight how teams can balance enforcement with velocity, evolve gates as technology and business priorities change, and maintain developer trust. While technical maturity is essential, the ultimate effectiveness of quality gates depends on the culture and organizational alignment that support their adoption and continuous refinement.

The next chapter will explore how to embed a quality-first mindset across teams, establish shared ownership of gates, and align incentives so that quality becomes a collective responsibility rather than a compliance checkbox.

Culture and Organizational Alignment

Purpose of chapter: This chapter explores how culture and organizational alignment shape the effectiveness of quality gates, emphasizing shared ownership, cross-team collaboration, and a mindset that makes quality a collective responsibility rather than a top-down enforcement.

Implementing quality gates in a CI/CD pipeline is not purely a technical exercise. While tools, tests, and thresholds are critical, the surrounding organizational culture often determines whether gates succeed or fail. Even the most rigorously designed gates can become ignored noise, sources of frustration, or bottlenecks if teams do not understand their purpose, trust the results, or feel empowered to act on them. Culture shapes how developers, testers, and DevOps engineers perceive and interact with gates, influencing adoption, adherence, and ultimately, the quality of software delivered.

A culture that values collaboration, transparency, and shared responsibility creates fertile ground for quality gates to thrive. When teams feel ownership over gate design, enforcement, and evolution, gates are treated as enablers rather than obstacles. Conversely, a culture that views gates as rigid mandates or punitive measures can lead to bypassing, ignoring failures, or gaming results, eroding both trust in the CI/CD process and confidence in software quality.

By aligning organizational practices, communication, and incentives with the technical implementation of quality gates, teams can ensure that enforcement supports learning, continuous improvement, and faster delivery. Culture and technical controls are inseparable: gates provide the rules and metrics, while culture provides the context, accountability, and motivation to use them effectively.

Shifting-Left Mindset

The "shift-left" mindset is about moving quality, testing, security, and compliance closer to the start of the software development lifecycle (SDLC). It's not just a tooling change, it's a cultural transformation. In the context of CI/CD and quality gates, shifting left means building quality into the pipeline, earlier in the workflow, and with everyone involved.

What "Shift Left" Really Means

Traditionally, quality assurance (QA) occurred after development, once features were built, they were tested. If problems were found, they were sent back to dev, often late in the cycle. Shift-left flips this model.

Traditional Workflow	Shift-Left Workflow
Code → Build → Test → Fix	**Design → Code → Test → Deploy**
Test late	**Test early and often**
Fix reactively	**Preventively build in quality**

How Shift-Left Shows Up in Practice

Building a culture of quality in CI/CD pipelines begins with embedding checks and best practices directly into developers' workflows. From pre-commit linting and unit tests to policy-as-code and security scans, these practices provide fast, actionable feedback and prevent issues from reaching later stages. Techniques like test-driven and behaviour-driven development, design reviews with quality considerations, and cross-role collaboration ensure that quality is not an afterthought but a shared responsibility. By integrating these practices early and consistently, teams can shift left on testing, security, and reliability, creating a pipeline where high standards are reinforced from the very start of development.

1. **Pre-Commit and Commit-Time Gates**
   - Linting, code formatting, unit tests, and secret scanning run locally or on commit
   - Developers get fast feedback before merging
2. **Infrastructure as Code & Policy as Code**
   - Security and compliance policies encoded as checks early in CI (e.g., Terraform plan reviews)
3. **TDD and BDD Practices**
   - Developers write tests before or alongside feature code, reinforcing quality from the start
4. **Security Embedded in Dev Workflows (DevSecOps)**
   - CVE scanning, SAST, license validation, and dependency checks integrated into early stages
5. **Design Reviews with Quality in Mind**
   - Teams assess observability, scalability, and testability before implementation begins
6. **Collaboration Across Roles**
   - QA, security, and reliability teams work with developers, not after them

Benefits of a Shift-Left Mindset

Embedding quality gates and practices early in the CI/CD pipeline delivers a range of tangible benefits, improving both technical outcomes and team collaboration.

- **Faster feedback loops** – Catch issues within minutes rather than discovering them post-release.
- **Lower cost of defects** – Fixing bugs before code is merged is far less expensive than addressing them in production.
- **Better security posture** – Identify vulnerabilities earlier in the software development lifecycle, reducing risk.
- **Higher confidence in releases** – Fewer surprises late in the pipeline lead to more predictable, stable deployments.
- **Shared ownership of quality** – Developers, testers, and operations teams all contribute to quality from day one, fostering collaboration and accountability.

Foundations for Adopting the Mindset

A strong organizational culture is critical to the success of quality gates in CI/CD pipelines. Beyond technical controls, teams thrive when developers feel empowered to own gate outcomes, when tooling is optimized for efficiency, and when cross-functional collaboration defines shared standards for quality. Education and enablement ensure all team members understand how to use and interpret gates effectively, while psychological safety encourages honest feedback and continuous improvement. Together, these cultural elements create an environment where quality is a collective responsibility, not just a set of rules to follow.

1. **Culture of Accountability & Empowerment**
    - Developers own quality gates and take pride in fast, reliable pipelines
2. **Investing in Developer Experience**
    - Tooling is fast, local-friendly, and integrated into dev workflows (e.g., pre-commit hooks, IDE plugins)
3. **Cross-functional Collaboration**
    - QA, Dev, Security, and Ops work together to define what "good" looks like
4. **Education and Enablement**
    - Teams are trained on how to write tests, understand CVEs, use CI tooling, and read pipeline outputs
5. **Psychological Safety**
    - Teams feel safe to surface flaws in gates or pipeline logic, without blame

Signs You Haven't Shifted Left (Yet)

Even with quality gates in place, many organizations struggle to fully 'shift left' if controls and accountability aren't embedded early in the development process. Signs of this include late discovery of bugs by QA, security checks occurring only post-deployment, developers disengaging from pipeline responsibilities, unexpected gate failures blocking releases, and costly rollbacks. Recognizing these indicators is the first step toward creating a truly proactive, integrated approach to quality and security in CI/CD pipelines.

- QA teams find issues that could have been caught in a unit test
- Security only runs post-deployment scans or annual audits
- Developers treat pipelines as "someone else's problem"

- Releases are blocked late in the process due to surprise gate failures
- Fixing issues often means rolling back weeks of work

Shifting left isn't just about moving tests, it's about moving mindset. It requires bringing quality concerns upstream, where they are cheapest and easiest to address, and building a culture where quality is everyone's job from the first line of code to the final deploy.

Making Quality Gates Seamless, Trustworthy, and Developer-Friendly

One of the biggest reasons quality gates fail isn't poor technical design, it's developer friction. Even the most effective gate is useless if it's seen as a blocker, a black box, or an unnecessary slowdown. To make quality gates truly successful, they must be engineered with empathy, embedded naturally into the development workflow, and provide fast, clear, and actionable feedback.

In short: *Good gates empower developers. Bad gates frustrate them.*

What Does "Friction" Look Like?

While quality gates are designed to enforce standards and prevent defects, poorly implemented or misaligned gates can create friction that slows development and frustrates teams. Understanding what this friction looks like helps organizations identify pain points and make targeted improvements.

Friction in CI/CD pipelines manifests in several ways. Slow feedback forces developers to wait excessive time for basic test or lint results, reducing productivity and breaking flow. Opaque failures leave engineers staring at cryptic logs with no clear root cause, increasing the time and effort needed to resolve issues. Noisy or flaky tests cause gates to fail intermittently, leading teams to ignore warnings or repeatedly rerun jobs.

Overly strict thresholds, such as blocking changes for a minor coverage drop, can prevent valid contributions and discourage developers from engaging with the pipeline. Lack of local replication means developers cannot verify gate checks on their machines, making them reliant on remote CI runs for validation.

Unclear ownership creates uncertainty about who maintains or configures gates, while gate overload, with dozens of simultaneous checks, adds cognitive load and leads to fatigue.

These friction points do more than slow pipelines; they erode trust in the CI/CD system, increasing the likelihood of bypasses, overrides, and workarounds. Addressing these issues requires a careful balance between enforcement, speed, clarity, and usability to ensure gates truly enable quality rather than obstruct it.

Common signs that gates are hindering rather than helping:

Friction Point	Symptoms
Slow feedback	Developers wait 15+ minutes for basic test or lint feedback
Opaque failures	Pipelines fail with cryptic logs or no obvious root cause
Noisy or flaky tests	Gates fail often, but are routinely ignored or retried
Overly strict thresholds	Gates block valid changes due to rigid rules (e.g., 1% coverage drop)

No local replication	Developers can't replicate gate checks locally before pushing
Unclear ownership	Developers don't know who maintains or configures the gates
Gate overload	Dozens of checks create cognitive load and pipeline fatigue

These pain points don't just slow things down, they degrade trust in the entire CI/CD system.

Principles for Low-Friction, High-Trust Gates

To ensure quality gates are effective without slowing down development, they must be designed for low friction and high trust. By following key principles, teams can create gates that developers respect, understand, and actively engage with, rather than circumvent.

Gates that are fast provide near-instant feedback, allowing developers to catch and fix issues quickly without disrupting their workflow. Actionable gates give clear guidance on what failed and how to resolve it, reducing guesswork and rework. Transparent gates are well-documented and visible to all stakeholders, so there's no ambiguity about their purpose or behaviour.

Gates that are replicable locally empower developers to validate changes on their own machines before pushing, minimizing pipeline surprises. Modular and configurable gates can adapt to the context of different services, risk levels, or environments, ensuring relevance without unnecessary blockage.

Well-communicated gates surface results in tools that developers already use, such as Slack notifications or pull request comments, so that feedback is timely and actionable. Finally, feedback-driven gates allow developers to suggest improvements or report issues, fostering a sense of ownership and continuous refinement.

By adhering to these principles, organizations create a CI/CD pipeline where gates enable quality, reinforce trust, and support fast, confident delivery rather than becoming points of frustration or avoidance.

To minimize friction and boost adoption, gates should be:

Principle	Why It Matters
Fast	Gates should run in seconds or minutes, not tens of minutes
Actionable	Output should clearly state what failed and how to fix it
Transparent	Gates should be visible, documented, and explainable
Replicable locally	Developers should be able to run checks before they commit
Modular and Configurable	Gates should adjust based on context (e.g., service, risk level)
Well-communicated	Gate failures should surface in tools devs already use (e.g., Slack, PRs)
Feedback-driven	Developers can suggest improvements or report issues

Practical Strategies to Reduce Friction

Reducing friction in CI/CD pipelines is essential for maintaining trust in quality gates while keeping delivery fast. The following strategies provide concrete ways to make gates more effective and developer-friendly:

Pre-Commit Hooks and Local Tooling

Allow developers to run linting, unit tests, security scans, and other checks before code is pushed to the repository. By catching issues early, developers can fix problems in their local environment, reducing pipeline restarts and wasted cycles. Tools like Husky, pre-commit, and Git hooks make it easy to integrate these checks seamlessly into everyday workflows.

Incremental and Selective Gating
Avoid running the full test suite or all gates for small or irrelevant changes, such as edits to documentation or minor config files. Techniques like file diffing, dependency analysis, or intelligent impact analysis can reduce the scope of checks, ensuring only relevant gates run and keeping feedback fast.

Fast-Fail Pipelines
Order gates strategically to surface likely failures quickly. For example, run linting first, then unit tests, then builds or integration tests, so pipelines fail early and cleanly. This minimizes wasted time spent running downstream jobs on code that is already failing a critical check.

Clear, Friendly Error Messages

Gate failures should be actionable and easy to understand. Include links to failing tests, relevant logs, documentation, or steps to remediate the issue. Avoid vague outputs like "build failed," which leave developers guessing and increase frustration.

Gate Dashboards

Provide visibility into gate outcomes over time. Dashboards can show failure history, trends, flakiness, and ownership, helping developers understand the intent and reliability of gates, not just the immediate results. This context builds trust and reduces the perception of gates as arbitrary roadblocks.

Developer Feedback Loops

Create channels for developers to flag false positives, flaky gates, or confusing messages using bots, forms, or chat commands. Review this feedback regularly in retrospectives or platform team meetings to identify and address the top sources of friction. Continuous feedback ensures gates evolve in alignment with developer workflows and maintain credibility.

Metrics to Track Developer Experience

Monitoring key metrics helps teams identify friction in CI/CD pipelines and ensure gates provide value without slowing development or eroding trust.

Metric	What It Measures	Why It Matters
Gate failure frequency	How often a gate fails	Indicates if the gate is too strict, noisy, or misaligned with real-world workflows
Re-run / retry rates	Frequency of pipeline retries due to failures	Reveals flakiness and potential gaming of the system, highlighting reliability issues
Time-to-feedback	Time developers wait for results from checks	Affects developer productivity and flow; faster feedback enables quicker fixes
Gate override frequency	Number and reasons for bypassing gates	Signals mistrust or friction in gates; helps prioritize improvements and enforcement adjustments
Developer satisfaction (via surveys)	Developers' perception of gates	Measures usability, trust, and overall acceptance of quality enforcement mechanisms

Gates should guide, not punish. The best quality gates don't feel like gates at all - they feel like helpful collaborators, quietly ensuring your code is safe, stable, and secure. By investing in developer experience, you not only make pipelines faster, you make teams more confident, productive, and aligned around quality.

Getting Buy-In from Leadership and Teams

Implementing quality gates in CI/CD is not just a technical change, it's a cultural shift. And like any meaningful transformation, success hinges on buy-in from both leadership and teams. Without it, even the best gates become brittle bureaucracy. With it, quality gates become trusted, respected, and deeply embedded in your delivery DNA.

Why Buy-In Matters

Gaining support from key stakeholders is essential for successful quality gate adoption, as each group influences how gates are designed, enforced, and trusted across the organization.

Stakeholder	Why Their Support is Critical
Engineering Teams	They must interact with the gates daily, adoption depends on ease and trust
Product Owners	They balance velocity and quality, support gates that protect roadmap integrity
Executives	They fund the investment, need to see how it mitigates risk or boosts delivery confidence
Security, QA, Ops	They help define and evolve gate policies, need a collaborative voice

Key Strategies to Get Buy-In

Successfully introducing quality gates requires more than technical implementation, it depends on clear communication, collaboration, and demonstrating tangible value. The following strategies help secure support and adoption across teams and leadership:

Frame Gates as Enablers, Not Barriers

Quality gates should be positioned as safety rails that accelerate confident delivery, not as arbitrary blockers. Highlight how gates prevent late-cycle failures, regressions, and security risks, and emphasize that faster feedback loops reduce surprises and enable more predictable releases. A simple mantra can resonate:

"Gates aren't about slowing teams down, they're about making fast, safe."

Connect to Business Outcomes

Leadership evaluates initiatives in terms of risk, cost, and velocity. Translate gate benefits into outcomes that matter to executives and product owners:

- **Reduced production incidents** → higher customer trust and satisfaction
- **Improved test coverage** → fewer bugs and faster delivery
- **SAST and license compliance gates** → readiness for audits and regulatory compliance
- **Increased release confidence** → fewer delays, more predictable timelines

Pilot Before You Preach

Prove the value of gates with a targeted pilot before rolling them out organization-wide. Choose a motivated team and introduce a few high-value gates, such as flaky test detection or security scans. Measure outcomes, like reduced rollbacks, faster MTTR, or improved feedback quality, and use the success story as a case study to demonstrate practical benefits to other teams.

Invite Collaborative Design

Involve engineers, QA leads, and team leads in deciding which gates to implement, setting thresholds, and reviewing results. When teams have a hand in shaping policies, they are more likely to trust and adopt them. Collaboration ensures gates are practical, aligned with real workflows, and seen as helpful rather than punitive.

Show the Before and After

Visual storytelling can make the impact of gates tangible. Highlight comparisons such as:

- Defect counts before and after gates
- Trends in incidents over time
- Improvements in pipeline stability or lead time

This approach makes invisible issues, like hidden quality debt or flaky test pain, visible and measurable, reinforcing the value of enforcement.

Address Concerns Proactively

Resistance is natural, particularly around perceived slowdowns or loss of autonomy. Prepare responses to common concerns:

Common Concern	Suggested Response
"Gates will slow us down"	"Gates prevent costly rework and late failures"
"We'll lose control over our pipeline"	"Let's make gates configurable and team-owned"
"It'll block innovation"	"We'll evolve gates based on risk and feedback"
"We already test locally"	"Gates ensure consistency across environments and teams"

Make It Visible at All Levels

Use leadership forums, demos, retrospectives, and dashboards to highlight successes and reinforce accountability. Show metrics tied to team OKRs, celebrate wins, and give platform or quality teams recognition for their contributions. Visibility strengthens buy-in and demonstrates that gates are aligned with both business priorities and developer needs.

Metrics That Build Confidence

These metrics help build confidence in your CI/CD pipeline by showing how quality gates are improving reliability, security, and developer experience, while providing data to guide continuous improvement.

Metric	What It Measures	Why It Matters
Reduction in post-release incidents	Number of bugs, outages, or regressions after deployment	Demonstrates that gates are preventing defects and improving release quality
Improved lead time and deployment frequency	Time from code commit to production release and number of deployments	Shows whether gates support fast, reliable delivery without creating bottlenecks
Security vulnerability closure rate	Percentage of identified vulnerabilities that are resolved within a target timeframe	Reflects effectiveness of security gates and risk mitigation
Gate failure / override ratios	Number of gate failures versus instances of manual overrides	Indicates gate reliability, credibility, and trust from developers
Developer satisfaction survey results	Engineers' perception of gates,	Helps understand adoption, morale, and areas for

	workflow friction, and usability	improvement in pipeline design

Getting buy-in isn't about forcing quality, it's about earning trust, showing value, and bringing people along for the journey. With transparent communication, real metrics, and inclusive design, quality gates become not just a platform team initiative, but a company-wide asset.

Aligning Quality with Incentives

Even the best-designed quality gates won't have lasting impact unless they're aligned with what teams are rewarded for. Incentives, whether formal (e.g., performance reviews, KPIs) or informal (e.g., recognition, praise, speed to delivery), shape behaviour. If the system rewards delivery speed but penalizes nothing for recurring production bugs, quality will always lose.

To make quality gates stick, organizations must align incentives to promote quality as a shared, valuable outcome, not an afterthought.

The Incentive Mismatch Problem

The incentives and measures an organization emphasizes directly shape developer behaviour, highlighting what gets rewarded or ignored reveals the habits and trade-offs teams are likely to adopt.

What's Rewarded	What's Ignored	Behaviour It Drives
Shipping features fast	Incident frequency	Risky releases, shortcuts around gates
Team velocity	Test coverage or stability	Less time invested in automation

Headline OKRs	Technical debt reduction	Code rot and brittle pipelines
Quantity of changes	Quality of outcomes	Frequent, shallow work instead of thoughtful delivery
Short-term fixes	Long-term reliability investments	Patchwork instead of architectural improvement

Without careful alignment, teams might see gates as obstacles to success, rather than tools that enable it.

Aligning Incentives: Strategies That Work

Driving adoption of quality gates isn't just about implementing technical controls, it's about aligning incentives so that developers, teams, and leadership see value in building and maintaining quality. Without the right signals, teams may prioritize speed over safety, resulting in shortcuts, flaky tests, or brittle pipelines. The following strategies help ensure quality is recognized, rewarded, and integrated into everyday work:

Make Quality Part of Performance Reviews and OKRs

Embed quality metrics into the way teams are evaluated. Include measurable indicators such as defect rates, test coverage, and gate stability in team or engineering OKRs. Recognize contributions beyond shipping features, like refactoring tests, improving CI reliability, or reducing flakiness during performance conversations.

As the saying goes: *"You get what you measure. Make sure you're measuring what you want to get."*

By tying quality to tangible goals, teams understand that reliability is just as important as speed.

Celebrate Quality Wins Publicly

Quality work is often invisible, yet it has a profound impact on the pipeline and end-product. Recognize developers who write solid tests, improve gate reliability, or optimize CI performance. Share dashboards, metrics, and before/after stories in team all-hands, newsletters, or internal demos. Public recognition reinforces the value of thoughtful, preventive work and encourages others to invest in quality initiatives.

Build Quality into Definition of Done

Ensure that passing gates is not optional. Integrate automated checks, like unit tests, static analysis, security scans, and policy validations, directly into the definition of done for each story or release.

For example: *"A story is only done when 90% unit test coverage is met and all gates pass."*

This formalizes quality as a core part of delivery rather than an afterthought.

Tie Quality to Business Risk

Translate technical measures into business language. Show how gate failures correlate with production incidents, customer dissatisfaction, compliance issues, or market delays. Frame adoption of gates as risk mitigation and trust-building, rather than purely engineering discipline.

For instance: *"Fewer vulnerabilities → higher audit scores → faster market access."*

By linking gates to tangible outcomes, leadership and teams alike see the strategic value in maintaining rigorous checks.

Make Quality Workload Visible in Planning

Avoid relegating quality work to "extra" or invisible labour. Treat test automation, gate maintenance, and tech debt reduction as integral tasks in backlogs and sprint planning. Allocate capacity explicitly, just like for new features. This not only prevents burnout but reinforces the message that quality is a core responsibility, not overtime or optional work.

Incentivizing Quality Across Roles

Aligning incentives across all roles ensures that everyone involved in the software delivery process is motivated to prioritize quality. When developers, testers, security teams, product owners, and leaders see tangible benefits from maintaining and improving quality gates, behaviours naturally shift toward safer, more reliable, and faster delivery.

Role	Aligned Incentives
Developers	Recognition for clean merges, test coverage, low bug rates
QA/Testers	Time to invest in automation and test design, not just manual validation
Security Teams	Partnership in gate design and CVE remediation loops
Product Owners	OKRs that reward stable releases and fast recovery metrics
Leaders/Execs	Confidence in delivery metrics, reduction in incident volume

Metrics That Reinforce Incentives

Tracking these metrics provides visibility into how quality gates are performing, where friction exists, and whether the pipeline is delivering reliable, high-quality software, helping teams build confidence and drive continuous improvement.

Metric	What It Measures	Why It Matters
Deployment success rate	Percentage of deployments that complete without rollback or failure	Indicates overall pipeline reliability and effectiveness of gates in preventing broken releases
Bug escape rate (post-prod defects)	Number of defects discovered in production after deployment	Shows whether gates are effectively catching issues before release, improving end-user quality
Gate pass/fail trends	Frequency of gate failures over time	Helps identify unstable or over-strict gates and guides tuning or improvement efforts
Gate flakiness and false positives	Instances where gates fail unpredictably or are overridden unnecessarily	Highlights gates that erode trust and create friction, signalling areas for refinement
Time-to-resolve for gate failures	Average duration from gate failure to issue resolution	Measures responsiveness and efficiency in addressing quality issues, impacting pipeline flow and confidence
Coverage or performance improvements over time	Trends in code coverage, SLO compliance, or performance metrics	Demonstrates that gates are driving measurable improvements in code quality and system reliability

Keep Incentives Evolving

Incentives should adapt as your quality maturity grows. Early on, you may reward the *act of writing tests*; later, you may reward *impactful improvements* like shrinking test execution time or refining gate thresholds.

Culture change doesn't happen by decree, it happens when incentives and expectations are aligned. By celebrating and rewarding the behaviours that lead to better quality, you make quality gates more than enforcement tools, they become badges of craftsmanship, symbols of trust, and accelerators of shared success.

Conclusion: Change and improvement is a culture not a technical skill

While technical implementation is critical, the success of quality gates ultimately depends on organizational culture and aligned incentives. Teams are more likely to adopt and maintain gates when developers, testers, security teams, product owners, and leaders all see clear value in them. Building a culture of accountability, collaboration, and psychological safety ensures that gates are not seen as arbitrary blockers but as enablers of fast, reliable, and secure delivery. Metrics, recognition, and thoughtful feedback loops reinforce the behaviours that support high-quality software, while visible leadership support and integration into performance goals make quality a shared responsibility.

With a strong cultural foundation in place, organizations are ready to design and implement a robust quality gate framework. The next chapter will explore how to structure gates across the CI/CD pipeline, define policies and thresholds, integrate them with tooling, and measure their effectiveness - turning cultural intent into concrete, enforceable practices that improve reliability, security, and developer confidence.

Building Your Quality Gate Framework

Purpose of chapter: This chapter guides teams on how to design, implement, and manage a practical quality gate framework that enforces standards, mitigates risk, and embeds quality directly into the CI/CD pipeline.

Now that we've explored the cultural foundations and organizational alignment required for quality gates to succeed, it's time to focus on how to implement a quality gate framework in practice. This chapter breaks the process down into clear, actionable steps that teams and organizations can follow, whether you're starting from scratch or evolving an existing CI/CD pipeline. The goal is not to prescribe a one-size-fits-all solution, but to provide a repeatable, adaptable approach that works across different team sizes, architectures, and levels of maturity.

Rather than treating quality gates as abstract policies or tooling decisions, we will walk through what implementation actually looks like day: assessing your current pipeline, selecting the right gates, defining thresholds, integrating with existing tools, and rolling out enforcement gradually. Each step emphasizes practicality - how to minimize friction, build trust with teams, and ensure gates deliver real value instead of becoming noise or bottlenecks. By the end of this chapter, you should have a clear blueprint for building a quality gate framework that is effective, scalable, and aligned with both engineering and business goals.

Example Project: Building a Quality Gate Framework – Step-by-Step

For this section, we will look at a specific scenario and then how we will approach building quality gates that address those challenges.

Scenario

Let's assume you're working at a mid-sized tech company called *CodeCurrent*, where multiple teams are pushing changes daily to a monorepo. Releases are frequent, but so are bugs, late-stage failures, and post-deployment issues. Leadership wants to improve software quality and reduce delivery risk without slowing teams down.

Your task: build and roll out a Quality Gate Framework across CI/CD pipelines.

Step 1: Define Objectives and Scope

You need to begin by making the initial goals clear and asking questions that can help to establish the scope and clarify any particular concerns a or questions that may be outstanding.

Goals:

- Prevent high-risk code from reaching production.
- Provide fast, actionable feedback.
- Ensure consistent quality across teams and services.

Key questions to ask:

- What are the most common causes of regressions?
- What tools are already in use for CI/CD?
- Which areas are most painful: security, test flakiness, slow pipelines?

Start small: Focus on one pilot team/service first before scaling org-wide.

Step 2: Choose Your Tools and Pipeline Platform

Once you understand what you want to gate and why, the next step is selecting the right tools and pipeline platform to enforce those quality checks consistently, automatically, and at scale across your delivery workflows. Below is an example of some tools and tech stack that apply to this particular example scenario:

CI/CD Stack: GitHub Actions

Testing Frameworks: Jest (unit), Cypress (E2E), JMeter (performance)

Security & Compliance: Snyk, Trivy, Licensee

Code Quality: ESLint, SonarQube

Observability: Datadog, Grafana for test/pipeline dashboards

Pro Tip: Create a shared pipeline library or template repo to version and distribute gates.

Step 3: Define Your First Gates (Minimum Viable Gate Set)

With the tooling in place, this step focuses on defining a minimum viable set of quality gates that protect commit-level quality, catch issues early, and establish consistent standards without overwhelming teams.

Build a first set of gates focusing on commit-level quality:

1. **Pre-Commit Gate:**
   - Linting (ESLint)
   - Secrets scanning (GitLeaks)
   - File size limits (no mega commits)
2. **Commit/PR Gate:**
   - Unit test pass with coverage >80%
   - Static code analysis via SonarQube
   - SAST via Snyk
   - Dependency license checks
3. **Build Gate:**
   - Compile/build must succeed
   - Artifact size validation

Gates must return clear pass/fail signals to GitHub pull requests, with links to logs.

Step 4: Integrate Gates into the CI Pipeline

Now that you have a clear plan of what your gates need to look like – you can begin to build them directly into your pipelines:

In .github/workflows/quality-gates.yml:

```
name: Quality Gates

on: [pull_request]

jobs:
  lint-and-test:
    runs-on: ubuntu-latest
    steps:
      - uses: actions/checkout@v2
      - name: Run ESLint
        run: npm run lint
      - name: Run Unit Tests
        run: npm run test:unit -- --coverage
      - name: Snyk Scan
        uses: snyk/actions/node@master
        env:
```

```
SNYK_TOKEN: ${{ secrets.SNYK_TOKEN }}
```

Step 5: Pilot and Iterate

Rather than rolling gates out everywhere at once, this step focuses on piloting the framework with a willing team and iterating based on real developer feedback and measurable outcomes.

Work with a volunteer team:

- Set up a Slack channel for fast feedback
- Track time-to-feedback and gate pass/fail rate
- Measure post-merge defect rate over 2–3 sprints

Use retrospectives to ask:

- Which gates were helpful?
- Which caused frustration or slowed us down?
- Are there any flaky tests or false positives?

Step 6: Expand with Additional Gate Types

After the initial success, progressively introduce new gates:

Gate Type	Tool/Strategy	Purpose
Integration Tests	Docker + Jest/Cypress	Catch API or DB-related issues
Security (DAST)	OWASP ZAP on staging	Dynamic web app security scan
Performance Tests	JMeter in pre-prod	Catch regressions before release
Release Approvals	Manual gate + Slack notification	Notify owners for high-risk deploys
Feature Flags	LaunchDarkly + gate for disabled coverage	Ensure flagged features are tested

Step 7: Visualize and Operationalize

To sustain adoption and trust, this step focuses on making quality gates visible and measurable through dashboards and alerts that help teams understand, improve, and own their pipeline quality.

Build dashboards and alerts:

- Gate pass/fail trends (Grafana)
- Flaky test heatmaps
- Time-to-pass per PR
- Gate duration and reliability

Goal: Teams feel like quality gates are their tools, not blockers.

Step 8: Define Governance and Continuous Improvement

As quality gates mature, this step focuses on establishing governance and continuous improvement practices that keep gates relevant, effective, and aligned with team maturity and business needs over time.

- Create documentation for all gates (thresholds, purpose, how to fix failures)
- Run quarterly reviews to revise thresholds (e.g., from 80% → 90% test coverage)
- Allow teams to suggest/remove gates based on maturity
- Introduce A/B testing of gate policies to validate effectiveness

- Template gates for small, medium, and enterprise teams

Template Gates for Small, Medium, and Enterprise Teams

We're now going to loo kat how certain quality gates methods should apply differently based on scale. Quality gates should be right-sized for the organization's size, complexity, and maturity. What works for a lean startup might choke a large enterprise, and what keeps a large enterprise secure might feel like overkill for a small dev shop.

To streamline adoption and avoid over-engineering, it's helpful to define template gate bundles, starting points tailored to the typical needs and constraints of teams at different scales.

Small Teams (Startups, Early-Stage Projects)

Focus: Speed with guardrails, minimal overhead

These teams typically value speed and simplicity, but still want protection from obvious mistakes. They benefit most from lightweight, fast-running checks.

Template Gate Set:

Gate Type	Tool/Method	Purpose
Linting	ESLint, Prettier	Catch syntax and formatting issues
Unit Tests	Jest, Mocha	Validate core logic with coverage check
Secrets Scanning	GitLeaks	Prevent accidental credential leaks
License Check	Licensee	Block problematic dependencies
Build/Compile Check	Native to CI (e.g., npm, Gradle)	Ensure it builds before merging

Optional: Add pre-commit hooks for fast local feedback (via Husky or pre-commit).

Medium Teams (Growing orgs, regulated industries, platform teams)

Focus: Balance between quality enforcement and team autonomy

These teams need greater consistency, governance, and risk coverage as the complexity of the product and team increases.

Template Gate Set:

Gate Type	Tool/Method	Purpose
All Small-Team Gates	—	Foundation layer
Integration Test Gate	Docker + test container	Ensure APIs and services play well together
Static Analysis (SAST)	SonarQube or Snyk	Catch code vulnerabilities
Dependency Scanning	Trivy, Dependabot	Detect vulnerable libs
Branch Policy Enforcement	CI rules or GitHub/GitLab	Prevent merge without gate passes
Code Coverage Threshold	Jest/coverage tools	Enforce minimum test standards

Optional: Add PR-based dashboards for gate results + trend reporting.

Enterprise Teams (Large-scale systems, multi-team CI/CD)

Focus: Reliability, governance, auditability, and scalability

Enterprises require **deep, layered gate policies** to ensure compliance, scalability, and service-level integrity across hundreds of services and contributors.

Template Gate Set:

Gate Type	Tool/Method	Purpose
All Medium-Team Gates	—	Base compliance and quality gates
Performance Test Gate	JMeter, k6, Gatling	Detect load regressions pre-release
SLA/SLO Validation	Prometheus, Datadog + gate plugin	Prevent deploys that degrade SLOs
Chaos/Fault Injection Gate	Gremlin, Litmus	Validate fault tolerance (stage/pre-prod)
Policy-as-Code Enforcement	OPA, Conftest	Enforce infra/security config rules
Feature Flag Verification	LaunchDarkly SDK + test injection	Ensure gated features are test-covered
Compliance Reporting Gate	License scanner + reporting tool	Audit trails and license risk controls

Optional: Add anomaly detection gates with ML-based telemetry (e.g., Prometheus + AI pipeline step).

Tooling Example: Azure DevOps, Jenkins + shared libraries, or enterprise GitLab runners.

Flexibility in Gate Templates

Each template should be:

- **Modular** – allow teams to opt into gates by need
- **Progressive** – support maturity growth (e.g., 80% → 90% test coverage)
- **Configurable** – allow thresholds and overrides per team or environment

Maintain templates as versioned CI pipeline modules (e.g., reusable workflows in GitHub Actions, pipeline templates in Azure DevOps).

Predefining quality gate templates makes it easier for teams to adopt good practices without reinventing the wheel. Whether you're a scrappy team deploying weekly or an enterprise team deploying 500x a day, right-sized gates offer scalable confidence, and let teams deliver quality at speed.

Reference Architecture: Scalable Quality Gate Framework

This architecture is intentionally designed to **scale quality without scaling friction**. It supports teams at different maturity levels while maintaining consistency, transparency, and governance across the organization. Specifically, it enables:

- **Easy onboarding of new services and teams**: New repositories can adopt a standard pipeline and gate set with minimal configuration, avoiding bespoke CI/CD implementations.
- **Progressive adoption of gates**: Teams can start with a minimum viable gate set and gradually enable stricter or more advanced gates as confidence and maturity grow.
- **Clear separation of concerns**: Pipeline orchestration, gate logic, and policy decisions are decoupled, allowing each to evolve independently without breaking delivery workflows.
- **Auditability, observability, and long-term maintainability**: Every gate decision is traceable, measurable, and reviewable, supporting compliance, continuous improvement, and operational insight.

Core Components

Pipeline Orchestrator

The pipeline orchestrator is responsible for executing CI/CD stages and coordinating gate evaluation, but not for defining gate logic itself.

Responsibilities

- Trigger builds on commits, pull requests, or schedules
- Sequence stages (lint → test → build → deploy)
- Collect and pass outputs to the gate controller
- Enforce pass/fail decisions

Tool Examples	Description
GitHub Actions, GitLab CI, Jenkins, Azure DevOps	Execute jobs, manage stages, and control workflow execution

Design Principle: Keep pipelines *thin*. They should orchestrate, not encode policy.

Gate Controller Layer

The gate controller acts as the central brain of the quality gate system. It defines *what* gates exist, *when* they run, and *how* success is evaluated.

Key Capabilities

- Shared, versioned pipeline templates
- Declarative gate definitions (YAML/JSON / policy-as-code)
- Configurable thresholds (coverage %, latency SLOs, vulnerability severity)

- Context-aware behaviour (e.g., stricter in main, looser in dev branches)

Benefits

- Consistent behaviour across repositories
- Easier governance and change management
- Reduced duplication and configuration drift

Example Gate Definition (YAML)

```
qualityGates:
  unitTest:
    enabled: true
    coverageThreshold: 80
  lint:
    enabled: true
  securityScan:
    enabled: true
    tools: [snyk, trivy]
  performance:
    enabled: false
    slaLatency: 500ms
```

This approach allows teams to opt into gates declaratively, while platform teams manage defaults and evolution centrally.

Policy-as-Code Engine

Policy-as-code introduces formal, testable governance into the delivery pipeline.

Purpose

- Encode security, compliance, and architectural rules as versioned code
- Evaluate changes consistently across services and environments

- Enable automated compliance checks without manual reviews

Tools	Purpose
Open Policy Agent (OPA), Conftest	Define and enforce policies using code

Typical Use Cases

- Blocking deployments with critical CVEs
- Enforcing encryption or logging standards
- Validating infrastructure or Kubernetes manifests

Gate Executors

Gate executors are specialized, plugin-like components that perform the actual checks. They are decoupled from orchestration and policy decisions.

Category	Tooling Examples
Code Quality	ESLint, SonarQube
Testing	Jest, Cypress, k6, Playwright
Security	Snyk, Trivy, OWASP ZAP
Licensing	Licensee, FOSSA
Performance	JMeter, Prometheus-based checks
Anomaly Detection	Prometheus + ML models (Prophet, Anodot)
Chaos Engineering	Gremlin, Litmus

Design Advantage

- Executors can be swapped, upgraded, or disabled without rewriting pipelines
- Enables best-tool-for-the-job flexibility

Observability and Feedback Layer

Observability ensures that gates are understood, trusted, and continuously improved, not just enforced.

What This Layer Provides

- Visibility into gate behaviour and trends
- Early detection of flakiness or excessive friction
- Data to support threshold tuning and governance decisions

Layer	Tools
Logging	ELK, Loki
Metrics	Prometheus, Datadog
Tracing	OpenTelemetry, Jaeger
Dashboards	Grafana, Power BI, Datadog
Notifications	Slack, Microsoft Teams, Email

Example Insights

- Gate pass/fail trends over time
- Flaky test heatmaps
- Average gate runtime per PR
- Gate coverage by repository or team

Gate Result Store & Audit Log

This component provides durable storage of gate outcomes for analysis, compliance, and historical insight.

Implementation	Notes
S3/GCS + DynamoDB/Firestore	Simple, scalable, event-driven
Elasticsearch	Excellent for searchable logs
SQL Stores	Ideal for audit reports and metrics dashboards

Why It Matters

- Enables post-incident analysis
- Supports audits and regulatory requirements
- Allows correlation between gate failures and production incidents

Developer and Admin Interfaces

These interfaces ensure gates remain team-owned and usable, not opaque platform mandates.

Interface	Purpose
CLI or Admin UI	Enable/disable gates, adjust thresholds
GitOps (YAML)	Declarative configuration with code review
Slack / ChatOps	Gate overrides, feedback, and alerts

Outcome

- Developers feel empowered to interact with gates
- Platform teams maintain governance without bottlenecks
- Quality becomes a shared responsibility

This architecture balances autonomy and governance, enabling teams to move fast while maintaining confidence, consistency, and compliance. By separating orchestration, policy, execution, and observability, quality gates evolve from rigid blockers into a flexible, trusted system that scales with both teams and ambition.

Progressive Architecture Across Maturity Levels

As organizations grow, so do the demands placed on their CI/CD pipelines and quality gates. What works well for a small, fast-moving team often breaks down at scale, where consistency, governance, and observability become critical. A progressive quality gate architecture allows teams to evolve naturally across maturity levels, starting with lightweight, team-owned gates and gradually introducing shared tooling, centralized governance, and enterprise-grade visibility, without disrupting delivery velocity or autonomy.

Layer	Small Team	Medium Team	Enterprise
Gate Invocation	GitHub Actions	GitLab templates	Central Jenkins/Templated CI
Config Mgmt	Hardcoded in YAML	Shared pipeline module	Declarative config with override
Observability	Console output	Basic dashboards	Advanced SLIs, audit trails
Gate Source of Truth	Per-repo scripts	Shared gate library	Gate registry & versioning
Gate Governance	By team	Quality/DevOps team	Org-wide policy board

High-Level Diagram

The following high-level diagram illustrates how quality gates fit into a modern CI/CD architecture, showing the flow from source control through pipeline execution, gate enforcement, and feedback. It highlights the separation between pipeline orchestration, centralized gate control, and specialized gate executors, while emphasizing how results and telemetry feed into shared observability and developer feedback loops to support continuous improvement.

Building Your Quality Gate Framework

```
            ┌──────────────────────┐
            │    Source Control    │
            │   (GitHub/GitLab)    │
            └──────────┬───────────┘
                       │
            ┌──────────▼───────────┐
            │    CI/CD Pipeline    │
            │  (GitHub Actions,    │
            │   Jenkins, etc.)     │
            └──────────┬───────────┘
                       │
      ┌────────────────▼─────────────────┐
      │     Quality Gate Controller      │
      │   (shared templates + config)    │
      └────────┬─────────┬─────────┬─────┘
               │         │         │
┌──────────▼──┐ ┌─▼──────────┐ ┌▼──────────┐
│ Lint/Test  │ │ Security  │ │ Perf/Load │ ← Gate Executors
└──────────┬──┘ └────────┬───┘ └────┬──────┘
           │             │          │
┌──────────▼─────────────▼──────────▼───────┐
│          Gate Results + Logs              │
│     (S3, DB, Prometheus, ELK)             │
└──────────┬────────────────────────────────┘
           │
   ┌───────▼──────────────────────────┐
   │   Observability & Dashboards     │
   │     (Grafana, Slack, etc.)       │
   └──────────────────────────────────┘
```

Design Goals for a Quality Gate Architecture

These core design principles ensure that a quality gate framework remains adaptable, trusted, and scalable, supporting teams as they evolve from simple checks to mature, enterprise-grade governance without sacrificing speed or autonomy.

Principle	What It Enables
Modular	Easily add/remove gates
Configurable	Tailor rules to team needs
Observable	Visibility into failures, trends, flakiness

Reusable	Share logic across teams and pipelines
Auditable	Log outcomes for compliance & learning
Progressive	Grow from simple to complex as teams mature

Common Pitfalls and Troubleshooting Tips When Implementing Quality Gates

Implementing quality gates can significantly improve your CI/CD pipeline and overall software quality, but it's not without challenges. Misconfigured, overly strict, or poorly communicated gates can create friction, delay deployments, or get bypassed altogether.

Below are the most common pitfalls, why they occur, and actionable troubleshooting tips to help you avoid them.

Overly Aggressive Gate Policies Too Early

Symptom: Developers constantly blocked, high gate failure rates, growing frustration

Cause: Starting with strict thresholds (e.g., 100% test coverage, zero vulnerabilities) before teams are ready.

Tip:

- Use progressive thresholds (e.g., 70% → 80% → 90%)
- Introduce gates in "report-only" mode first
- Start with non-blocking metrics to build awareness

Flaky or Slow Tests Breaking the Pipeline

Symptom: Inconsistent gate failures, pipeline times exceed tolerable limits

Cause: Unstable E2E tests, shared environments, long-running test suites.

Tip:

- Use a test flakiness tracker (e.g., retry with tags, flaky test dashboard)
- Implement parallel execution and isolate slow tests
- Introduce timeouts and ensure test cleanup routines

Gate Failures Are Hard to Debug

Symptom: A gate fails but provides vague logs or no actionable feedback

Cause: Poor logging, missing links to test artifacts or coverage reports.

Tip:

- Always output detailed logs to a known location
- Include links to dashboards or logs in gate outputs
- Normalize log output using a standard format (JSON, structured logging)

Ignored or Bypassed Gates

Symptom: Teams create workarounds or override failing gates without action

Cause: Low confidence in gate accuracy, pressure to deliver, poor gate governance.

Tip:

- Make override actions visible and auditable
- Use ChatOps or approval workflows for manual overrides
- Educate teams on the "why" behind each gate's purpose
- Track gate bypasses and review in retrospectives

Gates Not Environment-Aware

Symptom: Tests pass in staging but fail in production; security scans miss production-only issues

Cause: Gates applied inconsistently across environments.

Tip:

- Use environment-specific gates with configuration toggles
- Run destructive tests (e.g., chaos or load) only in isolated environments
- Ensure secrets and feature flags are injected correctly per environment

Gate Sprawl Without Ownership

Symptom: Too many gates, unclear rules, lack of maintenance

Cause: Gates added over time without central ownership or documentation

Tip:

- Define a gate registry with owners, descriptions, and contact info
- Regularly audit and remove obsolete or duplicate gates
- Appoint a "quality steward" per team or domain

Gates Slow Down Developer Feedback

Symptom: Builds take 30+ minutes to return results; velocity drops

Cause: Gates placed too late in the pipeline or running unnecessary checks every time

Tip:

- Follow the test pyramid and run fast gates early (lint, unit tests)
- Use event-driven triggers to avoid redundant work
- Cache dependencies and parallelize jobs aggressively

Gates Don't Align with Business Goals

Symptom: High-quality software still fails to meet customer expectations

Cause: Gates focus only on technical metrics (e.g., code coverage), not business outcomes

Tip:

- Introduce gates tied to SLAs/SLOs, feature flag validation, or business rule enforcement

- Involve product owners in defining high-impact quality gates
- Include real user metrics (e.g., latency, error rates) in release criteria

Fragmented Tooling and Poor Gate Integration

Symptom: Teams use different tools; no consistent pipeline or shared practices

Cause: Lack of centralized templates, gate libraries, or tooling guidance

Tip:

- Create shared pipeline modules or libraries (e.g., GitHub Actions templates, Jenkins shared libs)
- Standardize gate output and logging
- Encourage reuse over reinvention

No Feedback Loop or Continuous Gate Tuning

Symptom: Gates stagnate over time; false positives increase

Cause: No review process or evolution mechanism

Tip:

- Establish feedback channels (Slack, surveys, retros)
- Regularly review gate outcomes, success rates, and developer experience
- Track metrics like:
    - Time to pass/fail gate
    - Number of false positives
    - Frequency of override

Summary: Best Practices for Troubleshooting and Avoiding Pitfalls

Following these best practices helps teams troubleshoot effectively, avoid common pitfalls, and maintain quality gates that are trusted, actionable, and continuously improving.

Practice	Why It Helps
Start with soft gates	Build trust before enforcing strict rules
Provide clear logs and outputs	Speeds up debugging and builds developer confidence
Isolate flakiness	Prevents team-wide frustration
Make gates environment-aware	Increases accuracy and safety
Document everything	Promotes transparency and shared understanding
Assign ownership	Ensures gates evolve with the codebase and team needs
Monitor and improve	Keeps gates effective and relevant

Conclusion: From theory to practice

In this chapter, we've walked through the practical realities of implementing quality gates in real-world CI/CD pipelines. From defining a minimum viable gate set, choosing tools, and piloting with volunteer teams, to setting up dashboards, governance processes, and continuous improvement loops, the focus has been on creating a framework that is both effective and adoptable.

We've highlighted the importance of modularity, observability, and progressive adoption, ensuring that gates don't become blockers but instead serve as enablers of reliable, fast, and safe delivery. By combining technical architecture with governance, feedback loops, and developer-centric practices, organizations can embed quality as a shared responsibility while continuously refining their pipelines.

As we conclude the practical implementation discussion, the next chapter looks forward: the future of quality gates. We'll explore emerging trends, including AI-assisted gates, advanced anomaly detection, policy-as-code evolution, and how organizations can prepare for increasingly complex and automated CI/CD landscapes. This forward-looking perspective will help teams anticipate changes and design gates that remain relevant, scalable, and trusted in the years to come.

The Future of Quality Gates

Purpose of Chapter: The purpose of this final chapter is to explore emerging trends and innovations in quality gates, showing how organizations can evolve their CI/CD practices to stay ahead of growing complexity, leverage AI and advanced analytics, and maintain trust, speed, and reliability in their delivery pipelines.

As software delivery continues to accelerate, the landscape of CI/CD pipelines and quality gates is evolving at a rapid pace. Traditional approaches, manual thresholds, static analysis, and fixed test suites, can no longer keep up with the growing complexity of distributed systems, microservices, and hybrid cloud architectures. Organizations need to anticipate future challenges and adapt their quality gates to maintain speed, reliability, and security without creating friction for development teams.

This chapter explores the future of quality gates, highlighting emerging trends, tools, and practices that are reshaping how teams ensure software quality. From AI-driven test prioritization to automated anomaly detection and adaptive thresholds, these innovations are helping teams balance confidence in their releases with the need for velocity.

We'll examine how predictive analytics, observability integration, and increasingly sophisticated policy engines can transform quality gates from static checkpoints into dynamic, context-aware safety mechanisms. By looking ahead, organizations can prepare their pipelines and teams for the next generation of continuous delivery, where quality gates are not just controls, but intelligent enablers of faster, safer software delivery.

AI in Quality Prediction and Risk Scoring

As CI/CD pipelines become faster and software delivery grows more complex, traditional quality gates, based on binary rules (pass/fail thresholds), are reaching their limits. The future lies in predictive quality assurance powered by AI and machine learning (ML).

By analysing historical data, patterns, and contextual signals, AI can help teams anticipate failures before they occur, score the risk of code changes, and make gating smarter and more dynamic.

What Is Predictive Quality?

Predictive quality is the concept **of** forecasting the likelihood of defects, instability, or regressions based on various signals, even before a test or deploy step is executed.

Instead of asking:

"Did the code pass the test?"

We begin to ask:

"How risky is this change based on historical and behavioural signals?"

How AI Powers Quality Prediction

AI/ML models can consume and correlate large volumes of data from across the SDLC, including:

Signal Type	Examples
Code change metadata	PR size, complexity, churn, ownership patterns
Historical test outcomes	Flaky tests, failure frequency, time-to-fix
Commit history	Bug density by file, blame history
Pipeline behaviour	Build time, pass/fail trends, anomalies
Usage data	APM logs, production exceptions, traffic shifts

These signals feed into trained models (e.g., gradient boosting, random forest, or deep learning), which can produce:

- **Risk scores** (e.g., "This PR has a 72% chance of introducing a regression")
- **Failure prediction** (e.g., "This test will likely fail due to flakiness")
- **Anomaly detection** (e.g., "This build duration is 40% longer than average")

Example Use Cases

AI and machine learning are increasingly being applied to quality gates to make them smarter, more predictive, and context-aware. The following use cases illustrate practical ways these technologies can enhance CI/CD pipelines.

Use Case	AI/ML Application

Change Risk Scoring	Predict regression likelihood before merge
Smart Test Selection	Run only the tests likely affected by the PR
Flaky Test Detection	Identify non-deterministic test patterns
Gate Threshold Tuning	Adjust pass/fail criteria based on context
Failure Root Cause Prediction	Suggest likely fault area based on logs/code
Early Alerting for Hotspots	Predict which components need extra attention

From Binary Gates to Intelligent Gates

Traditional quality gates operate in a binary fashion: a threshold is set (e.g., 80% test coverage or zero critical vulnerabilities), and if the criteria aren't met, the build or deployment is blocked. While simple, this rigid pass/fail approach doesn't account for context or nuanced risk, every failure is treated the same, and every success may mask underlying issues.

AI-enhanced gates take a more intelligent, data-driven approach. Instead of simply blocking or allowing a change, these gates generate contextual insights:

- **Risk scoring:** Assign a likelihood that a change will introduce regressions or defects (e.g., Risk Score: 78/100).
- **Entropy or variability metrics:** Evaluate factors like security exposure, code churn, or test flakiness.
- **Actionable recommendations:** Suggest next steps, such as additional manual review, targeted testing, or proceeding with a caveated approval or rollback plan.

By moving from rigid thresholds to context-aware intelligence, AI-driven gates enable more informed decision-making. Teams can balance speed, risk, and quality, reducing unnecessary blocking while still catching critical issues. This evolution turns gates into advisory systems that guide developers and release managers, rather than blunt instruments that simply allow or deny changes.

Real-World Tools and Ecosystem

Several tools and platforms are beginning to leverage AI/ML to enhance CI/CD quality gates, providing predictive insights, smarter test selection, and actionable recommendations for engineering teams.

Tool/Platform	Capability Example
GitHub Copilot/TestPilot	AI-assisted PR and test suggestions
Harness SRM	Risk scoring based on pipeline signals
Launchable	Predictive test selection from ML models
CodeScene	Hotspot analysis using behavioural code patterns
Sentry + ML insights	Predictive exception patterns from telemetry data

Feedback Loops & Continuous Learning

AI-enhanced quality gates are not "set and forget" tools. To remain accurate and relevant, they must continuously learn from real-world feedback. This ensures that the system adapts to evolving codebases, team practices, and emerging risks, rather than relying on static rules.

Key inputs for training and refinement include:

- **Actual production incident data:** Feeding post-release defects, outages, or rollback events back into the model helps the gate better predict risky changes.
- **Developer feedback:** Reports of false positives or overly strict gate failures inform the AI which signals were noise versus meaningful.
- **Merge outcomes and defect leakage rates:** Tracking which changes pass gates yet cause downstream issues allows the system to recalibrate thresholds and prioritization.
- **User behaviour and test effectiveness data:** Metrics such as flaky test frequency, test coverage gaps, or critical paths influence which signals the gate weights more heavily.

By incorporating these inputs continuously, AI-based quality gates evolve into a self-improving quality engine. Over time, they become increasingly precise, reducing unnecessary blocks, catching true risks earlier, and aligning with both engineering workflows and business priorities.

Benefits of AI in Quality Gating

AI and intelligent quality gates provide measurable benefits by making pipeline enforcement smarter, faster, and more context-aware, improving both risk management and developer experience.

Benefit	Description
Proactive risk reduction	Surface high-risk changes early
Faster pipelines	Test only what matters, reduce gate bloat
Better developer experience	Fewer false alarms, less gate fatigue
Adaptive thresholds	Tune gates to context instead of rigid policies

Smarter decisions	Augment judgment with data-driven insights

Challenges and Considerations

While AI-enhanced quality gates offer powerful insights, careful attention to explainability, bias, integration, and governance is essential to ensure they support, rather than replace, responsible engineering decisions.

- **Explainability**: Developers need to trust and understand predictions
- **Bias**: Training data can reinforce biases if not curated carefully
- **Integration**: Seamless fit into CI/CD tooling and workflows is critical
- **Governance**: Risk scoring should inform, not override, responsible ownership

The Future: Autonomous Quality Guardrails

Looking ahead, the evolution of quality gates points toward intelligent, adaptive systems that proactively guide engineering decisions, enabling safer, faster, and more resilient software delivery.

As models improve, the long-term vision includes:

- Fully self-healing pipelines that rerun/retry based on signal confidence
- Context-aware gates that evolve with codebases and usage patterns
- AI co-pilots for QA that recommend test cases, identify coverage gaps, and flag anomalies in real-time

Rather than static "blockers," quality gates will act as real-time decision support systems, guiding safe, confident, and efficient software delivery.

Predictive Gates Based on Historical Trends

Predictive gates bring a proactive, data-driven approach to CI/CD pipelines, using historical insights and trends to anticipate risks and guide smarter, context-aware decisions.

What Are Predictive Gates?

Predictive gates are dynamic checkpoints in your CI/CD pipeline that leverage historical data and trend analysis to decide whether a build, test, or deployment should proceed. Unlike static gates (e.g., "block if code coverage < 80%"), predictive gates ask:

"Based on how similar changes behaved in the past, what's likely to happen if we ship this now?"

They move quality control from reactive to proactive, helping teams make smarter decisions and reduce failure rates without hardcoded thresholds.

How Historical Trends Enable Predictive Gating

By analysing past builds, test executions, deployment results, and production incidents, predictive gates can learn patterns and identify outliers or elevated risk.

Here's what they might evaluate:

Historical Signal	What It Reveals
Code churn and complexity	Highly volatile files may introduce bugs
Past test flakiness	Tests failing intermittently ≠ reliable signal

Previous commit failure rate	Developer/area-specific stability trends
Time-of-day / release timing	Certain windows may show higher rollback rates
Deployment durations	Spikes may indicate hidden issues
Post-deploy incident rates	Early indicators of bad releases

Example: What a Predictive Gate Might Say

"This commit touches historically volatile files, comes from a high-risk contributor context, and lacks sufficient test deltas. Based on past trends, the chance of regression is 62%. Suggest additional review or limiting rollout exposure."

Rather than outright blocking, predictive gates can:

- Flag for manual review
- Route through a canary or feature flag path
- Trigger additional tests or chaos experiments
- Log the risk for future audit

Enabling Predictive Gates in Practice

Implementing predictive quality gates requires more than dropping an ML model into your pipeline. It's about building a reliable feedback system that turns historical delivery data into actionable, real-time signals during CI/CD execution. At a high level, predictive gating rests on four foundational capabilities: data collection, signal shaping, risk scoring, and policy enforcement:

Data Collection Layer

Predictive gates are only as good as the data they learn from. You need to systematically capture signals across the full delivery lifecycle, including:

- **Build and pipeline data:** job duration, failures, retries, flaky test occurrences
- **Test reports:** pass/fail rates per test, historical stability, coverage deltas
- **Deployment metadata:** environment, rollback events, blast radius
- **Production signals:** incidents, alerts, MTTR, user-reported defects

This data should be stored in a structured and queryable form, such as a time-series database, centralized metrics platform, or data lake. Consistency matters more than volume early on, start with a small, high-signal dataset and expand as maturity grows.

Feature Engineering

Raw data rarely tells a useful story on its own. Feature engineering transforms noisy events into trends and patterns that predictive models can reason about. Common examples include:

- **Stability trends:** flaky rate per test over time, failure frequency per service
- **Change velocity signals:** commit frequency, size of change, churn rate
- **Pipeline health indicators:** rolling averages for lead time, queue time, or retry rates
- **Human factors:** author or team historical defect leakage (used carefully and ethically)

Techniques such as moving averages, rolling windows, standard deviation bands, and decay factors help emphasize recent behaviour while still learning from the past. The goal is to detect meaningful drift, not punish normal variation.

Scoring Engine

The scoring engine converts engineered features into a single, interpretable risk signal. This can range from simple statistical models to more advanced ML approaches:

- **Baseline models:** logistic regression or weighted scoring for transparency
- **Rule-augmented models:** decision trees combining heuristics with learned signals
- **Advanced approaches:** ML classifiers trained on incident and deployment outcomes

Risk scores are typically composed of weighted contributors, such as:

- The nature of the code change (size, complexity, affected components)
- The confidence of the test suite (historical flakiness, coverage relevance)
- The deployment target (production vs. staging, criticality)
- Optional contextual signals (time of day, release window, recent incidents)

Transparency is critical here, teams must understand *why* a score is high, not just that it is.

Gate Policy Evaluation

Finally, predictive signals must translate into clear pipeline behaviour. Gate policies define how risk scores influence flow:

- **Thresholds and bands:**
  - Low risk → auto-proceed
  - Medium risk → warn, require acknowledgment or extra tests
  - High risk → block or require manual approval
- **Tooling integration:** expose decisions directly in CI tools like GitHub Actions, Jenkins, or GitLab CI
- **Observability:** publish scores, contributing factors, and outcomes to dashboards and logs

Importantly, predictive gates should augment decision-making, not replace ownership. The intent is to provide earlier, smarter signals, giving teams the context they need to slow down when it matters and move fast when it's safe.

Example Predictive Gate Criteria

These trend-based gate rules illustrate how predictive and historical signals can be translated into concrete, automated decisions that adapt to real system behaviour rather than relying on static thresholds alone.

Gate Metric	Trend-Based Rule
Test Flakiness	Fail gate if flake rate > 25% over past 30 runs
File Volatility	Flag if commit touches top 10% most changed files
Commit Complexity	Gate if >100 lines changed + >5 files affected

Incident Correlation	Alert if changed area has recent high-severity incidents
Risk Delta	Block if risk score increases >2 std deviations vs. average

Feedback Loop for Continuous Learning

This concept highlights how modern quality gates shift from fixed, one-size-fits-all rules to adaptive controls that learn from past behaviour, using real trends and predictive signals to guide smarter, context-aware pipeline decisions.

As more builds and releases go through the pipeline, the system learns:

- What changes led to rollbacks or production bugs
- Which test suites provide good predictive signal
- Which contributors or files tend to correlate with failures

This continuous feedback loop makes the predictive gate smarter and more reliable over time.

Benefits of Predictive Gates

Predictive gates introduce *foresight* into the CI/CD pipeline by identifying risky changes before failures occur, rather than reacting after something breaks. By analysing historical patterns, such as defect leakage, flaky tests, or incident-prone components, these gates can surface early warnings that traditional, static rules would miss.

They also enable *faster and smarter feedback*. Instead of treating every change equally, predictive gates help teams prioritize deeper testing and stricter scrutiny only where risk is high. Low-risk changes can flow through with minimal friction, while high-risk changes receive the attention they deserve. This targeted approach keeps pipelines fast without compromising quality.

Another key advantage is *adaptive decision-making*. Predictive gates move beyond one-size-fits-all thresholds like "80% coverage" or "no critical CVEs" and replace them with context-aware assessments. A small change in a stable area may pass easily, while a similar change in a historically volatile component might trigger additional checks or manual review.

Importantly, predictive gates are trust-building rather than punitive. Instead of hard-blocking by default, they often warn, recommend, or suggest next steps, empowering developers to make informed decisions. This shifts gates from being perceived as obstacles to being seen as intelligent advisors.

Over time, this approach contributes to a *reduced incident rate*. By catching regressions and risky patterns that static gates routinely miss, predictive gating improves release quality while preserving delivery speed.

Benefit	Description
Foresight	Catch risky changes before failure occurs
Faster feedback	Prioritize high-risk changes for deeper testing
Adaptive decisions	Move beyond one-size-fits-all rules
Trust-building	Warn rather than block, empowering developers
Reduced incident rate	Catch regressions missed by traditional gates

Where Predictive Gates Fit in the Pipeline

Predictive gates can operate at multiple points in the delivery lifecycle, adding intelligence wherever decisions are made.

Early in the workflow, such as pre-commit or pull request stages, they can alert developers that a change resembles past regressions or touches high-risk areas, allowing issues to be addressed before merge. During build and validation phases, predictive signals can be used to skip expensive tests for low-risk commits or, conversely, trigger broader test coverage when risk is elevated.

Before deployment, predictive gates become especially valuable as safety mechanisms, preventing high-risk changes from reaching production without additional review or safeguards. After deployment, they continue to learn by correlating release data with SLIs, SLOs, and incidents, feeding new insights back into future predictions.

In this way, predictive gates don't replace existing quality controls, they enhance them across the entire pipeline.

Pipeline Stage	Predictive Gate Use Case
Pre-commit	Alert on risky changes before merge
Build validation	Skip expensive tests for low-risk commits
Pre-deploy	Block high-risk changes from hitting prod
Post-deploy	Correlate with SLIs/SLOs for continuous learning

Real-World Tools and Patterns

Many teams are already using predictive techniques, even if they don't label them explicitly as "predictive gates." Tools like Launchable apply machine learning to select only the tests most likely to fail based on historical data. CodeScene analyses codebase evolution to highlight hotspots and areas of rising technical risk.

On the platform side, teams often rely on ML platforms such as MLflow or SageMaker to train, version, and deploy risk-scoring models. Observability stacks, combining systems like Prometheus with anomaly detection, help surface unusual behavioural trends in performance or reliability data.

In more advanced setups, organizations build homegrown ETL pipelines that aggregate build logs, test results, and incident data into a central store, feeding custom models tailored to their architecture and delivery patterns.

Tool/Pattern	Use
Launchable	Predictive test selection
CodeScene	Historical hotspot analysis
MLflow / SageMaker	Model tracking and deployment
Prometheus + anomaly ML	Behavioural trend alerting
Homegrown ETL pipelines	Feed custom models with build / test data

Challenges and Considerations

Predictive gates are powerful, but they introduce new responsibilities. Models can suffer from *drift* as systems, teams, and architectures evolve, requiring regular retraining and validation. *Interpretability* is critical, developers must understand why a gate flagged a change, or trust will quickly erode.

Data quality is another major factor. Poor or incomplete data leads to poor predictions, and false positives can be just as damaging as missed risks if not carefully tuned. Predictive gates should be introduced progressively, with clear feedback loops and conservative enforcement until confidence is established.

- **Model drift**: trends change, retrain frequently
- **Interpretability**: developers must understand risk scores
- **Data quality**: garbage in = garbage predictions
- **False positives**: can erode trust if not tuned carefully

Predictive Gates Add Intelligence to CI/CD

Predictive gates represent a shift from static quality checks to historically informed, context-aware decision support. They don't simply say *yes* or *no*, they say *"this looks risky, and here's why."*

When used correctly, predictive gates help organizations minimize risk, improve confidence in every release, maintain speed without sacrificing safety, and foster a culture of continuous learning. Rather than acting as rigid blockers, they become intelligent partners in delivering high-quality software at scale.

Adaptive Pipelines

An adaptive pipeline is a CI/CD pipeline that dynamically adjusts its behaviour based on real-time signals, context, and historical insights. Unlike traditional pipelines that follow fixed sequences of steps for all changes, adaptive pipelines optimize the path to production by:

- Skipping irrelevant steps

- Scaling testing based on risk
- Altering behaviour based on environment, author, or time
- Making decisions informed by AI/ML or rules engines

In short, adaptive pipelines respond intelligently to what's happening, not just what's configured statically.

What Makes a Pipeline Adaptive?

An adaptive pipeline is one that responds intelligently to context rather than treating every change the same. Instead of running a fixed, linear set of steps for every commit, an adaptive pipeline continuously evaluates *what changed, how risky it is,* and *what level of assurance is actually required.* The goal is simple: apply the right checks, at the right time, with the right level of strictness, no more, no less.

At the core of adaptiveness is context-aware execution. The pipeline understands the nature of a change, whether it's a documentation update, a small configuration tweak, or a major refactor in a critical component, and tailors its behaviour accordingly. This avoids wasting time on low-value checks while ensuring that high-risk changes receive deeper scrutiny.

Closely related is risk-based decisioning. Adaptive pipelines don't rely on binary pass/fail rules alone; they adjust gating behaviour based on predicted risk. A low-risk change might pass with lightweight checks, while a high-risk change may trigger additional testing, tighter thresholds, or manual review. This allows teams to maintain speed without sacrificing safety.

Another defining trait is dynamic gate selection. Gates are no longer static fixtures hardcoded into the pipeline. Instead, they can be enabled, disabled, or reconfigured at runtime based on policies, signals, or historical data. Thresholds can flex, tests can be added or skipped, and enforcement levels can change without rewriting the pipeline.

Adaptive pipelines also deliberately create optimized fast paths. Safe, routine changes are prioritized for rapid feedback and deployment, reducing lead time and developer friction. Rather than slowing everyone down to accommodate worst-case scenarios, adaptiveness ensures that only changes that *need* heavy validation pay that cost.

Finally, truly adaptive pipelines are feedback-driven. They learn over time by correlating pipeline decisions with real outcomes, such as incidents, rollbacks, or customer impact, and use that data to refine future behaviour. This turns the pipeline into a living system that improves as the organization learns.

Characteristic	Description
Context-aware execution	Executes different gates/tests based on change context
Risk-based decisioning	Adjusts gating strictness based on predicted risk
Dynamic gate selection	Turns gates on/off or alters thresholds at runtime
Optimized fast paths	Prioritizes safe changes for quick deployment
Feedback-driven learning	Adjusts over time based on outcomes and telemetry

Examples of Adaptive Behaviour

In day-to-day workflows, adaptive behaviour often shows up in small but powerful ways. A documentation-only commit might skip build and test stages entirely, providing near-instant feedback. On the other hand, a pull request that modifies a historically unstable or business-critical module may automatically trigger a full regression suite and performance tests.

When flaky tests are detected, an adaptive pipeline may retry the test or allow the build to proceed with a warning instead of hard-failing, preventing unnecessary disruption. Operational context also matters: a nighttime deployment to a staging environment might defer heavy load testing until business hours, while a release to a low-traffic region could run minimal smoke tests paired with heightened monitoring.

Even contributor context can influence behaviour. A pull request from a new or infrequent contributor might automatically add extra static analysis checks or require additional reviewer approvals, not as punishment, but as a safety net.

These behaviours illustrate how adaptiveness balances speed, confidence, and pragmatism.

Situation	Adaptive Behaviour
Small doc-only commit	Skip build and test stages
PR modifies high-risk module	Trigger full regression + performance tests
Flaky test failure detected	Retry or bypass with warning instead of hard fail
Nighttime deploy to staging	Defer heavy load tests until business hours
Release to low-traffic region	Run minimal smoke tests with monitoring
New contributor PR	Add static analysis and reviewer reminders

Key Components of Adaptive Pipelines

Adaptive pipelines are enabled by a small set of foundational components working together.

At the centre is a **policy engine**, which may be rule-based, ML-powered, or a combination of both. This engine evaluates metadata such as PR size, files touched, commit history, test health, and risk scores, then decides which gates to run, skip, or modify. It acts as the "brain" of the pipeline.

Supporting this is a **dynamic orchestration layer** capable of expressing conditional logic. Modern CI/CD platforms, such as Jenkins, GitHub Actions, GitLab CI, and Azure DevOps, provide constructs like rules, expressions, and conditions that make this orchestration possible without excessive custom scripting.

Adaptive decisions rely on **real-time signal inputs**, including change metadata, historical risk indicators, test flakiness trends, and observability metrics like performance or error rates. The richer and cleaner these signals are, the smarter the pipeline can be.

Finally, a **feedback loop** closes the system. Pipeline outcomes, successful releases, incidents, overrides, and developer feedback, are tracked and fed back into the policy engine. This enables continuous tuning, ensuring the pipeline evolves alongside the codebase, teams, and business priorities.

In summary:

Policy Engine

- Rule-based or ML-powered

- Evaluates metadata (PR size, files touched, test results, etc.)
- Decides which steps to run, skip, or modify

Dynamic Orchestration Layer

- Orchestrates conditional logic
- Tools: Jenkins pipelines, GitHub Actions expressions, GitLab rules, Azure DevOps conditions

Real-Time Signal Inputs

- Change metadata
- Historical risk scores
- Test health dashboards
- Performance and observability metrics

Feedback Loop

- Tracks outcomes
- Feeds data back into the policy engine
- Enables continuous improvement

Adaptive vs. Static Pipelines

The table below contrasts traditional static pipelines with adaptive pipelines, highlighting how adaptive approaches use context, risk, and feedback to deliver faster, smarter, and more resilient CI/CD workflows.

Static Pipelines	Adaptive Pipelines
Same steps for every commit	Steps vary by risk, context, history
Hardcoded thresholds	Thresholds shift based on real-world data

Delays from unnecessary gates	Skips or condenses low-impact steps
Require manual tuning to improve	Self-optimizing through feedback
All-or-nothing test execution	Smart test selection or test bucketing

Benefits of Adaptive Pipelines

Adaptive pipelines deliver tangible benefits by tailoring checks and decisions to real-world context rather than applying the same rules everywhere. Key benefits include:

- **Faster feedback loops** – Saves time by skipping unnecessary checks and prioritizing only what's relevant for the change.
- **Reduced noise and friction** – Developers aren't blocked by irrelevant failures, false positives, or low-value gates.
- **More accurate gating** – Tests and quality controls align with actual risk, impact, and intent of the change.
- **Self-improving behaviour** – Pipelines evolve over time by learning from outcomes, trends, and feedback.
- **Contextual release decisions** – Balances quality, speed, and risk intelligently instead of relying on rigid pass/fail rules.

Common Challenges

While adaptive pipelines offer significant advantages, they also introduce new challenges that teams must address to ensure flexibility doesn't come at the cost of clarity, trust, or control.

- **Complexity**: Conditional logic must be carefully managed
- **Observability**: Harder to trace full execution paths across commits
- **Trust**: Developers and teams must trust the pipeline's intelligence
- **Tooling support**: Not all CI tools offer easy dynamic behaviour
- **Governance**: Need clear rules to avoid unpredictable or risky shortcuts

Building Adaptive Pipelines: Step-by-Step

To successfully introduce adaptability without losing control, teams should approach adaptive pipelines incrementally, layering intelligence and feedback into the pipeline in a deliberate, observable way rather than attempting a big-bang redesign.

1. **Start with classification**:
   - Define commit types: low-risk vs. high-risk
   - Add labels, tags, or metadata to signal change types
2. **Add conditional execution logic**:
   - Use pipeline rules, `if` statements, or policy-as-code tools
   - Examples: Skip deploy if tests haven't changed
3. **Integrate historical risk signals**:
   - Pull in test flakiness, code churn, incident history
4. **Tune based on feedback**:
   - Use telemetry and team feedback to adjust thresholds and logic
5. **Visualize and audit behaviour**:
   - Build dashboards that explain why steps were run or skipped

Adaptive Pipelines in the Bigger Picture

Adaptive pipelines are a cornerstone of modern DevOps maturity because they fundamentally change how teams balance delivery speed with confidence. By responding to context, risk, and real-world feedback, they reduce unnecessary friction while still protecting critical systems. This makes pipelines more developer-centric, lays the groundwork for AI-enhanced automation, and creates a virtuous cycle of continuous improvement that strengthens release reliability over time.

Adaptive pipelines are a cornerstone of modern DevOps maturity. They:

- Bridge the gap between speed and safety
- Enable developer-centric workflows with fewer roadblocks
- Prepare pipelines for AI-enhanced automation
- Drive continuous improvement and release resilience

Autonomous Remediation and Self-Healing Systems

Autonomous remediation refers to the automatic detection and correction of faults, failures, or misconfigurations **in** CI/CD pipelines or production environments, without requiring manual intervention.

In other words, it's when your delivery system says:

"I've identified the problem, applied the fix, and everything is stable again, no need to wake anyone."

This concept is a core enabler of self-healing systems, which aim to maximize uptime, maintain quality, and reduce operational toil by proactively resolving issues as they arise.

Why It Matters

Modern software delivery is fast, complex, and increasingly continuous. As systems scale:

- Failures become inevitable
- Manual responses don't scale
- Delays in remediation impact customer experience and SLAs

Autonomous remediation helps organizations move from reactive firefighting to proactive stability, freeing up engineering time and reducing incident severity.

How Self-Healing Works in CI/CD

Self-healing in CI/CD refers to pipelines and automation that can detect failures or deviations and automatically take corrective actions without requiring human intervention. This approach increases reliability, reduces mean time to recovery, and allows teams to focus on building features rather than firefighting broken pipelines or environments.

Self-healing can operate across multiple stages of the pipeline and across different layers of the software delivery stack.

Examples of Self-Healing Behaviour by Stage

Self-healing behaviour manifests differently across stages of the CI/CD pipeline, with automated detection and remediation tailored to the specific type of failure or risk at each point.

- **Pipeline Execution:** Automatically retry flaky or transient failures, re-run failed stages with adjusted parameters, or dynamically reorder steps to reduce impact.
- **Test Failures:** Detect non-deterministic or flaky tests, quarantine them, and optionally re-run only the affected tests to minimize developer disruption.
- **Environment Drift:** Identify missing configurations, inconsistencies, or unhealthy services and reapply or restart them automatically.
- **Security Scanning:** Auto-update vulnerable dependencies or trigger re-scans to validate that fixes are effective before merging.
- **Infrastructure:** Detect unhealthy nodes or pods and automatically replace them using orchestration tools like Kubernetes or autoscaling groups.
- **Deployments:** Roll back failed releases, trigger fallback strategies, or deploy to safe environments automatically to prevent customer impact.

Common Remediation Patterns

Several common remediation patterns help pipelines recover automatically from failures, reducing manual intervention and minimizing disruption to developers and end users.

- **Test Flake Isolation:** Flag, quarantine, or selectively rerun flaky test cases to prevent blocking the pipeline.
- **Auto-Retry Logic:** Retry failed builds with exponential backoff or parameter adjustments to recover from transient failures.

- **Rollback Automation:** Revert to the last known good deployment automatically when critical failures are detected.
- **Security Auto-Fixes:** Patch known vulnerabilities or update dependencies without human intervention, then re-run validations.
- **Package Conflict Healing:** Detect and resolve dependency clashes or rebuild artifacts dynamically.
- **Service Restarts:** Restart failed containers, pods, or microservices automatically using orchestration tooling.

AI and ML in Autonomous Remediation

Modern self-healing pipelines increasingly leverage AI/ML to make remediation smarter and faster:

- **Predictive Fixes:** Models analyse historical incidents to propose the most likely successful remediation.
- **Confidence Scoring:** AI evaluates the reliability of proposed fixes and chooses actions based on risk level, context, and time of day.
- **Contextual Decisioning:** Actions are prioritized based on business impact, system criticality, and environmental conditions.
- **Continuous Learning:** Reinforcement learning improves remediation strategies over time, learning from successful interventions.

Examples of AI-assisted self-healing include identifying a flaky test and automatically quarantining it, suggesting dependency upgrades to prevent future CVE failures, or recommending a pre-emptive rollback before a deployment reaches production. By combining automated detection, intelligent remediation patterns, and learning algorithms, self-healing pipelines help teams maintain high release confidence while reducing manual intervention and operational overhead.

Examples of Self-Healing Tools & Platforms

Modern CI/CD pipelines increasingly rely on automated remediation to recover from failures with minimal human intervention. A variety of tools and platforms support this self-healing behaviour across deployment, testing, infrastructure, and monitoring layers:

- **Argo Rollouts** – Automates canary deployments and rollbacks in Kubernetes, enabling pipelines to safely revert changes without manual intervention.
- **Keptn** – Implements event-driven remediation workflows triggered by SLO violations or pipeline anomalies.
- **GitHub Actions / Jenkins** – Provides retry plugins and conditional recovery logic to re-run failed stages automatically.
- **Chaos Mesh + Prometheus** – Injects controlled failures and monitors system responses, allowing pipelines to auto-tune for resilience.
- **PagerDuty + Rundeck** – Connects alerts to remediation scripts, ensuring automatic recovery for predefined incidents.
- **LaunchDarkly** – Implements "kill switches" using feature flags to disable problematic code paths during regressions.

Business Benefits

Implementing automated remediation delivers tangible business value:

- **Reduced MTTR** – Failures are resolved faster, often without human intervention.
- **Fewer overnight pages** – Known failure patterns are addressed automatically, reducing on-call fatigue.
- **Less manual toil** – Engineers can focus on improvements rather than firefighting recurring issues.
- **Lower incident impact** – Quick rollbacks or automated mitigations help maintain customer SLAs.
- **Improved feedback loops** – Systems learn from recurring issues, enabling continuous improvement of gates, tests, and operational logic.

Building a Self-Healing Foundation

To implement reliable autonomous remediation, teams should focus on six key pillars:

1. **Instrumentation** – Collect detailed logs, metrics, traces, and quality data across pipelines, tests, and deployments.
2. **Observability Tools** – Detect failures, anomalies, and drift using tools like Prometheus, OpenTelemetry, or custom monitoring dashboards.
3. **Automation Triggers** – Use pipelines, event buses, or workflow tools (e.g., Keptn, Argo) to initiate remediation automatically.
4. **Remediation Playbooks** – Encode known fixes in scripts, bots, or runbooks to standardize responses to common failures.
5. **Confidence Boundaries** – Only trigger automated fixes when signals are clear and confidence is high to avoid unintended consequences.
6. **Feedback Loop** – Measure success, audit outcomes, and refine remediation logic based on real-world results.

Cautions and Challenges

While self-healing pipelines offer major benefits, teams must be mindful of potential pitfalls:

- **Remediation confidence** – Avoid auto-fixing changes without verifying the correct target.
- **Logging and traceability** – Every automated action must be visible and auditable for accountability and troubleshooting.
- **Blast radius** – Ensure remediation actions are scoped appropriately to prevent cascading failures.
- **Security** – Automation scripts and bots must run with minimal permissions necessary to operate safely.
- **Cultural readiness** – Teams need time to trust automated systems; start small, show reliable results, and expand gradually.

The Future: Self-Governing Delivery Systems

Autonomous remediation represents a major step toward self-regulating CI/CD ecosystems, where pipelines adapt in real time, failures are anticipated and pre-empted, and systems heal and evolve without waiting for human intervention. By enabling this level of automation, developer time is preserved, systems become more resilient, and software delivery achieves a higher level of reliability and confidence than ever before.

Conclusion: The Future is Rapidly Evolving

This chapter has explored the evolving landscape of quality gates, from traditional static checks to AI-enhanced predictive gates, adaptive pipelines, and self-healing CI/CD systems. We've seen how emerging technologies enable context-aware, risk-driven decision-making, faster feedback loops, and autonomous remediation that reduces manual toil while increasing reliability and trust in software delivery. By integrating predictive analytics, historical trends, and real-time signals, organizations can move beyond rigid pass/fail rules to a smarter, continuously learning quality ecosystem that balances speed, safety, and developer experience.

As we close this chapter, the focus naturally shifts toward reflection and synthesis. The next, and final, part of our book will summarize the key insights from this book, highlighting practical takeaways, overarching principles, and lessons learned along the journey of designing, implementing, and evolving quality gates in modern software delivery. It's a moment to step back, see the full picture, and consider how to carry these practices forward into your own teams and pipelines.

The Journey Through Quality Gates in CI/CD

Throughout this book, we've navigated the full spectrum of quality gates in modern software delivery, beginning with the **Introduction to Quality Gates** and their role in enforcing trust, consistency, and reliability in CI / CD pipelines.

We built a foundation by exploring **CI/CD Pipelines** and understanding how continuous integration and delivery underpin fast, safe, and repeatable software releases. From there, we defined **Quality in Software Delivery**, framing it not just in terms of defects or test coverage, but as a combination of reliability, security, performance, and maintainability.

The middle chapters explored the practical mechanics of implementing quality gates. We examined the **Types of Quality Gates**, from **Static Code Analysis**, **Test Automation**, and **Security/Compliance Gates**, to **Performance and Reliability Checks**, and even **Custom, Contextual Gates** tailored to organizational needs.

We delved into **Designing Gate Policies and Thresholds** and integrating gates into **Pipeline Orchestration**, while highlighting the critical importance of **Observability and Feedback Loops** to ensure actionable insights and continuous improvement. Handling failures thoughtfully was also emphasized, illustrating that gates are most effective when combined with clear remediation and exception strategies.

Practical, real-world applications were reinforced through **Case Studies and Real-World Implementations**, showing how teams evolve gates over time, measure impact, and iterate safely. Equally important, the **Culture and Organizational Alignment** chapters reminded us that technical controls alone cannot guarantee quality, adoption, trust, and shared ownership across developers, QA, security, and leadership are vital for success.

We then explored **Building Your Quality Gate Framework**, providing step-by-step guidance for establishing, piloting, and evolving a robust, maintainable gate system. Finally, **The Future of Quality Gates** looked ahead to AI-driven predictive gates, adaptive pipelines, and self-healing CI/CD, emphasizing that quality enforcement is increasingly intelligent, context-aware, and autonomous.

Taken together, this book paints a comprehensive picture: quality gates are not mere blockers, but essential enablers of reliable, secure, and high-performing software delivery. They empower teams to balance speed and safety, transform data into actionable insight, and foster a culture of accountability and continuous learning.

As you close this book, the key takeaway is clear: the journey to effective quality gates is iterative, grounded in technical rigor, enriched by organizational alignment, and enhanced by emerging technologies. Whether you're starting small with commit-level checks or aiming for AI-assisted predictive gates, the principles, practices, and frameworks presented here will guide you in evolving your CI/CD pipelines toward resilience, efficiency, and confidence in every release.

Final Thoughts

Quality gates are more than rules, they're the guardians of trust in your CI/CD pipelines. When designed thoughtfully, implemented wisely, and embraced culturally, they transform chaos into confidence, risk into insight, and friction into speed. As you return to your own pipelines, remember: every gate is an opportunity, to catch errors early, empower your teams, and deliver software that's reliable, secure, and high-performing. Build them with care, evolve them with data, and watch your software delivery soar.

Bibliography

No effort like this is complete in isolation and draws upon a lot of the great work done by others. Below are some important resources that helped form a lot of the work in this book.

Books on CI/CD, Quality Gates, and DevOps

Continuous Delivery: Reliable Software Releases Through Build, Test, and Deployment Automation

- **Authors:** Jez Humble & David Farley
- **Publisher:** Addison-Wesley Professional
- **Publication:** 2010
- **ISBN-13:** *978-0321601919*

A foundational text for modern software delivery automation and pipeline design, covering end-to-end CI/CD concepts and practices.

Continuous Integration: Improving Software Quality and Reducing Risk

- **Authors:** Paul M. Duvall, Steve Matyas & Andrew Glover
- **Publisher:** Addison-Wesley Professional
- **Publication:** 2007
- **ISBN-10:** *0321336380*
- **ISBN-13:** *978-0321336385*

Classic practical guidance on CI best practices which underpin quality gates and automated testing workflows. Amazon

GitHub Actions in Action: Continuous integration and delivery for DevOps

- **Authors:** Michael Kaufmann, Rob Bos & Marcel de Vries
- **Publisher:** Manning Publications
- **Publication:** 2024
- **ISBN-13:** *978-1633437302*

Focused tutorial and practical guide to CI/CD with GitHub Actions, useful for implementing quality gates in real workflows.

Hands-on GitHub Actions: Implement CI/CD with GitHub Action Workflows

- **Authors:** Chaminda Chandrasekara & Pushpa Herath
- **Publisher:** Apress
- **Publication:** 2021
- **eBook ISBN:** *978-1-4842-6464-5*
- **Softcover ISBN:** *978-1-4842-6463-8*

Practical exercises and examples for building CI/CD workflows with GitHub Actions.

Accelerate: The Science of Lean Software and DevOps

- **Authors:** Nicole Forsgren, PhD; Jez Humble; Gene Kim
- **Publisher:** IT Revolution Press
- **Publication:** 2018
- **ISBN-10:** *1942788339*
- **ISBN-13:** *978-1942788331*

Research-based exploration of what makes high-performing software teams, including CI/CD and quality practices measured across organizations.

Recommended Complementary Reads

Note: These don't focus purely on pipelines, but give excellent context for culture and adoption.

- **The DevOps Handbook: How to Create World-Class Agility, Reliability, & Security in Technology Organizations**: Gene Kim, Jez Humble, Patrick Debois, John Willis, Nicole Forsgren (IT Revolution Press, various editions).
- **The Phoenix Project: A Novel About IT, DevOps, and Helping Your Business Win**: Gene Kim, Kevin Behr & George Spafford (IT Revolution) .
- **The Unicorn Project** : Gene Kim (IT Revolution) .
- **Team Topologies** - Matthew Skelton & Manuel Pais (IT Revolution) .

These contextual books help *why* quality gates matter organizationally and culturally.

Web References and Online Resources

Practical Articles & Community Guides

- **InfoQ: Pipeline Quality Gates & Implementation Patterns** – A practical overview of CI/CD gating strategies ideal for pipeline design.
- **Testkube Glossary: Quality Gates** – Concise definition and typical use cases for quality gates.
- **DZone: DevOps Pipeline Quality Gates – Benefits and Pitfalls** – Community article discussing real challenges and considerations.

Additional Online Materials (Vendor/Tool Docs)

Even though not "books," official documentation and tutorials are essential for hands-on work:

- **GitHub Actions Official Docs** – Workflows, gating examples, and pipeline integrations.
- **GitLab CI/CD Docs** – Pipeline rules, quality gate examples, and security gating best practices.
- **Jenkins Pipeline Documentation** – Scripted & declarative pipelines, retry logic, and integration examples.
- **Azure DevOps Pipeline Docs** – Environment approvals, conditions, and multi-stage gating.

Tips for Using These Resources

- **Start with foundational texts** (e.g., *Continuous Delivery, Continuous Integration, Accelerate*) for *conceptual grounding.*
- **Use practical guides** (e.g., *GitHub Actions in Action, Hands-on GitHub Actions*) for *hands-on pipeline implementation,* including quality gates.
- **Complement with culture and performance books** (e.g., *The DevOps Handbook, The Phoenix Project, Accelerate*) to understand the *people and process dimensions* that make quality gates succeed.
- **Leverage research papers** for *evidence and data* that justify investments in CI/CD improvements or predictive gating strategies.

Terms of Reference

Below is a summary of common terms used through this book with brief descriptions of what they mean:

A

- **Agile** – Iterative software development methodology; basis for DevOps/CICD practices.
- **Ansible** – Infrastructure as Code (IaC) tool for configuration management and deployment.
- **Artifacts** – Build outputs (binaries, Docker images, packages) stored in repositories for deployment.

B

- **Blue/Green Deployment** – Deployment strategy minimizing downtime and risk by running two production environments.
- **Branching Strategies** – Git workflows (GitFlow, trunk-based) that impact CI/CD pipelines.
- **Build Automation** – Tools and scripts to compile, test, and package code automatically.

C

- **CI (Continuous Integration)** – Merging code changes frequently, with automated builds and tests.

- **CD (Continuous Delivery / Deployment)** – Automated delivery of changes to staging/production environments.
- **Canary Deployment** – Releasing changes gradually to a subset of users to test production impact.
- **Containers / Docker** – Packaging applications with dependencies for reproducible builds and deployments.
- **Code Coverage** – Metric for percentage of code exercised by automated tests.
- **Code Review / Pull Requests** – Key collaboration step for quality, often integrated into pipelines.

D

- **DevOps** – Culture and practices bridging development and operations for fast, reliable delivery.
- **Docker Compose** – Tool for defining multi-container applications, often used in testing environments.
- **Dependency Management** – Tools like Maven, npm, or pip that manage libraries for builds.

E

- **Environment Promotion** – Moving artifacts through dev, test, staging, and production environments.
- **Elastic / Kubernetes** – Container orchestration and scaling for CI/CD pipelines.

F

- **Feature Flags** – Mechanism to control features at runtime without redeploying; enables safe experimentation.
- **Flaky Tests** – Tests that fail intermittently; critical to manage in quality gates.

G

- **GitOps** – Git-driven infrastructure deployment and configuration approach.
- **GitHub Actions / GitLab CI** – Popular CI/CD platforms.

H

- **Helm** – Kubernetes package manager, used for deploying complex services.
- **Hotfix** – Immediate, often small, production fixes handled through pipelines.

I

- **IaC (Infrastructure as Code)** – Automated provisioning and configuration of infrastructure.
- **Immutable Infrastructure** – Concept of replacing rather than modifying running systems.

J

- **Jenkins / Jenkins X** – Popular open-source CI/CD automation server.
- **Job Orchestration** – Controlling sequence and conditions of CI/CD tasks.

K

- **Kubernetes** – Orchestration platform for containerized workloads.
- **Kanban** – Visual workflow method often paired with Agile for CI/CD visibility.

L

- **Linting / Static Analysis** – Automated code checks for style, quality, and potential bugs.
- **Load Testing** – Performance evaluation often integrated as a CI/CD gate.

M

- **Microservices** – Architectural style impacting pipelines, deployment strategies, and testing.
- **Monitoring & Observability** – Metrics, logs, tracing to observe system and pipeline health.
- **MTTR (Mean Time to Recovery)** – Key reliability metric used to measure pipeline effectiveness.

N

- **Nightly Builds** – Scheduled CI jobs for long-running validation, security scans, or regression tests.
- **Notification Channels** – Slack, Teams, or email alerts integrated into pipelines for gate results.

O

- **Open Policy Agent (OPA)** – Policy-as-code engine used for enforcing security/compliance gates.
- **Observability Dashboards** – Grafana, Datadog, or Kibana dashboards for pipelines and application metrics.

P

- **Pipeline as Code** – Declarative CI/CD definitions (e.g., Jenkinsfile, GitHub Actions YAML).
- **Predictive Gates** – AI/ML-informed gates based on historical data and risk scoring.

- **Pre-commit Hooks** – Local checks before committing code to reduce errors early.

Q

- **Quality Gates** – Automated checks in CI/CD pipelines to enforce standards (tests, coverage, security, performance).
- **Quarantine Tests** – Isolating flaky or failing tests without blocking pipelines.

R

- **Rollback / Rollforward** – Mechanisms for handling failed deployments safely.
- **Release Orchestration** – Coordinating deployments across multiple services/environments.

S

- **SAST / DAST** – Static / Dynamic Application Security Testing integrated into pipelines.
- **Smoke Tests** – Minimal tests to validate new deployments quickly.
- **SonarQube / ESLint** – Tools for code quality analysis.

T

- **Test Automation** – Unit, integration, E2E tests integrated in CI/CD.
- **Trunk-based Development** – Branching strategy that enables continuous integration.

U

- **Unit Testing** – Automated tests verifying small pieces of functionality.

- **UI / E2E Testing** – End-to-end checks of full system or user interface.

V

- **Versioned Artifacts** – Tracking build outputs with unique identifiers for reproducibility.
- **Vault / Secrets Management** – Secure handling of credentials in pipelines.

W

- **Workflow / Orchestration** – Defining sequences, dependencies, and conditions for pipeline jobs.
- **Webhooks** – Event-driven triggers for CI/CD actions.

X

- **X-Ray / Tracing** – Observability for distributed applications and pipelines.

Y

- **YAML Pipelines** – Declarative pipeline definitions for GitHub Actions, GitLab, or Azure DevOps.

Z

- **Zero Downtime Deployments** – Deploying updates without service interruptions, e.g., via blue/green or canary strategies.

www.ingramcontent.com/pod-product-compliance
Lightning Source LLC
LaVergne TN
LVHW052016200926
848481LV00005B/1511
* 9 7 8 1 0 4 9 2 9 2 9 0 8 *